Social Class and Social Policy

SOCIAL CLASS

AND

SOCIAL POLICY

S. M. Miller

&

Frank Riessman

Basic Books, Inc., Publishers

NEW YORK   LONDON

HN
65
M5

Jean
and
Jon and Ned

Cathy
and
Robin, Janny, and Jeffrey

PREFACE

This book is a product of more than twenty years of friendship and intellectual camaraderie. We first met as graduate students at Columbia University in an economics class. Over the years we changed our sights, Miller from economics to sociology and back toward the newly developing field of social economy; Riessman from sociology to social psychology. Throughout this period we have shared three common concerns: The first is to see that social science grows in usefulness to those in action—to distill ideas, orientations, strategies, and techniques which are to be effective for people engaged in various kinds of applied work.

The second is to develop social-science theory by applying it. Our aim is not only to test theory by its utilization; more importantly, it is to deepen theory by the probing of its application. An effective applied social science should create new theoretical perspectives.

The third is an abiding concern for those who are not doing so well as the rest of society. Here our interest has been initially in the working classes and then, more and more in recent years, we have centered on those at the bottom of the society, those now termed the poor. We have always felt that the understanding of the non-middle classes has been marred by stereotyping and by inadequate appreciation of their positive characteristics. Consequently, much of our writings over these decades have been centered on the problems of trying to clarify their strengths in order to provide a base for action. At the same time, we consciously reject a sentimental portrayal of the disadvantaged. We do not believe that the poor want to be poor or that being poor is an exciting way of life. But we do believe that the poor, or at least segments of the poor, have something to offer to the main stream of American life and that in many ways they are an important irritant for progress.

Thus, it is the poor who are basically challenging our educational system and are indirectly producing the demand for changes in educational technology and organization that will be of benefit to all, disadvantaged and advantaged. It is the minority groups who are leading the way in the removal of discrimination and prejudice in our country so that we can realize the dream deferred of a democratic, equalitarian United States. It is the poor whose need for decentralized, reachable, humane, informal service has led the way to the development of a community mental-health approach, the humanity of which can benefit all and help to counteract the bureaucratizing trends in the society.

We believe that it is only through an understanding of these strengths and potential contributions of the poor that we can establish a meaningful relationship with them. It is not through an emphasis on pathology, deficit, or the supposed nonadaptive culture of poverty. These foci lead to an attack on the victims of the system rather than an indictment of the system itself. The pathology approach does not lead to institutional or structural change, but rather to an emphasis on changing presumably disturbed, deprived individuals so that they can utilize the inadequate services and opportunities inappropriately offered by the educational and social-service systems.

We started in the 1940's with a then unpopular concern with factory workers. In recent years, we have moved our analysis of classes to center upon those nearer the economic bottom of our society. But we feel that there is cohesiveness in our writing about these various social segments. Indeed, one of our greatest difficulties in preparing this book has been to decide whether or not to include our older essays on the organized working class. We have finally decided to exclude most of them and to concentrate on the essays of more recent days which focus on the new working classes or the new poor. But we feel that the outlook that we have developed has been a rather consistent one over these decades—to look for the positives in the underclass, to stress the differentiation within it, to look for the levers of change, and critically to appraise institutional and professional inadequacies that prevent effective work with this particular group. Our stress has been much more on the problems of professional and institutional inadequacies than on an arraying of pathological deficiencies of the underclass.

In developing the ideas in this book, we have been much influenced by our experiences as consultants and administrators of programs. We have attempted to maintain the outlook, which we developed early, of an applied social science. Our orientation has been to learn from practice as well as to contribute to it. We have always assumed that from the analysis of experience one can learn much that has great social-science significance. In turn, we continue to feel that social science has much to contribute to practice, even if the contribution is mostly in the form of ways of thinking rather than in packaged recipes for action.

The book, then, represents a bridge between our concern with the world of action and our roots in the world of social science. In the present work we have not been sufficiently able to distill the implications of our analysis for general social-science theory. That is our next objective, but we hope that the book conveys our continuing endeavor to show how social science can contribute to action and may be molded and developed through the attempt to utilize it.

We start with the hope that much can be accomplished in the 1960's and 1970's. Whether or not it is depends on developing the kind of political strength to change institutions in ways which will be more effective to those who are part of the institution. While we do not discuss all aspects of social class but rather concentrate upon those at the bottom, we feel that the issues of institutional inadequacy, inappropriate relationship to the outlook of the clientele, and similar problems permeate the institutions of social welfare today in our country. Consequently, although we have concentrated on this underclass, we feel that the mode of analysis has wider implications. This mode is to look at the setting in which a class or stratum functions, to look at the particular forms of its outlook (not to deduce them from the various external constraints but actually to see the various coping mechanisms which have developed), to search for the nature and the impact of the professional and his institution upon those who may presumably be serviced, and to accent positive characteristics in terms of change and development of the population at risk.

In this book we have attempted to make a distinction between strategy and policy on the one hand and technology on the other. By the first set of terms we refer to the analysis of the underlying issues involved in a problem or to the depicting of the social-class dynamics that have to be considered in developing a particular program. By technology, we refer to activities which would increase the effectiveness of practitioners. Our orientation is that much more can be accomplished if practitioners have a clearer perspective of what can be achieved and a line of action laid out. Rather than offering some vague general mandates, we feel it is possible to be more specific in terms of the kinds of practices which are effective with today's poor. This book aims at sharpening some social-policy issues and shaping technology so that needs and values are more effectively met.

The chapters were originally written in response to issues of the day. Most of them were not written collaboratively. We have tried to rework them into a book that is a joint enterprise and now is relevant to underlying rather than topical issues.

In a book of this kind that has accreted over twenty years, we are indebted to many people. In the development of our basic viewpoint, we had the advantage in our graduate and early postgraduate days of continuing and exciting discussions with Bert Alpert, Lloyd Barenblatt, Leslie Beheunek, Seymour S. Bellin, Alvin W. Gouldner, Sol Levine, Elliot Mishler, Morris Rosenberg, Mae Stern, and Bruce Young. More recently, we have learned much from Arthur Pearl, Martin Rein, Robert Rieff, and Richard Titmuss.

In addition, we have had the opportunity to speak with many others, too many to list, whose comments and criticisms, not always politely offered or received, have sharpened our thinking about both action and theory. Though we argued, we also listened.

A grant from the Louis M. Rabinowitz Fund permitted the development of a number of the ideas presented here. Riessman's work at Mobilization for Youth and in the Lincoln Hospital Neighborhood Service Center Program led to many of the formulations. Miller's research on school dropouts, social services, and poverty, supported at various times by the Stern Family Fund, the Ford Foundation, Social Security Administration, and the New York State Division for Youth, shaped a number of the major themes. The Syracuse University Youth Development Center provided a most hospitable environment for this work.

Pamela Roby's aid has been enormous. She has welded articles into a book, forced us to give up the more commonplace, and resolved or reduced the differences in viewpoints between two old friends who have always prided themselves on their independence of view.

We have led extraordinarily busy lives in attempting to be academics and activists. Our wives, professionals in their own right, have made this possible. And they have infused our lives with their grace and hope. Sharing our ideals, they are the co-producers of this volume.

New York City S. M. MILLER
July 1968 FRANK RIESSMAN

CONTENTS

I
POLICY OBJECTIVES

II
SOCIAL CLASS: THE POOR TODAY

III
EDUCATION

IV
MENTAL HEALTH

V
POVERTY AND
COMMUNITY ACTION

VI
SOCIAL SCIENCE AND
SOCIAL POLICY

I

Policy Objectives

I

THE NEW INCOME

THE RELATIVE VIEW OF POVERTY

To examine poverty is to examine American society. A realistic, up-to-date, relevant analysis of poverty cannot be separated from a search for understanding of what are the important changes in American life.

Most of those Americans we label as "poor" are not on near-starvation diets. Nor do most live on city streets, lacking a roof over their heads. Both conditions characterize the poor in many places. In what sense, then, are most of the poor of contemporary America (or England or France) poverty stricken?

They are poor because they have fallen far behind the rest of society. This is the meaning of poverty in the affluent society as it seeks to become "the great society." Not that individuals are facing starvation and physical destruction—although some of our poor do—but that they are not full members of society.

We can see this clearly if we review the changes in thinking about poverty. In the nineteenth-century studies of poverty in England, the effort was to discover the basic ingredients of life and to estimate the ability of populations to obtain or adequately to use these ingredients. Those who fell below the sustenance band were the poor. Today, 79 per cent of poor husband-wife families have a television set, 57 per cent a telephone, 73 per cent a washing machine.[1]

The standards of society obviously change with place, time, and possibilities. As a society advances economically, new standards emerge. Those whose positions have not improved or have advanced slightly have suffered a relative loss. With economic growth not only do the standards improve quantitatively as increased amounts are consumed, but the standards change and expand as new items are added to the welfare of individuals. The failure to gain these new items is part of falling behind.

In different societies, different standards emerge. These are more related to the conditions of society than they are to the "basic" definition of life sustenance. For example, Peter Townsend has pointed out that the nutritional level deemed necessary for life differs widely in Britain and in India. In Great Britain, it takes 50 per cent more calories to provide "basic maintenance" than it does in India. At least that is what the British nutritional experts seem to be saying when their statement about nutritional needs in Britain is compared with the estimates for India made by Indian nutritional experts.[2] Obviously, cultural factors intrude in defining the needed caloric intake level, although the lower the economic output of a society the more likely it is to be closer to a basic "subsistence" level.

We see another illustration of the difficulty in determining a "subsistence level" in the World War II estimate that less than one hundred dollars was required to purchase an adequate diet for the entire year. This low sum was the result of estimating the number of calories needed for survival and then pricing the cheapest bulk basket of goods —e.g., wheat, potatoes, etc.—that would provide these calories. Following this logic and allowing for price changes since 1944, less than $300 a year would cover the food needs of a family today.

Obviously, the definition of poverty is not a world-wide or a permanent specification. It is relative to time and place. Those who are labeled poor today would certainly not be poor by the standards of 1870, when telephones did not exist and running water in homes was uncommon. To say "relative to time and place" implies that what we define as poverty is affected by the conditions and possibilities of society. The poverty line is "determined by prevailing standards of what is needed for health, efficiency, nurture of children, social participation, and the maintenance of self-respect and the respect of others."[3]

As a society changes in the quantity and kind of production and in the "prevailing standards" of life, the definition of poverty changes. Poverty, thus, is not a fixed position. It is relative to the possibilities of society and the "average" standard of life in a society, although we can have sharp disagreements about the level of the relationship.

This point is not novel: Our practices in estimating the costs of minimum budgets reflect changing conditions of life:

> . . . postwar costs of "modest but adequate" budgets for self-supporting families, roughly deflated for price change, range from about 30 to 60 per cent higher than the "minimum comfort" budgets of the early '20s.[4]

This statement means that between the twenties and the post-World War II period our nominally acceptable basic standard of living, as measured by governmental agencies, increased by at least 30 per cent and possibly by more than a half, depending on which estimates are used. Although we are not always clear about this point today, a century ago it was recognized that "as a society advances, the standard of poverty rises."

The situation of poverty means that a family is falling behind other families in access to the resources of society:

> People are poverty-stricken when their income, even if adequate for survival, falls markedly behind that of the community . . . they are degraded, for in the literal sense they live outside the grades or categories which the community regards as acceptable.[5]

COMMAND OVER RESOURCES

In an affluent society such as the United States, if we are to meet the problems of poverty of the present rather than those of the past, we must have a vision of poverty which relates it to current conditions. The contemporary discussion of poverty has been in terms of an insufficiency of income. It is important to see the inadequacies of this view. Our discussion will consequently center on the broadest issues of inclusion or participation: economic, service, political, psychological, and social. As we shall see, each of these dimensions of "the standards of society" is, in turn, many-sided.[6]

To some extent, monetary income can buy some of the other aspects of economic inclusion and the other forms of inclusion. But this is not always or completely true, especially for those with limited incomes. Consequently, we shall have to discuss each of the dimensions and subdimensions of "the command over resources" in its own right. Obviously individuals may wish to make certain kinds of bargains and choices, trading off one kind of inclusion against another. But first we need an understanding of the significance of these varied aspects of the contemporary standard of living to be able to discern the permutations which are possible.

While our discussion is mainly in terms of the poor, the concepts of well-being that we outline apply to other groups in society. Although the plight of the poor highlights the analysis of what is involved in well-being today, the issues have wide relevance in our rapidly changing society, not only for the near-poor but frequently as well for the better off.

Economic Inclusion

We believe that the new forms of our economy require us to break out of the mold of thinking that sees economic well-being as solely related to annual monetary income. As we shall point out, the latter computation is much more shaky and difficult to make than is customarily realized. Furthermore, a modern conception of the standard of living requires that we go beyond income to the accumulation of assets and the access to various kinds of services that are important parts of one's command over resources. Consequently, in discussing "economic inclusion," we shall analyze income, assets, and services.

THE INCOME COMPONENT

Income has a dollar-and-cents sign on it. Consequently, it is easy to believe that it is a definite and reliable figure. Actually, its calculation is complicated and subtle.

Price-level changes affect the purchasing power of each dollar of income. Modifications in the level of structure of taxes reduce or expand what is available for personal expenditures. Obviously, statements about adequate income have to take into account prices and taxes. Many high-income individuals transfer their flow-over money into capital gains so as to be able to reduce their taxes. Obviously, then, the asset level has to be considered in appraising what is "current" income as well as in measuring the more important indicator of command over resources.

THE POVERTY INCOME LINE

The stability of income is also important. Individuals whose incomes are precarious may be in much more difficult economic and psychological straits than individuals whose average level of income may be lower but more assured.

Since a high percentage of those who are below the poverty income line do not suffer this condition for two years in a row,[7] the length of time under the poverty line is important. We might distinguish between the chronically poor, the frequently poor, the sporadically poor. In dealing with the frequency of low income we should be aware of the wide disparity of situations among the poor and non-poor.

At what level to peg the poverty income line will obviously vary by the size of the family, its composition (presence or absence of the father), ages, area of country, and type of community. The emphasis on a solitary poverty line (first given as $3,000) has been very misleading. Some families can be poor despite incomes of more than $5,000 because there are many children in them or heavy medical bills. The cost of living varies some 20 per cent among major cities in the United States and even more when Southern rural and Northern or Western metropolitan areas are compared. Consequently, we need many definitions of the poverty income level, which adjust for familial and areal differences.

The poverty income line is a band rather than a line. Exactly what the level should be will vary a good deal by social values, not just technical decisions. The poverty-deprivation line for a family of four ranges from $1,000 to $6,000. What we need is a recognition of degrees or depths of poverty from the extreme poverty of the American family on $1,000 whose conditions rival those of the Calcutta poor, to the milder poverty of those just below the poverty line for its particular familial or residential characteristics, to the near-poor, a perilous notch above the poverty line.

THE ASSET COMPONENT

Titmuss has stressed that in contemporary economies much income is disguised as wealth or asset accumulation in order to reduce taxes.

Consequently, we must look at assets when we try to get an understanding of income. But this view must be broadened to recognize that the accumulation of a certain level of assets is a needed part of the standard of living. We shall distinguish four dimensions of assets: the accumulation of pension reserves; housing; consumers' durable goods; liquid reserves.

Pension Reserves

One out of eight adults in the United States is past the age of sixty-five; those who live to the age of twenty-five can expect to live to age sixty-five and those who live to be sixty-five can expect to live another fifteen years. Thus, perhaps a quarter of adult life is lived in old age. Consequently, increased attention must be paid to the adequacy of the income during this period. As a person grows older during his working life, he should be accumulating sufficient pension reserves to insure a decent style of life after retirement. The assurance of this future income is an important part of one's current situation.

Consequently, the accumulation of assets in pension funds—governmental and private—has become an important part of one's current command over resources. Obviously, the accumulation can be lower for a young person than for an older person and still provide a feeling of security. But with the years, pension rights should be increasing.

What level would be considered the poverty line for the accumulation of pension rights? We would need to provide a basic minimum level and a certain percentage of current income. The asset accumulation should advance with age at a certain rate, perhaps accelerating in the later years.

Liquid Reserves

The possession of some ready cash for emergencies and special needs is increasingly an important part of one's standard of living. Emergencies become less terrifying and oppressive with monetary protection. Few families escape emergency or special needs. Consequently, some liquid reserves are part of the new standard of living.

The minimum liquid reserve level at the lower-income levels should be twice current income, the ratio of savings to income going down as income rises. There should likely be a minimum level, perhaps $3,000. The funds could be in the form of cash, bank deposits, liquid stocks, etc.

Consumer Durables

Some minimum level of household durables would seem to be part of the basic American standard of living. While there might be disagreement on what durables should be possessed by all families, obviously some household items such as a toaster and a washing machine would be included by most.

While some low-income families have high assets, this is not true of all. The level of income, the availability of credit, and welfare regulations affect the ability to accumulate household durables, as they do the style of life. Various ways of getting low-interest credit to the poor and near-poor have to be developed. Public-assistance standards should permit the purchasing of important consumer durables.

Housing

The availability of housing for families is largely but not completely determined by their incomes. Negroes pay more for comparable housing than do whites and therefore expend a higher proportion of their income on housing. Low-income families face greater shortages of adequate housing; marginal increases in their incomes do not guarantee that they can obtain decent housing. It therefore is especially important that we recognize that the adequate command over resources requires that families have decent housing. This can be provided by public housing, private housing, publicly subsidized private and cooperative housing.

A question can be raised as to why we have listed housing adequacy under assets. If most—rather than a majority of Americans—lived in owned homes, the reason would be less obscure. For then we would see housing as an asset. Looking upon housing as a stock—not as a payment even when rented—which yields utilities to families, we decided that it best fits under assets, although it could be discussed under services, as we do discuss neighborhood amenities.

What are the standards of decent housing? Obviously, these vary by size and composition of family and area of the country, since cultural tastes would be important. The standards of public housing—a kitchen, living room, a bedroom for the parents, and no more than two children in one bedroom—could be utilized. Minimum levels of square feet space should be observed. The absence of a need for major repairs and the presence of running water, an indoor toilet, and hot and cold water would seem to be part of today's basic requirements. (A troublesome issue is to what extent are racial and class integration an important part of contemporary housing standards.)

These standards mean that some whose incomes were above the income poverty line were below the housing poverty line, especially in particular areas.[8] This would be important to recognize, for it might lead to development of a comprehensive program to upgrade the housing in particular areas and regions which have fallen behind the great housing advance of the rest of society.

Both private and public housing activities can improve the situation. We do not see advancing along the varied dimensions of well-being as the narrow function of the public sector alone. For example, public support of various kinds could aid the construction of private housing.

The housing situation points up an issue already mentioned. To some extent, improvement along one dimension of the command over resources is not automatically or easily transferable or translatable into improvement along others.

Services

Increasingly, a large part of our command over resources is in the form of services. For example, as medical science progresses, our ability to prolong our lives seems to depend somewhat on access to medical services. In some cases, the service is a nondivisible item—we are dependent on the cumulative development of a field. In general, the lower the income the greater the reliance on public services to provide resources, although for most of the population (except the very rich) public services are of great importance.

We tend to think of these services as publicly provided, but this is not always true. For example, many individuals have the assurance of and ready access to high-grade medical care through employer-financed (in whole or part) health plans. These fringe benefits are occupationally connected and not publicly offered. In defining levels of adequacy, to some extent private and public goods are exchangeable. It has been Titmuss's contribution to show the common function of the activities of quite different types of organizations and policies.[9]

But in general it is misleading to think of publicly provided services as distinct from an individual's income. This type of thinking leads to a sharp dichotomization between the public and private sectors, rather than recognizing that a good part of our command over resources comes out of things we consume collectively. The command-over-resources theme leads us to realize that we are dealing with new forms of income rather than a sharp division between public and private production and expenditures.

The issue of what is an appropriate standard is particularly acute in the area of services. A "minimum" level and an "adequacy" level compete with each other, usually with the victory of the former. The result is to a large extent owing to the outworn notion that services are a residual activity rather than a basic component of the command over resources.

In discussing services, the quality question comes to the fore. How good a service is may be as important as how much of it is delivered. Frequently, what differentiates an inadequate from an adequate service is not the quantity or expenditure but its quality. The difficult but important task is to define a minimal level of adequacy in terms of the quality of service, even though this can sometimes be defined only in terms of expenditures.

We shall discuss only four aspects of services: education, medical care, neighborhood amenities, transportation.

EDUCATION

In today's society, education is important to an individual both in terms of gaining access to income and in terms of building satisfactions in life. Education is an economic good affecting the productivity of labor and the job possibilities of individuals. Economists, consequently, currently stress that education is an investment in human capital. But in our kind of society, education also is a consumption good in the language of the economists. That is, education adds enjoyment values to individuals who possess it, apart from the economic gains that they may receive because of it. Our discussion will consider education in terms of both production and consumption.

In today's society, a person is socially and economically excluded if he does not have at least a high-school diploma. Soon, some college or a college diploma may be the passport to full participation in society. Already the income gap between the diploma elite and the rest of society is widening. The gap in income and social relations will probably deepen in the next years.[10] To move low-income dropouts to high-school graduates is an important but inadequate goal. The aim should be to increase the college-graduating achievements of the children of the poor. An interim goal should be to reduce the educational differences between the poor and non-poor so that the rate of college graduation among the poor is 50 per cent that of the rate of the non-poor.[11]

In the affluent society, those with "limited" education defined in contemporary terms are not fully included in the society. Not only are they barred from a growing number of jobs, but they are not able to enjoy a variety of benefits of the society; they are singled out for poor treatment by various types of agencies, both public and private. They lack the information and confidence needed to manage the network of governmental and quasi-governmental agencies. A society truly concerned about the elimination of poverty and the extension of social inclusion is interested, consequently, in the improvement of educational achievement among large groups of the poor. The aim here is not necessarily to improve the economic situation, although that probably would follow, but to provide education so that low-income groups have a greater chance of participating in a variety of new forms which have developed in the affluent society. Education then becomes an important way of becoming included in the society.

Those with low education fall further and further behind those of higher education not only in terms of income but in terms of their ability to use a variety of leisure and other new advantages in society.

In an important sense, people are culturally excluded in this nation if they do not have a fairly high level of literacy. If they lack access to or find it difficult to utilize newspapers, magazines, radio, television, theaters, movies, they are missing important elements in the new standard of life. While education does not determine the availability of these resources, it does deeply affect the ability to use them.

Consequently, a social inclusion program must advance beyond thinking of education in narrow terms and stress education as a way of gaining entrance into the rapidly broadening society; or begin to develop other mechanisms which reduce the social role of education— effective informational and advocate measures to get services to the low-educated and the humanization of bureaucracy so that the low-educated are well treated, receiving services as rights and entitlements rather than as charity or good fortune.

MEDICAL CARE

The quality of medical care has enormously improved in the United States with the advances in medical discoveries, but the distribution of this care has not much improved. Large numbers of Americans have limited physical access to a physician or hospital. They cannot afford adequate medical care and receive inadequate attention under uninviting conditions in public clinics. The result is that there is a large, if diminishing, gap between the health conditions of the low-income and the rest of society, especially in regard to infant mortality and life expectancy.

The adequacy line of medical services should include the availability of a physician for every 700 persons in every part of the United States, the underwriting of health costs so that families can afford full utilization of medical services, programs of early identification of problems and their care (which would be public programs), and emphasis on prevention of illness through public-health measures.

These measures are indicators of medical activity; the eventual appraisal of adequacy is in the morbidity and mortality data themselves, reducing the gap between the poor and the rest of the society. In making the output criteria so concrete and visible, we will become more aware of the problem of quality of medical care.

To some extent, increasing income alone solves problems of gaining access to quality medical services alone. But this is not completely true where adequate facilities and services are unavailable in particular areas. Further, the general advance of medical services is increasingly underwritten by government funds (51 per cent of medical school funds were supplied by the Federal government). Medical services, an important part of our income, are to some extent an indivisible good; for some to benefit, all must benefit.

NEIGHBORHOOD AMENITIES

Sound physical structure is not enough to provide a decent housing environment. The kind of neighborhood one lives in matters. Neighborhood security and attractiveness are things which may be provided to a large extent only on a community-wide basis. Therefore, the provision of neighborhood and leisure facilities and amenities is a separate condition of well-being. Individuals cannot provide adequately on their own for police and fire protection, clean streets, and recreational facilities.

Minimal levels in terms of open area per individual, density of housing, fire and police services for structures, frequent garbage pickup, and the like are needed. Low-income areas are notoriously underserviced in this regard: Government authorities have contributed to the development of slums by reducing garbage collections.

TRANSPORTATION

The transportation plight of the low-income city dweller was dramatized by Watts. After the 1965 Los Angeles riots, some jobs were made potentially available to residents of the Watts district. But it would take two or more hours each way to get to these jobs in other parts of Los Angeles. Many Watts residents could not afford cars; public transportation is scarce in Los Angeles, and the end result is that to be poor means to be stuck.

In other large cities and in rural areas, the poor face similar immobility because of the scandalous underdevelopment of public transportation in this country. In many cases, as in Watts, the transportation failure results in lost economic opportunities; in most cases, it means cultural and social isolation.

The availability of low-cost transportation is now an important component of life in these mobile United States.[12] To be neighborhood bound is to be cut off from many possibilities and delights. In many areas, an automobile should be part of the package of minimum consumer durables we spoke about earlier. If the expansion of mass transportation eventually reduces the need for private transportation, then the need for private assets such as a car would be reduced. Unfortunately, present indications are that public transport is only slowly advancing, if at all.

Political Inclusion

In the truly "great society," the elimination of poverty requires more than bringing up a particular group to a minimum level of income, assets, and public services. It requires attention to the achievement of new rights of political and social inclusion. For the poor are the excluded—not only from economic affluence but from other possibilities in society.

In the political realm, inclusion has these four dimensions: (a) legal protection, (b) the exercise of voting, (c) bureaucratic protection, (d) political participation.

LEGAL PROTECTION

The case of *Gideon* vs. *Wainwright* has highlighted the mistreatment accorded to many of the poor in the administration of justice. Some have argued that there is "class justice" and that the poor are actively discriminated against in the process of arrest and adjudication. The Kennedy-Johnson administrations have highlighted this issue, particularly in their measures and proposals for the poor.

The efforts to reduce incarceration because of inability to raise bail are an instance of the reduction of income-discriminatory justice. Police behavior in low-income neighborhoods gives rise to frequently justified complaints of police brutality, the new rallying cry of the disinherited. The differential treatment of juveniles is a striking illustration of class justice: the number of youth stopped by police does not differ much in low-income and high-income neighborhoods, but the number of arrests is much greater in the former, indicating the differential and negative treatment of low-income youth.[13] The "midnight raids" of the homes of women on welfare to see if a man is present have been a frequent invasion of the privacy of the poor.[14]

In the realm of justice there cannot be a level of protection for the poor which differs from that of the better off. The impartial and full protection of the law for all is involved, although many parts of the law apply principally to the poor. The general rule should be—would this have happened to this individual if he had a higher income or education?

THE EXERCISE OF VOTING

One important area of social inclusion is the development and extension of citizenship rights. In our country, all citizens legally have the right to vote, although this is obviously a reduced right for Negroes in the South. For the poor generally throughout the society voting rates are very low. A realistic and close look at political inclusion or citizenship rights means that the poor must have a much more effective voting situation than they do now. The acquisition of formal rights without their actual use does not mean much in present-day society.

An active program to increase the voting rates of low-income groups is necessary. This would mean making it easier to be able to vote, by decentralizing registration offices, by having year-round registration, by increasing registration and voting hours, by active campaigning to bring out the potential voters. The general climate should facilitate and encourage voting.

The target should be to achieve among the poor almost the same rate of voting as among other income groups in society. "Apathy" or nonvoting is a characteristic of social deprivation and as such should be combated in a full-scale war on poverty.

POLITICAL PARTICIPATION

The concept of "maximum feasible participation" in the interpretation of the Economic Opportunity Act of 1964 forges beyond voting rights and their exercise and protection from bureaucratic harshness. In requiring that the poor participate in the drawing up and conduct of programs in their behalf, the relationship between the individual and the service bureaucracies which impinge upon him is brought to center stage. To a large extent these bureaucracies have treated individuals as clients and unqualified, rather than as citizens and competent. As a citizen, the individual has rights vis-à-vis the agencies; as a citizen, he should have a role in policy determination.

The formula of "maximum feasible participation" has introduced a needed note in the welfare state—new forms of political rights are required which not only protect the citizen but give him greater scope in affecting policy. The citizens of low-income areas have largely been acted upon rather than actors in the crucial decisions which affect them. The new political rights of self-determination and participation should not be restricted to the war on poverty but should be extended to all the other agencies which affect the individual—the conduct of city agencies such as housing and health departments, the operation of schools, the behavior of police.

There will be a tense tug among professional outlook, central political responsibility, and citizen participation. But these agencies of education and welfare are extraordinarily important today and cannot be left untouched by the spread of citizenship rights. The right to vote was an important achievement for the working classes in England; the right to participate in decision making will require new creative organizational and governmental inventions and will be the important political battleground for the poor in the coming years.

The issues of control and participation are especially important for today's poor since they are most vulnerable to the service agencies. But all groups in society are now deprived of effective mechanisms of participation in the education and welfare arena. The effort to achieve greater participation of the poor as we move from a clientele to a citizenship outlook will involve molding new forms of political rights that will be of great importance for all Americans.

Professionals and politicians may assert that the citizen, particularly the poor citizen, is not competent to make difficult decisions. But cannot he contribute to the decision makers, and cannot organizational structures be changed so that they are more sensitive to community needs and quests? Perhaps he cannot make all, but certainly some; perhaps not always alone, but with useful assistance he can find direction and understanding. At the very least he can contribute to the decision-making level. We are just beginning to address ourselves to the problems of organizational relevance, structure, and performance. The effective strengthening of citizenship rights will require organized power of the poor and creative organizational forms and styles. The effort will be a long step toward the humanization of organization and welfare.

BUREAUCRATIC PROTECTION

The great growth in governmental services to the poor (as well as to other groups in society) means that they are highly dependent upon procedures, policies, and personnel of the agencies with which they deal. Since many practices and policies of agencies are not defined by statute, full legal protection of the poor is missing or not easily available. Bureaucratic excesses take place; slowness of bureaucratic action handicaps the poor; interpretation of law and policy so that they are disadvantageous to the poor frequently occurs; petty and vindictive personal behavior by officials victimize the poor. The poor frequently find themselves in the role of K in Kafka's *Trial*—accused without clarity; jeopardized without recourse.

Because of the great growth in "administrative justice and injustice," it frequently has been suggested of late that the ombudsman concept be adopted in this country—as an intermediary for the poor. There has been fear that a public official would be limited in what he can do. Alternatively, organizations of the poor can effectively voice complaint and grievance and demand and receive action. But the important thing in the present discussion is that the poor be treated by agencies as they would be if they were better off, and that agencies raise the level of humanity with which they treat those who have to deal with them.

Psychological Inclusion

AUTONOMY

We have discussed self-determination in political terms—participation in public and private agency decisions. But there is a psychological side which deserves independent attention. That is the overcoming of the feeling of powerlessness and the contrary development of the feeling of autonomy, of control over one's destiny. To some extent, poverty has the mark of apathy and withdrawal; the affluent can hope to control some of the events that impinge upon them.

As we have freed ourselves from the vicissitudes of famine and climate, the lives of many give them the feeling that they are controlling to some extent the forces that affect their lives. Some measure of destiny control becomes an important command over resources in a psychological sense. For then one can hope and plan without falling into fantasy.[15]

Social Inclusion

SOCIAL CONTRIBUTION

Earlier we discussed the level of income, assets, and services needed to move above the poverty line. But the source of these elements is significant in our society. Receiving income from the private-enterprise economy is favored; receiving income from "government" (unless presumably purchased through insurance or a return for military contribution) is not. Stigma attaches to those who receive "welfare," affecting an important slice of the poor. A quarter of the poor presently receive public assistance; an adequate welfare system would increase this percentage. Most of those now receiving or who should be receiving welfare assistance may not be temporary recipients but may need aid for long periods. Giving them income through the welfare system aids them financially (though inadequately) while punishing them socially in terms of the non-poor society. They are in but not of the society.

As a result, many are now advocating a guaranteed annual income as a matter of right without the debasing apparatus of the means test. Some movement in the direction of this social invention is desirable, but the core principle should always be clear: to provide adequate income in ways that are not demeaning to the individual.

To do this may mean reassessing what is a contribution to society. Instead of thinking of usual employment situations as the only ones which "contribute" to society, we should begin to revalue the activity of the husbandless mother who brings up children, the indigent aged, and others. Labeling the unemployed dropout a "trainee" changes his status. The opportunity to participate in useful ways—and broadening the concept of usefulness—is important in improving the social position of all Americans, especially the poor.[16]

SOCIAL DISTANCE

Social inclusion of the poor requires changing the patterns of social distance and deference. This may be the most difficult kind of change and represents the final and deepest meaning of the elimination of poverty.[17]

In our society, where caste and estate privileges have been largely eliminated except for Negroes, it is difficult to talk precisely about social distance. But obviously individuals in different occupations have different levels of prestige and social acceptance. We are not only interested in improving the well-being of people but reducing stigma, the disrespect for particular groups, and increasing the status and privilege of the once lowly. To improve the economic situation of the poor, that is, to bring them up to a higher economic level, does not automatically guarantee that they will have a different social position in terms of the way we look upon them and their children. No one should have a social position which produces anguish and disturbance because of the negative assessment of that position. We are engaged in a long-term struggle toward acceptance of people with diverse contributions to make to society and with diverse rewards from society.

To talk about the reduction of social distance, to ask that individuals mingle more freely regardless of their economic background, does not necessarily mean the homogenization of society. Rather, it could mean that we recognize diversity without placing as significant deep and pervasive markers of good or bad, high or low, positive or negative, evaluations upon these differences. *We seek differentiation without stigma.*

Improvement in the situation of the poor, then, is not only an economic phenomenon but an important event in the nature of the human relations between the poor and other groups in society. It is not only in terms of the mingling of individuals, that is the existence of interactions among them, but also in the quality of these interactions. The diminution of stigma, the acceptance of diversity, the willingness to recognize that those at the bottom are not necessarily limited individuals, are significant in the development of new forms of inclusion into the affluent society.

To some extent this requires changes in the hearts of men. This is what some civil-rights activists have asserted. They are concerned about an exclusive concern with the elimination of discrimination and the development of physical integration. They are concerned also with the character of the relationships among individuals and groups. To some extent the same kind of concern is exhibited in the discussion of social-distance and social-deference changes. It is not only that we want the poor to be better off economically so that they do not trouble us with their plight, but that they should be included in the society in terms of the character of our attitudes toward them and the acceptance of them in our social relationships.

This may sound terribly utopian and removed from the present-day situation but, if we look at the historical sweep, we recognize that the exclusion of various groups has been greatly reduced. The phrases "kikes," "hunkies," "wops" no longer have the impact that they once did, and surely they are much less used than ever before. In a sense, then, ethnic groups have been more and more included in American life, as perhaps symbolized in the failure of Al Smith to be elected in

1928 and the success of John Kennedy in 1960. This election marked the social inclusion of Catholics and specifically Irish Catholics in the United States.

Similarly, we will have to move toward the inclusion not only of Negroes specifically but the poor generally. They will be less and less stigmatized and more accepted into the bosom of the family if we really are sincere and effective in trying to eliminate poverty and discrimination.

Our aim should be that people of varying backgrounds, concerns, and outlooks live together in harmony and that we recognize and appreciate the differences among them. We seek not a homogenized society but a highly differentiated society where individuals of varied backgrounds, races, and experiences can live useful lives in quite different ways. Not all will wish a high degree of social inclusion; they should be free to choose or resist inclusion. Today only the rich or intellectuals (with other kinds of resources) have the luxury of this choice. The poor do not.

POVERTY AMID AFFLUENCE

The implication of the discussions of social inclusion is that we must go beyond the narrowly economic side of income in discussing the improvement of the situation of the poor. This is particularly true as we attempt to advance into a great rather than an affluent society. As we attempt to change the conditions of society qualitatively, then we have to make sure that the poor are included in these qualitative gains in society. To look at poverty only in narrow economic terms overlooks much of the anguish, strain, and dismay which poverty produces. What we are concerned with is not only a striking economic advance for the poor—which is basic, of course, to any program of improvement—but with advances in other areas of life as well.

To be poor is to fall behind the rest of society. This lag is not only an economic lag but a lag as well in developing political rights, in the character of social relationships, in the nature of the homes and neighborhoods in which one lives, the advantages of education in terms of daily life.

We cannot assume that an improvement in economic conditions will automatically produce improvements in these other areas. Indeed, they may not. Consequently, we must pay specific attention to attempts to try to improve the situations in the various dimensions of poverty.

The affluent society has greatly enlarged the possibility and arena of choice of the non-poor. In this society, poverty represents the great deprivation of having only limited possibilities of making selections, of deciding among a variety of interesting and/or useful alternatives. Reducing poverty, to a large extent, involves today increasing the possibilities of choice.

PRIVATE AND PUBLIC

The view of income and poverty that we have espoused contests the now-traditional sharp dichotomy between the public and the private sectors. Regarding income as the command over resources requires the recognition of the diversity of resources which are important in one's well-being. Income in the resources-command sense can be augmented, even when personal dollar income is not directly increased. If we are able to solve present-day poverty and deprivations rather than yesterday's, our view of poverty must be contemporary, recognizing the varied ingredients of the standard of living and the new conditions of life.

Poverty consists of falling behind the shifting standards of society. As such, we must be aware of the new and great advances in many areas of human life and an inadequate stretching out of these amenities.

Our economic perspective on poverty must be broader and more subtle than it has been. In an economy where the gross national product is expected to double every twenty-four years, a poverty level cannot be a fixed point. But in some ways even more important than the relative view of economic conditions is the broadening of our understanding of poverty to include the political and social dimensions. To gain in some areas, such as in the economic, and not in others could lead to that unevenness of development which is productive of great unrest.

DIFFERENT TYPES OF POOR

The view of income that we have presented implies that there will be great variations in the nature of families' command over resources.

Partly this occurs because of the variety of consumption styles—e.g., the limitation of liquid assets in order to have high consumers' durables. But beyond this, individuals, because of their economic, regional, and political situations, differ very widely. Two individuals of the same education and annual income may differ very much in terms of their pension accumulations because of different employer policies about fringe benefits. The available education or medical services in one community may be much better than those available to individuals of another community whose incomes are similar in other respects.

If we could aggregate the various parts of the command over resources, individuals would be at the same over-all level, but the components of the level might well differ. We should welcome and encourage diversity as a measure of the heterogeneity of desires, needs, and styles which make up a society of great possibility in which individuals are able to live out their lives in ways that most please them rather than commissars or neighbors.

The strategy that we have suggested is to examine the poor in terms of their economic, political, social, and psychological losses or deprivations. Each of these dimensions has new contours in the affluent society.

To understand the plight and progress of the poor, we have to understand the rest of society, in particular, the new forms of necessities and of social stratification. The definition of poverty and the possibilities of reducing it are interwoven with the general and changing nature of the larger society.

In the succeeding sections of the book we take up some of the implications of the new income point of view for social policy today. In sections III through V we discuss current policies in education, mental health, poverty, and community action against the backdrop of our perspective in section II on what the poor are like.

NOTES

1. S. M. Miller and Martin Rein, "Poverty, Inequality and Policy" in Howard S. Becker, ed., *Social Problems* (New York: John Wiley and Sons, 1966).

2. Peter Townsend, "The Meaning of Poverty," *British Journal of Sociology* (1963).

3. U.S. Bureau of Labor Statistics, "Workers' Budgets in the United States," *Bulletin No. 927,* p. 6.

4. Helen H. Lamale, "Changes in Concepts of Income Inadequacy over the Last Century," *American Economic Review*, LXXVIII (1958), 297.

5. John Kenneth Galbraith, *The Affluent Society* (New York: Houghton Mifflin, 1958).

6. The concepts of "command over resources" and "social inclusion" that we develop are based on the pioneering work of Richard Titmuss of the London School of Economics who has insisted on the importance of "the command over resources" idea and the significance of assets and welfare services as parts of income. This analysis was pushed along by Bertram Cross of the Maxwell School who showed how it could be used to define a poverty line. Everett Reimer of the Department of Education of the Commonwealth of Puerto Rico extended the Titmuss-Gross notions by centering on "social inclusion rights." This direction revitalizes the historic issues of citizenship rights and voting for the disenfranchised. T. H. Marshall's work on citizenship is important here, as are Charles Reich's works on rights and subsidies. In fusing these ideas, we have built on the work of Martin Rein and the foregoing, although they are not responsible for our particular formulations. We are grateful for the ethos of the community of scholars which fostered discussion among us. See S. M. Miller, Martin Rein, Pamela A. Roby, and Bertram M. Gross, "Poverty, Inequality and Conflict," *Annals* (September 1967).

7. *Economic Report of the President, 1965.*

8. The majority of those living in substandard housing were not below the poverty income line. See Alvin Schorr, "National Community and Housing Policy," *Social Service Review*, vol. V (1965).

9. Richard Titmuss, "The Social Division of Welfare" in his *Essays on "The Welfare State"* (New Haven: Yale University Press, 1958).

10. Miller and Rein, *op. cit.*

11. Using indicators such as "graduation" may be inadequate. For the rate of accession of diplomas may increase as the diploma becomes less meaningful in gaining economic or social inclusion.

12. We are indebted to Bertram Gross of Syracuse University and to Vivian Henderson of Clark College for pointing out to us the significance of transportation as a component of the command over resources.

13. Robert H. Hardt, "Delinquency and Social Class: Studies of Juvenile Deviations or Police Dispositions," Syracuse University Youth Development Center, December 1964.

14. Charles Reich, "The Midnight Searchers, *Yale Law Review* (1963).

15. A strong case for the importance of overcoming feelings of powerlessness is made by Warren Haggstrom, "The Power of the Poor" in Frank Riessman, Arthur Pearl, and Jerome Cohen, eds. *Mental Health of the Poor* (New York: The Free Press of Glencoe, 1964).

16. A neglected area in contemporary discussion is that of work enjoyment or satisfaction. Surely a rich society can pay more attention to this than it has in the past.

17. Our analysis here has been stimulated by discussions on personal relations and race relations with Rudolph Lombard, formerly national vice president of CORE and a graduate student at Syracuse University. He is not responsible for the formulations presented.

I I

Social Class:
The Poor Today

2

☙ ☙ ☙

THE "NEW" WORKING CLASS

A few short years ago little attention was devoted to poverty and the poor. It was widely assumed that poverty was rapidly declining in "the affluent society," and that comparatively few people were touched by it. Indeed, it appeared that to think about the poor was to reveal that one was caught in a repetition compulsion, unable to overcome the trauma of the 1930's despite the advent of prosperity and well-being. The great improvement in levels of living was presumed to have all but eliminated the vestiges of poverty among a "hard core."

A spate of books upset this complacent picture of the United States. Michael Harrington feelingly portrayed the strain of poverty; Lampman, Kolko, Morgan, and Keyserling revealed its extent.[1] The "income curtain" which separated the American "haves" from the American "have-nots" has been drawn back, and we can no longer assume that poverty affects few, that it is rapidly dwindling, or that it is far less destructive than the poverty of old. Nor do current trends furnish much optimism. The income of the poor generally, and of Negroes in particular, is not increasing relative to that of those who are better off. World War II stimulated a great economic change in the United States to the advantage of low-income groups.[2] But since 1944 the income gap between the poor and better off has not been closing.[3] Income and wealth inequalities seem to be increasing rather than decreasing.

The Background of the Poor

In American life, the poor are probably a more varied group than ever before. The farm poor live in areas where the economic sustenance has withered with the technological development of agriculture and its economic concentration. The rural nonfarm, small-town, and small-city poor suffer from the demise of local industry, whether it be the coal mines of West Virginia or the dead one-industry textile towns of the East. The poor of the industrial centers such as Detroit and Pittsburgh suffer from high productivity and limited demand. The youthful poor possess limited or outmoded skills and inadequate educational credentials in a high-technology, certificate-demanding economy.

Farms and small-town America are large producers of the poor; the big cities are increasingly the receivers of the poor (as well as generating a poor themselves). Many from "old America" move to the slum areas of large cities, where they join the leftover third-generation immigrant population and the other poor of the metropolis.[5]

Although farm and rural areas are pushing people toward the cities, the metropolises are not prepared to accept them. There is no pull from most of the urban centers. In contrast, an urban labor force was needed in the beginning stages of Britain's industrial progress and, as E. H. Carr argues, it was governmental policy to permit market forces to starve people off the land. In the contemporary case, our cities do not need the labor of the migrants or of the older urban poor. (We do not want to paint a gilded picture of industrialized Britain, for the urban jobs there provided a level of living that has been characterized as "grinding poverty.")

Poverty is sad (and, in our kind of society, unforgivable) wherever it takes place, but we want to concentrate on the urban poor, particularly those in large cities. This urban poor is composed of many strands: refugees from the land and older settlers of the urban slums, Southern mountaineer whites and Southern Negroes, Puerto Ricans, and Mexican Americans.

The "New" Working Class

Despite their diversity, the poor in the largest urban centers are rapidly evolving into a "colored" poor of Negroes and the Spanish-speaking (Puerto Ricans and Mexican Americans).[6] It is these groups who are most likely to be politicized. The confluence of class and race issues gives the poor a much greater political potential than is usually true of low-income, depressed populations. Obviously, the term "colored" describes perceptions of and attitudes toward these groups rather than biological phenomena.

We shall be referring to the poor as the "new" working class.[7] The "old" working class, who still are the bulk of skilled and semiskilled union members as well as the majority of blue-collar workers, is made up of "old-settler" Protestant recruits largely from farm and rural areas and the second- and third-generation Catholic emigrants from Eastern Europe. Unfortunately, social scientists have tended to classify people who are members of families where the bread-winner is not involved in some kind of white-collar (middle-class) occupation as "lower class." This category is then considered to have high homogeneity and treated as though it constituted a group with great centrality of attitudinal and behavioral patterns. A distinction between the old and the new working classes has only slowly been made.

Let us try to clarify how we see the relationship between the "new" working class and the poor, for a way of classifying a population is a way of thinking about them.

The poor are frequently referred to, following the lead of sociologists, as "lower class." For a variety of reasons, we are avoiding this designation. First, it has a negative connotation which an analytic term, at least, should avoid. Second, it is not a term that people use to designate themselves. This was sharply shown in Richard Centers' study of social-class identification which made an important discovery by offering people four choices for their social class (upper, middle, working, and lower) rather than three (upper, middle, and lower); in the *Fortune* study which employed three categories, most people, including the poor and manual workers, put themselves in the middle class; in Centers' investigation, a slight majority of the total American

population called themselves "working class," and an overwhelming
proportion of the manual workers, including the poor, chose this term.[8]
Third, "lower class" has been used to refer to a wide gamut of people
from relatively highly paid, fairly well-educated workers to third-
generation welfare families where the head of the household has only
intermittently worked and then in low-paid marginal jobs.[9]

We prefer to use the term "new" working class in talking of the
poor; the "old" working class largely includes those whose families
have been urban manual for at least a generation. This "old" working
class is more likely to be white, engaged in semiskilled and skilled
occupations, and employed in high-wage construction and manufacturing industries in the main economy than is the "new" working class.
The latter is more frequently "colored," unskilled, in low-wage service
and nonunionized industries (for example, hospitals) in the marginal
economy of present-day United States. These distinctions are overstated, for obviously there are Negroes in unionized, skilled manufacturing occupations. (The election in 1962 of the first Negro to the
executive board of the UAW is indicative of the importance of
Negroes in the high-wage, predominantly semiskilled and skilled
manufacturing occupations covered by the contracts of this union.)

This formulation runs into another difficulty, because (using
Keyserling's standards) 35 per cent of the heads of low-income
families are not in the labor force—that is, they are not classified by
census statisticians as currently employed or actively engaged in
looking for work if they are unemployed. This is not the place in
which to analyze labor-force concepts, but we would emphasize that
many of the adult poor who are outside of the labor force have
worked and would work if jobs were available. The aged poor—a
large percentage of the nonworkers—are less characterized by the
orientation to work. They continue, nonetheless, to have many
economic and political interests in common with the new working
class. The welfare poor (particularly in families headed by women)
are again probably limitedly oriented to working (but the reluctance
should not be so casually assumed as it seems to be by many commentators today). Here again the long-run economic and political
interests are frequently in common with the new working class. Moreover, when the welfare poor work, they are in the occupations which
characterize the new working class. Many of the poor will be shifting
back and forth between low-level unskilled work and government

support; in both activities they will have common interests in banding together to improve their conditions.

The concept of the "new" working class is more a fishing net than a hard container. Nevertheless, we prefer it to terms such as lower class, the lumpen proletariat, skid rowers, and the like, because it points to economic and political issues rather than to personality deficiencies. It indicates that the poor are not a narrow segment of psychologically damaged individuals. The stratification term emphasizes common economic issues which many low-income people face in affluent America; it raises the possibility that they might move politically to do something about it. A less invidious term such as "new" working class implies that low-income people are trying to get a foothold into urban industrial life. We should not ignore them by acting as though their plight were little involved in the basic economic situation of America.

Harrington has pictured the poor as passive, inert, and apathetic, lacking generally the capacity for action. We find this portrait misleading. The aged have been active in political movements—from the Townsend Plan to the fight for Medicare. Mexican Americans in the early sixties won political control in Crystal City, a small Texas town. In many cities, the young and adult poor have organized to protest their conditions, as in Chicago, where women on welfare strongly demonstrated against the cessation of allowances. We shall be concentrating on the political possibilities of Negroes, because they are a sizable proportion of the under-sixty-five, large-city poor, and because they are especially likely to become politicized.

Negroes, then, are developing a political "clout" which will give them the ability to demand and get services and help at both the federal and local levels. We are witnessing the extension of citizenship rights to a new group and their groping utilization of the potential effectiveness of these rights. Historically, the trend in this nation has been toward the spread of citizenship rights. Formally, these rights have almost always been available to all; in practice, they have been accessible only to whites and more slowly to working-class whites. The white ethnics—first the Irish, later the Jews, and still more recently the Italians (the first Italian did not arrive in the United States Senate until shortly after World War II)—strengthened their citizenship rights through organization and pressure. They were able, consequently, to obtain a more equitable distribution of political and economic rewards. The same process is beginning with Negroes, and, at a slower rate, with many other members of the new working class. It promises to be the decisive political condition of the 1960's and 1970's in this country.

A large-scale politicalization of Negroes and others of the poor is a real possibility because of the interweaving of class (economic) factors with ethnic and racial issues. The intermeshing of these concerns is leading to political mobilization. The racial-ethnic factors cement solidarity within some of the groups of the poor. Usually, the long-term, economically depressed are unlikely candidates for a dynamic political movement, but the racial-ethnic dimension, as well as the economic factor, is propelling the poor, whether Negro, Mexican American, or Puerto Rican.

Many of the leaders of the new working class will probably come from middle-class families of the racial-ethnic group, providing qualities and abilities that may not early emerge among the poor. E. Franklin Frazier's notion of a "black bourgeoisie," who in rising had cut itself off from feeling, contact, and identity with the mass of Negroes, was probably overstated when he expressed it a few years ago; it undoubtedly is today. Less and less does "going up" mean "going out" of the Negro community: even those who are able to and do move out of the Negro ghetto frequently maintain ties with it and are deeply and actively concerned about the black poor. A generational factor is involved: the older, successful Negroes are less likely to be identified with poor Negroes and are more likely to emphasize "progress" than are younger, middle-class Negroes. But even the older frequently are being pushed along by the dynamism and pressure of the young and of the Negro community generally.[10]

The cohesion which comes from the racial-ethnic issues may also separate each of the poor ethnic groupings from one another, leading each to be concerned only with issues particular to it. This self-centering pressure and inter-ethnic hostility may be overcome by the large number of issues which are common to all of the poor.

The high rate of unemployment among the new working class, their low wages, their inadequate housing as they suffer the bulk of the ravages (and reap few of the benefits) of urban redevelopment, the poor schooling offered their children, the neglect of public services in their neighborhoods, the frequent callousness of the police and welfare departments, their bilking by merchants—in short, their second-class economic and political citizenship—provide the issues which may mold the new working class into a potent political force.

But the poor will not be able to gain powerful political leverage without allies and without joint action with other groups. Professionals, liberals, and the conscience-stricken can join, at least on particular issues, with the poor to fight for larger resources and better programs devoted to the new working class.

Many of the issues that we discuss in later sections of the book might be considered by some as "professional" problems, coming under the exclusive purview of high-educated, trained specialists. Increasingly, however, these problems are embedded in deep political issues. Consequently this book—dealing with many issues of professional practice and choice—is inevitably a political book.

The very discussion of the characteristics and outlook of the new working class is a profound question affecting policy. We have stressed in this chapter the potential political force of the poor and their non-apathy primarily because powerlessness and apathy have occupied center stage in most poverty analyses. The two succeeding chapters attempt to shape a point of view that is not only at variance with many popular social-science views about poverty, but one that we feel is much closer to the actual perspectives of the poor.

NOTES

1. Conference on Economic Progress, *Poverty and Deprivation in the United States* (Washington, 1961); the main author of this analysis is Leon Keyserling, and it is known as the "Keyserling Report." Michael Harrington, *The Other America: Poverty in the United States* (New York: Macmillan, 1962). Gabriel Kolko, *Wealth and Power of the United States* (New York: Frederick A. Praeger, 1962). Robert J. Lampman, "The Low Income Population and Economic Growth," *Study Paper No. 12*, Joint Economic Committee of Congress, December 16, 1959. James N. Morgan *et al., Income and Welfare in the United States* (New York: McGraw-Hill, 1962).

2. Lampman, *op. cit.,* p. 12.

3. Herman Miller, "Is the Income Gap Closing? No," *New York Times,* Magazine Section, November 11, 1962.

4. S. M. Miller, "Youth and the Changing Society," in Irwin Deutscher and Elizabeth Thompson, eds., *Among the People* (New York: Basic Books, 1968).

5. See the rich discussion in Richmond A. Cloward and Lloyd E. Ohlin, *Delinquency and Opportunity: A Theory of Delinquent Gangs* (New York: The Free Press of Glencoe, 1960), pp. 193–211.

6. Seymour Martin Lipset and Reinhard Bendix, *Social Mobility in Industrial Society* (Berkeley: University of California Press, 1959), p. 106.

7. In Great Britain the term *new* working class has been used to refer to the more affluent manual workers. David Lockwood and John Goldthorpe of Cambridge University have carefully analyzed this group. The differences in immigration history and working-class economic and social conditions in the two countries have led to the contrasting usages of the term.

8. Richard Centers. *The Psychology of Social Classes* (Princeton: Princeton University Press, 1949).

9. For a more extended analysis of the omnibus character of the term *lower class*, see S. M. Miller and Frank Riessman, "The Working-Class Subculture: A New View," *Social Problems*, IX (1961), 86-97, reprinted in Frank Riessman, *The Culturally Deprived Child* (New York: Harper, Row, 1962).

10. Obviously, contrasting patterns exist among Negroes and other ethnic groups of the poor. The middle-class Negro who does not want his children to have contact with low-income educationally deficient Negro children is a frequently cited example of change within an ethnic group. Our impression is that the general sweep of ethnic movement is today more compelling than interclass antagonism.

3

❀ ❀ ❀

VARIATIONS AMONG THE POOR

Many discussions of the poor assume a high degree of homogeneity among those who suffer from inadequate income. A major step in policy formulation is to recognize and react to the diversity among the poor. Unfortunately, social-science information is very deficient. This chapter is consequently a beginning effort to provide a way of thinking about the heterogeneity of the poor in affluent America.

Two approaches, not always clearly noted, are employed in defining the new working class. One approach emphasizes the definition of groups in terms of "class" characterizations, especially economic role or income. The other employs "cultural" or "status" criteria such as style of life. The Hollingshead index—occupation, education, place of residence—is in the tradition of the first approach.[1] Walter Miller's discussion[2] of "the lower-class subculture" is along the lines of the second. Social workers' discussions of the "lower-class client" and the "multi-problem family" almost always employ style-of-life indicators.

The two approaches intertwine but seem to make independent contributions to clarifying the characteristics of the new working class. Consequently, we have brought them together in an effort to move away from a broadly and vaguely defined "lower class" into a specification of types of new working-class individuals. The effort is to utilize class and status variables in categorizing a population. The combination of the two produces problems, but these may be overweighed by the difficulties and obscurities produced by the current shifting between the two sets of dimensions in discussing groupings and issues: Walter Miller's "lower class"[3] is not Lee Rainwater's nor Oscar Lewis'.[4]

Obviously other dimensions such as education or region should also be employed. Class and status dimensions should be more carefully marked off than in the following discussion. Unfortunately the material to do an adequate job is still lacking. Our purpose here is to begin to approach the problem of specifying the differentiation within the poor.

The Class Criterion

The advantage of using an economic indicator in defining the new working class is that it specifies a political-economic category to which legislation and other remedial programs could be devoted. Emphasis on style-of-life indicators can be confusing because the meaning of an attitude or behavior or what it leads to can be quite different for the rich, for the middling well off, for those "getting by," and for the poor. The same behavior may have different roots and consequences in varying milieus.

On the other hand, the class or occupational criterion is not so clear cut as it appears. Some unskilled workers have stable, fairly well-paid jobs and are thus not a pressing social or economic problem. (This is particularly true where the unskilled worker is employed in a unionized, mass-production factory.) Many semiskilled and fewer skilled workers suffer some degree of irregularity of employment, especially because of seasonal factors. Another problem is that a considerable number (35 to 50 per cent) of poor families, as we have noted in Chapter 2, have no member in the labor force.[5]

Consequently, we would suggest that today an income criterion is more useful than an occupational criterion in the definition of the new working class. The recent analyses of poverty in the United States can be employed for this purpose. The level of income defining poverty varies depending on family size, composition, age, region, type of community. For our purposes, we can handle some of these complexities and follow Orshansky who puts the poverty line around $3,000, adjusted for several family characteristics.[6] The Orshansky lines are probably too low. It is this population which could be called "low income."

The advantage of utilizing the economic criterion, and particularly the income definition, is that it specifies a socioeconomic category toward which policy can be directed. For example, Morgan reports,[7] following Lampman's earlier lead, that $10 billion would bring all spending units now below the poverty line to an income level above poverty. Questions of the distribution of income and of social services can be pinpointed then in terms of how they affect this population.

Obviously, income levels and sources of incomes vary considerably among the "low-income" population. Keyserling distinguishes between the very poor, the poor, and a higher-income group who suffer what he terms "deprivation" but not outright poverty. The low-income are not basically a "welfare poor." Only one-fifth of Morgan's poor receive welfare assistance. Social scientists and social-service specialists who write of the "welfare poor" are discussing only a slice of the poor; those concerned with "hard-core" and "multi-problem families" are, in turn, analyzing only a very thin wedge of this small slice.

The income criterion has several components: the level of income, the stability or regularity of income, the source of income (employment or welfare). A number of observers believe that it makes a difference, holding income constant, whether a family is supported by welfare or not. The knowledge to make a fine classification of these components is lacking. We have resorted, therefore, to combining them into one indicator of economic security (roughly combining income and stability), and then split this indicator into the two simple dimensions of high (security) and low (insecurity). This procedure is inadequate.[8] But we cannot at present describe each permutation of what should be a set of eight or sixteen possibilities. We think, however, that four types can be usefully discussed. These four types should rapidly be expanded and refined as we acquire more knowledge and understanding.

The Style-of-Life Criterion

The style-of-life variable also offers difficulties. It refers at least to attitudes and behavior in the areas of family relationships and consumption patterns. Evaluative judgments (as implied in the concepts

of "family disorganization," "social disorganization," or "family instability") are invariably involved. As yet, it is not possible to formulate
a clean-cut classification which avoids cultural biases and still is able
to render a judgment about the impact of life style on individuals.
For example, does the absence of a permanent male figure mean that the
family is inevitably "unstable" and that children are necessarily
psychologically deformed by living in such a family? Assessments
such as these are difficult to make because much of our knowledge and
theorizing about fatherless families is based on middle-class situations.

We employ the notion of "familial stability-instability" to sum-
marize a variety of elements in the style of life. Familial-stability
patterns are characterized by families coping with their problems—the
children are being fed, though not necessarily on a schedule; the family
meets its obligations so that it is not forced to keep on the move;
children are not getting into much more trouble than other children
of the neighborhood. These are not satisfactory indicators; they are,
at best, suggestive of the kind of behavior which is characteristic of
stability among the "low-income." The aim is to be able to describe
the degrees of effectiveness of different styles of life in handling the
same environment. Our vocabulary is inadequate for this task.

Class and Status

The two approaches can be welded together by cross-tabulating the
two dimensions of the two variables of economic security and familial
stability in a two-by-two table:

Types of Economic Security and Familial Stability

			Familial	
			Stability	Instability
			(+) High	(−) Low
Economic	Security	(+) High	++(1)	+−(2)
	Insecurity	(−) Low	−+(3)	−−(4)

Cell 1 is referred to as the stable poor; cell 2, the strained; cell 3,
the copers, and cell 4, the unstable.

To some extent, life-cycle stages may be involved here, as some young people escape from cell 4 via cell 2 or cell 3 to cell 1, a more stable pattern, and beyond. Or families may drop with age from cell 1 to cell 3, where they have lower economic security but maintain family stability.

Each of the cells contains many variants. While we believe the four types are an improvement over analysis in terms of "*the* lower class" or "*the* poor," it is important to recognize that each type has many variations. One difference, of course, is whether the family is stationary in its particular pattern or moving to greater or less security stability. Our general orientation is to emphasize flux rather than assuming a permanent position in a pattern.

THE STABLE POOR

Cell 1, *the stable poor,* is characterized by stability, economically and familially. This cell points to the regularly employed, low-skill, stable poor families.

Farm and rural nonfarm persons undoubtedly make up the bulk of the stable poor since they are the majority of the American poor: a recalculation of Morgan's data suggests that only 30 per cent of the poor live in metropolitan areas. The majority of all the poor and of the stable poor are white rural Southern populations. In addition, the nonurban poor are probably represented in this cell to a greater extent than they are among all the poor. Aged persons are also over-represented and constitute a large part of the downwardly mobile since most of them were better off at earlier points in their lives. Leftover second- and third-generation immigrant populations in large cities are probably underrepresented.[9]

A number of Negro families are of the stable poor. They have higher social status in the Negro community than their economic counterparts have in the white community because of the general scaling down of incomes and occupational levels of Negroes in the United States. For reasons discussed in the previous chapter, Negroes and other discriminated groups are probably becoming more important politically as well as in relative size among the urban stable poor.

The children of cell 1 families are most likely of all the children of the poor to be educationally and occupationally mobile. Cell 1 might be the "takeoff" cell, the phase necessary before many can really make a big advance. But this is a dangerous metaphor, for obviously many youth from families in more difficult circumstances are able to make considerable gains.

The stable poor, then, are a varied group; one component, the aged, has a poor economic future, except to the extent that social-security and old-age payments improve, and a declining future as an intact family unit.

THE STRAINED

Cell 2, *the strained*, portrays a secure economic pattern, but an unstable family one. This might be a life-cycle problem, i.e., at certain points the families of low-wage, unskilled workers are likely to exhibit unstable patterns. Examples might be "wild" younger workers or alcoholic older workers who disturb family functioning. Or the pattern could manifest the beginning of a move into cell 4, as a low-income family finds increasing difficulty in maintaining its economic security because of family and personal problems or the economic situation. Obviously, the two possibilities may be closely connected.

Movement may be viewed inter-generationally as well as in terms of life-cycle patterns. Many of the offspring of strained families may fail to match the economic security of their parents and experience inter-generational skidding.[10]

Strained familial relations may not, however, result in skidding. In earlier periods, immigrant groups faced considerable internal strain arising from the conflict between the younger and older generations in the course of acculturation. Nonetheless, the second generation generally improved its economic circumstances. The instability of today's strained families is regarded as more "pathological" than that of the immigrant populations, although some social-work accounts of families at the turn of the century differ little from current reports of "poor family functioning." The current analysis stresses fighting and drinking of adults, illicit sexual relations of parents, and neglect or brutality toward the children. Whether the economically secure and familially unstable are characterized by these patterns is not clear. If they are not, then, the offspring of the strained family may not be a prey to skidding. Further, not all children of deeply conflicted or hostile families are inevitably unable to maintain or improve their economic position.

We have looked at cell 2 as a transitional condition. This view may be misleading: many families persist with a low but steady income and a great deal of internal strain.

THE COPERS

The copers of cell 3 manifest economic insecurity and familial stability—families and individuals having a rough time economically but managing to keep themselves relatively intact. This group probably increases considerably during extensive layoffs. Probably a considerable number of Negroes are in this group and their children are more likely to be mobile than those living in strained situations.

The copers probably contain a disproportionate number of families which have been downwardly mobile. Both Morgan[11] and we[12] have shown the sizable number of sons of nonmanual workers who end up in manual (and sometimes low-income) positions. In Great Britain, 40 per cent of those born in nonmanual families move into manual occupations. Many of these downwardly mobile are probably more likely to retain a stable family style than others in the same economic predicament. As in many other situations, however, a minority of the downwardly mobile may manifest extreme familial instability, which would place them in cell 4. Limited data suggest that children of downwardly mobile families have a better chance of rising occupationally than children of families which have been at this low level for some generations.[13]

THE UNSTABLE

In cell 4 *the unstable* have neither economic nor personal stability. It is this group which is probably most generally called "the lower class" by sociologists and regarded as "the poor" by the public. Within the unstable group there are degrees of stability and strain—not every family is a "hard-core case" nor has a "multi-agency problem." Nor do we have sufficient long-term data to assert that once in cell 4, always in cell 4. The citing of data on "the inheritance of welfare" as evidence of the perpetuation is frequently naïve. Those children who leave poverty are ignored in centering on those who do not. The former group is undoubtedly larger than the latter.

It may be that families and individuals occasionally manifest both economic and personal instability, then overcome these problems for a while. Later they may again suffer from illness, unemployment, emotional upset, or familial instability.

As important in some ways as distinguishing cell 4 from the other three cells which make up the new working class is to note that cell 4 is a very varied grouping. In it are partially urbanized Negroes new to the North and cities, remaining slum residents of ethnic groups which have largely moved out of the slums, long-term (inter-generational) poor white families, the déclassé of Marx. Also included are the physically handicapped and the aged who have dropped through the class structure. The low-income class generally and the unstable in particular are a category of unskilled, irregular workers, broken and large families, and a residual bin of the aged, physically handicapped, and mentally disturbed.

Prospects

In some cases, social characteristics handicap low-income groups: recent rurality (unfamiliarity and lack of skills with urban problems) and discrimination. These groups—Negroes, former mountaineer whites—would have the worst problems. They would also have per-haps the greatest potential because removing their social limitations would lead to big change. Their handicaps are less self-inflicted and self-sustaining. This may not be so true for mountaineer whites as for Negroes. Aside from people dropping into the poverty class along the life-and-physical cycle, the whites in the lower class who have no good, i.e., social, reason for being there are likely to be slowest to advance environmentally.

Hylan Lewis[14] has suggested the categories of clinical, preclinical, and sub-clinical to delineate patterns among the poor. We would substitute the word "chronic" for "clinical." The chronics refer to long-term dependents, part of whom would be the "hard core"; the pre-chronics would be a high-risk group which is moving toward a chronic situation but have not yet become chronically dependent. The sub-chronics are those who have many characteristics of dependence but have a greater ability to cope with their problems.[15]

A number of forces can lead individuals into chronic dependence.

New working-class life is crisis life, constantly trying to make do with string where rope is needed. Anything can break the string. Illness is one of the most important—"Got a job but I got sick and lost it"; "We managed until the baby got sick." The great incidence of physical afflictions among the poor—frequently unknown to the victim—is obvious to any casual observer. Particularly striking are the diseased teeth of many. The tendency of poor people to somaticize their emotional difficulties may be influenced by the omnipresence of illness.

Familial and personal instability may be the sources as well as the consequences of difficulties. While some frequent concomitants of low-income life such as matrifocality (dominating mother—weak or absent father) do not inevitably produce grave difficulties in family life, they frequently do. Alcoholism, an inability to handle aggression, hostility, or dependence—one's own or other's toward one—can deeply disturb family functioning. A variety of direct personal aid may be necessary.

Sophistication along these lines of analysis has frequently tended to denigrate the importance of structural or social factors in producing "personal inadequacies," "social disabilities," "familial instability." The work of Raymond Smith[16] and Edith Clarke[17] strongly suggests that illegitimacy is related to economic conditions—the better the economic conditions among the "lower-class" Negroes of the Caribbean, the lower the rate of illegitimacy. Kunstadter[18] similarly argues that matrifocality as a "lower-class" trait is related to a particular set of economic characteristics.

Prolonged unemployment, irregular employment, and low income are important forces leading to a chronic pattern. Low-paid and irregularly employed individuals do not develop an image of the world as predictable and as something with which they are able to cope. Controlling or directing events appears (and frequently is) an unattainable achievement. When they suffer long-term unemployment, they are less likely than other unemployed who have had the experience of fairly regular employment to maintain a personal stability. (Maslow[19] has argued that those who have had a stable past are more able to manage in disastrous circumstances than those who have had considerable prior deprivation.) A high-employment economy has relatively fewer "hard-core" cases than a low-employment economy. The American community studies suggest that the "lower class" is smaller in times of prosperity than in periods of depression. Peter Townsend has noted that during the 1930's in England it was believed that 500,000 to 1,000,000 of those not working were "unemployable."

In 1940, with the pressures of the war, it was discovered that only 100,000 were really unemployables. Structural changes would be of great importance in reducing chronic dependence.

Strategies

Three basic policies are possible: (1) direct economic change, such as providing better employment, or directly raising incomes through the provision of a national minimum level of income; (2) direct services, such as case-work activities to strengthen the ego functioning of the individual or family assistance through homemaker help or job training; (3) indirect change by affecting the climate—social, psychological, political—of the neighborhoods in which the poor live.

What would lead one type of a low-income population in a given direction would not work at all for another type. A panacea does not work because there is no one thing which will have a pervasive impact in all cases. What is dynamic for one type may be insignificant for others.

We find the concept of elasticity useful here.[20] It points to the amount of change resulting from additional services or income. Some types of the poor have high-income elasticity—a little change in income produces a big change in behavior; other types may have low-income elasticity but have high-education elasticity or high case-work elasticity. Still other types will respond rapidly and deeply to new housing, to a steady job, to counseling, or a package of such ingredients rather than to, say, case work. The concept of elasticity introduces frontally the issues of variable remedies for different types. The issues of costs, substitution and choice of different services or resources are made vivid by the notion of elasticity and productivity (the return per unit of expenditure).

The stable, those in cell 1, would be immediately helped if their incomes were raised so that they came closer to the American standard of life. Unionization of their industries (especially in service trades and occupations) shifts from low-productivity land and industries to high-productive industries, and occupational retraining would be important. In some situations, individuals have to be prepared for retraining (where, for example, the level of literacy is low) or aided in moving to new localities where opportunities are greater. They may need help in adjusting to new urban conditions, but this adjustment would probably not be very difficult where jobs and housing were adequate. The stable poor, in short, would have a high-income elasticity, rapidly improving and adjusting to increases in their income.

The inadequacy of social services and payments in the United States forces many into cell 1. Improving and extending welfare and social-security payments, which keep many in penury and are unavailable to many others, would move many from cells 2, 3, and 4 into cell 1 and lead many of the stable poor into the main society. A guaranteed income would alleviate many though not all of the problems of many of the poor. Harrington[21] and Titmuss[22] have pointed out that social services in the United States and Britain do not seem to be benefiting the poor as much as the middle classes. Obviously, changes in social policy are necessary here.

Some of the strained of cell 2 might require some case-work help in improving family conditions and operations, but other approaches might be effective. If they live in a locality that manifests high rates of disturbances, they might be helped by moving to new areas. For some, an improvement in economic conditions may be necessary in order to get deeper family changes. Undoubtedly, a number are not sensitive to income changes or to neighborhood climate change and sustained case-work help would be necessary.

Familial instability may be a carry-over from an earlier period when the family suffered from economic insecurity; the family has not caught up with its economic improvements. But, as Seymour S. Bellin and Jerome Cohen have pointed out, in some families where economic conditions have improved after a long period of economic deprivation and family difficulties, withdrawing the stress of economic insecurity may be insufficient. The toll of the stress frequently must be overcome. Special help may be necessary to bring about familial changes of great importance. The adaptation of social agencies would be important so that they are able to meet the requirements of these families at the time of need and to provide aid in ways which fit the family's outlook.

The copers of cell 3, who maintain family stability in the face of grave economic difficulties, obviously need economic aid. Many of them would be helped by improvement in income programs; others, where there is a working head of household, would be advanced by regularization of work and/or shifting to more remunerative fields. The needs of the stable and the copers would seem to be similar. Improvement on the economic dimension would push more of the copers into the mobility possibilities of the stable poor of cell 1 and beyond.

Cell 4, the unstable, is the most-discussed grouping of the poor today. Many, if not most, are on welfare allotments; women head many of the family units. A general improvement in economic conditions would not have much economic impact on the unstable because they are largely out of the labor force and out of the economy. It is widely believed that unstable families do not have a high-income elasticity, but the evidence is not strong. Specific programs aimed at this group would be important. Present-day welfare services are insufficient since they have largely been budgetary and policing activities. Concentration on improving the educational achievement of the youth of these families would be more important, perhaps, than a diffuse effort to achieve better family functioning.[23] A number of interesting and aggressive case-work services have been offered; their degree of long-term success is unclear. A variety of direct services may be effective with some of these families—including continuous homemaking and baby-sitting services, provisions of nurseries, all-day schools, and consumer buying protection.

It may be that a less direct approach would be effective. It would involve trying to mobilize politically the communities in which the unstable live with the more stable poor so as to provide greater feelings of strength and control. The anticipated but side effect would be the improving of family conditions. A general change in a low-income community precipitated perhaps by the mobile, the strained, and the copers, may spread to affect the unstable of the community. But feelings of powerlessness will be produced if a movement does not produce material improvements. Actions in the mid-sixties along these lines were frequently miscued, as we learn in section IV. The social actionists, of whom Saul Alinsky is the best known, have this implicit strategy of strengthening feelings of control.

In all of the strategies it is necessary to be clear about who exactly is the target population. This is frequently determined on the basis of the numbers involved, although there is always the delicate choice of helping a lot of people a little or a few people a lot. The second step is to discover what works with whom. There is probably nothing that will help all of the poor in one move although, as suggested above, a steady, meaningful, well-paid job as a general base of action should not be underestimated. A decent level of living as the minimal responsibility of an affluent society, no matter what people do around this level, may be an important point to maintain in a period when government welfare payments are under criticism. But there are some things that will help certain types. We have to find the right things for the right groups at the right time.

Cause and Consequence

A good deal of the tone of discussions of the new working class, even by sociologists, has a negative quality. On the other hand, a few seem to have a romantic feeling about the "lower class," particularly their juvenile delinquents, and see them as rebels against the horrors of middle-class conformist America. The former view suffers from the assumption that they have little potential for change; the latter, that there is nothing better in present-day America to which they can change.

Among other things, the glorification theme ignores the impact on the new working class of its limited education. [24] The negative view frequently confuses, as Keyserling has noted, cause and consequence. The personal instability of many new working-class persons may be a consequence of economic instability as well as a cause of it. The chain of cause and effect over time frequently becomes blurred. Where is there an effective way of cutting into the chain so that change will occur? That becomes the issue. Our feeling is that structural forces have been underplayed recently while "the culture of poverty" has been overstressed.

The negative view has the danger of not seeing positive elements in the new working-class life. By ignoring these elements, social policies can frequently worsen them. For example, in an exciting study of a Puerto Rican slum, Helen Icken Safa has reported the community and familial solidarity of the residents of a slum barrio. When families were moved into public housing, community ties were weakened. The project social workers centered on the wife. The husband's role and responsibility in the family and community diminished.[25]

It is perhaps a "heuristic" fallacy to believe that low-income people are willing and capable of positive change. This is not always true, but if professionals and social reformers lack confidence in the poor, little can be accomplished in the social services or in political action. One might fail with this optimism—as we frequently do—but without it, it is doubtful if anything can be moved. Frequently, disenchantment and cynicism capture accurately a slice of life. They are also immobilizing, for they ignore the constructive and energizing role of hope.[26]

Conclusion

A clearly defined poverty class does not exist—it is a varied, changing group as Peter Townsend has noted:

> A misconception is that in a relatively prosperous society most individuals have the capacity to meet any contingency in life. Only a poor and handicapped minority need special protection or help. This ignores the infinite diversities and changing conditions to be found in any population. Men gain or fall in status and living standards; at one stage of their life their dependencies are minimal, at others unduly numerous; sometimes they need exceptional help to achieve qualifications and skills held to be desirable by society; and at all times they are susceptible to the vicissitudes of prolonged ill-health, disability, redundancy of unemployment, and bereavement, which they are usually powerless to control or even reasonably anticipate. Unanticipated adversity is not the peculiar experience of one fixed section of the working class.[27]

In England, Dahrendorf contends,[28] the unskilled category is a temporary position—individuals at various stages of the life cycle may drop into it, but only for a comparatively few is it a permanent position. In the United States, this is not so true, and if caste pressures grow, it will be even less true.

The changing economy of America is producing new property relations; at the same time it is producing new working classes and lower classes.[29] The analysis of data and the development of our concepts have not kept up with the increasing differentiation within these populations. Many pressures and counterpressures exist in every stratum. Despite a modal pattern, considerable variety in values and behavior occurs. Since cross-pressures affect the "lower class" to a considerable extent,[30] we should look for types of behavior patterns even among people apparently very similar in objective characteristics. Those at the social bottom see only a vague and ill-defined "them" up there—and those above believe that those below are all rather similar. But the tops know how much differentiation within the top actually takes place; the bottoms are aware of much more differentiation than are the outsiders looking in. In particular, what has been taken as typical of the most unstable bottom group has been generalized to apply to all who are poor or manual workers.

We must begin to demarcate types of poor people more sharply if we are to be able to understand and interpret behavior and circumstance and to develop appropriate social policies. Evaluations of commentators are frequently masked as description. Ways of coping with hard reality are interpreted as normatively prescribed when they frequently are weakly dissanctioned behavior.

The resurgence of interest in the poor augurs well for a rethinking of the new kind of poverty in the "Welfare State," which is unlike the mass unemployment of the 1930's or the grinding poverty of the employed workers of the nineteenth century. Our "received wisdom" should be superseded by new categories and concepts. New wine is being poured into old conceptual bottles and the specialness of the new is being lost.

NOTES

1. August B. Hollingshead and Fredrick C. Redlich, *Social Class and Mental Illness: A Community Study* (New York: John Wiley & Sons, 1958), pp. 387–397.

2. Walter Miller, "Lower Class Culture as a Generating Milieu of Gang Delinquency," *Journal of Social Issues*, XIV (1958), 6, footnote 3. In his penetrating analysis, Miller notes the existence of "subtypes of lower-class culture" but does not pursue this point. While his emphasis is on cultural characteristics such as "female-based" household and "serial monogamy" mating patterns, he elsewhere employs educational, occupational, and income variables to define the lower class. See his "Implications of Urban Lower-Class Culture for Social Work," *Social Service Review*, XXXIII (September 1959), 229ff. His major stress is on cultural or status characteristics as defining the lower-class culture.

3. Miller, "Lower Class Culture."

4. Lee Rainwater assisted by Karol Kane Weinstein, *And the Poor Get Children* (Chicago: Quadrangle, 1960). Oscar Lewis, *The Children of Sanchez* (New York: Random House, 1961). See also the distinctions made within the lower-lower class by Martin Loeb, "Social Class and the American Social System," *Social Work*, VI (April 1961), 6.

5. Conference on Economic Progress, *Poverty and Deprivation in the United States*, Washington, D.C., 1961; the main author of this analysis is Leon Keyserling, and it is known as the "Keyserling Report." Robert J. Lampman, "The Low Income Population and Economic Growth," Study Paper No. 12, Joint Economic Committee of Congress, December 16, 1959. Mollie Orshansky, "Who's Who Among the Poor: A Demographic View of Poverty," *Social Security Bulletin* (July 1965).

6. Mollie Orshansky, *ibid.*

7. James N. Morgan *et al.*, *Income and Welfare in the United States* (New York: McGraw-Hill, 1962).

8. Not all families receiving welfare assistance should automatically be classified in the economically insecure category. For the aged, perhaps, welfare assistance does not constitute a lack of security. In general, however, the fact of welfare assistance would put a family in the economically insecure category.

9. Richard Cloward and Lloyd Ohlin, *Delinquency and Opportunity* (Glencoe, Ill.: The Free Press, 1960).

10. Dennis Wrong, in a personal communication, has influenced this and the following paragraph. "Skidding" is discussed in Harold Wilensky and Hugh Edwards, "The Skidder: Ideological Adjustments of Downward Mobile Workers," *American Sociological Review*, XXIV (April 1959), 215–231.

11. Morgan, *op. cit.*

12. S. M. Miller, "Comparative Social Mobility," *Current Sociology*, IX (1960), 1–89.

13. *Ibid.*, 32–33.

14. Hylan Lewis, "Child Rearing Among Low Income Families," Washington Center for Metropolitan Studies, June 8, 1961. This paper and others by Lewis are among the most stimulating on the problems of low-income patterns. Also see Hyman Rodman, "The Lower-Class Value Stretch," *Social Forces*, vol. XLII (December 1963).

15. We have used the terms "dependent" and "dependence" here for want of a sharper term; we find the concept of dependence murky and frequently used to cover a variety of conditions which a writer does not like.

16. Raymond T. Smith, *The Negro Family in British Guiana* (London: Routledge & Kegan Paul, 1956).

17. Edith Clarke, *My Mother Who Fathered Me* (New York: Humanities Press, 1957).

18. Peter Kunstadter, "A Survey of the Consanguine and Matrifocal Family," *American Anthropologist*, LXV (February 1963), 56–66.

19. A. H. Maslow, *Motivation and Personality* (New York: Harper & Bros.), pp. 80–106.

20. Carlsson has introduced the concept of elasticity into sociological thinking. Gosta Carlsson, "Okonomische Ungleichheit und Lebenschanchen," *Kolner Zeitschrift fur Soziologie*, V (1961), 189–199.

21. Michael Harrington, *The Other America: Poverty in the United States* (New York: Macmillan, 1962).

22. Richard Titmuss, *Essays on "The Welfare State"* (London: George Allen & Unwin, 1958), Chapter 2, "The Social Division of Welfare"; and *Income Distribution and Social Change* (Toronto: University of Toronto Press, 1962). Although Titmuss is a seminal thinker in analyzing changes in the social structure of the modern society, he has been largely ignored by American sociologists.

23. Miller, "Poverty and Inequality in America."

24. Frank Riessman, *The Culturally Deprived Child* (New York: Harper & Bros., 1962).

25. Helen Icken Safa, *"From Shanty Town to Public Housing,"* Syracuse University Youth Development Center, 1962. The peculiar stresses of public housing life may be functional equivalents of the economic conditions of matrifocality discussed by Kunstadter.

26. See S. M. Miller and Frank Riessman, "Working Class Authoritarianism, A Critique of Lipset," *British Journal of Sociology* (September 1961).

27. Peter Townsend, "Freedom and Equality," *New Statesman*, LXI, No. 1570 (April 1961), 574.

28. Ralf Dahrendorf, *Unskilled Labor in British Industry*, unpublished Ph.D. thesis in sociology, London School of Economics, 1956, pp. 429–430.

29. S. M. Miller, "Poverty, Race and Politics," in Irving Louis Horowitz, ed., *The New Sociology: Essays on Social Values and Social Theory in Honor of C. Wright Mills* (New York: Oxford University Press, 1964).

30. See Miller and Riessman, "The Working-Class Subculture," and Hylan Lewis, *op. cit.*

4

"THE CULTURE OF POVERTY": A CRITIQUE

Social policies reflect social values, and social values reveal what is important to a group or a nation. Policies toward the outsiders, the poor, are especially revealing in depicting what is important to the predominant groups:

> The attitudes that Society adapts to its deviants and especially its poor and politically inarticulate deviants, reflects its ultimate values. . . . We must learn to understand the moral presuppositions underlying our action.[1]

For example, the British refused to offer much aid to the colony of Ireland during the potato famine of 1848 because aid was seen as interfering with the natural forces of economic law.[2] Economic myth permitted the triumph of disease and malnutrition over human life. Approximately 25 per cent of those seen by the voluntary agencies in England during this period were Irish vagrants. These agencies defined poverty as pauperism, a condition of moral defect which inhered in the individual. Only at the turn of the century was poverty as a condition of society discovered.

Even in our sophisticated society, we aim at providing minimum rather than adequate levels of financial aid to those who cannot support themselves because we are still fearful of sapping morale and incentive to work.

Views of the Poor

The way one looks upon the members of the new working class and how one regards the sources of their difficulties will affect the kinds of proposals one makes to improve conditions and how one implements proposals once they are made. Four major views of the poor seem to prevail: (1) the undeserving poor; (2) the self-defeating poor; (3) the victimized poor; (4) the culture of poverty.

The Undeserving Poor

Some believe, as Gladwin has commented,[3] that only selected segments of the poor are deserving of help. Others, as Alfred Doolittle declares in Shaw's *Pygmalion,* and in Lerner and Loewe's *My Fair Lady,* are an "undeserving poor," content in squalor, resistant to work, sponging off society. This view of the poor leads to efforts to reduce payments to the poor and to make them as uncomfortable as possible. The "Newburgh Incident" in that upstate New York town in 1961 illustrates the harshness that can prevail when the poor are considered as undeserving. Aged citizens on welfare were "mugged" (photographed) and forced to appear at the police station in order to get their checks as though they were committing an economic crime. Welfare assistance to young fathers of growing families was discontinued even when no work was available for them.

Some poor may be "undeserving" in the sense that they are not interested in being self-supporting, but this stricture is hardly relevant to the aged and the young children who made up more than 75 per cent of the almost 8 million welfare cases in this country.[4] Further, since less than a quarter of the new working class are supported by welfare, clearly most poor are "deserving." Nonetheless, the view of the poverty stricken as undeserving is undoubtedly common in the United States, affecting the extent and character of aid to the poor.

Present legislation supports this position. The 1962 and 1967 amendments to the Social Security Act are committed to the reduction of dependency, which is viewed as a personal defect and not as a consequence of the character of the economic organization of society.[5]

The Self-Defeating Poor

A variant of the "undeserving-poor" argument is that many, if not most, of the difficulties of the poor arise from the way in which they deal with their problems. Poverty becomes equated with incompetence.[6]

An essential part of this view of the new working class is the contention that they lack the ability to defer gratification.[7] This statement is a comparative one, with the middle classes as the contrasting standard-bearer. The middle classes are believed to be distinguished by the presence and significant operation of the ability to defer gratification, to accept later rewards instead of immediate satisfactions, to bank their impulses, and to plan effectively for the future. The non-middle classes are believed to be characterized by the absence of these abilities. To some extent, then, the deferred gratification pattern (DGP) statements are relative statements: the middle classes have more of the deferred patterns than do other classes (the upper classes are usually ignored in these discussions). Consequently, an examination must not only weigh the existence of the patterns among the poor but the degree of deficiency when compared with the middle classes.[8]

An undertone of the non-DGP analysis is that the pattern is not temporary nor easily overcome. Indeed, the assumption is that the ability or inability to defer gratification is deeply embedded in the personality dynamics of the individual, performing an important role in his psychodynamic economy. The picture seems to be that both the DGP and the non-DGP are developed through early life experiences: they become incorporated in the personality and are relatively impervious to situational factors.

There is growing evidence that the DGP analysis is not valid.[9] In addition to direct empirical questioning of the thesis, conceptual problems abound. First, in general statements about the absence of the DGP among the poor, the middle classes are frequently perceived in an outmoded way. They are regarded as delighting in hard work, frugally and carefully planning and budgeting activities and expenditures, abjuring debt, and constantly foregoing the indulgence of present gain in order to reap future rewards. It is hard to recognize this "Protestant Ethic" pattern in the new middle classes possessed by "other direction" and pursuing the consumption euphoria of today. The rise of consumer debt among the middle classes, the refrain of "not being able to make ends meet" despite affluent income levels, the competition between work and the coffee break, suggest that important changes have taken place in many sections of the middle classes—or is it that the middle classes were never quite as described? Consequently, the actual behavior of the poor is frequently compared with the official norms rather than the actual practice of the better off. Some official middle-class norms also may have changed, compounding the unreality of the comparison.[10]

Moreover, in order to compare the two groups' capacity to defer, one has to assume that they equally desire the deferred objectives, that they are making equal sacrifices in deferring, and that they have equal opportunity to realize success at the end of the deferment period.[11]

While the notion of a psychodynamically-based inability to defer gratification is probably not valid, it is true that low-income people have a shorter time span, and that they expect rewards to be visible, concrete, and soon. In our view, the narrowed time pattern arises from immediate conditions of life and is readily changeable. In the non-deferred view, this would be difficult to achieve because of the deep roots of the life pattern.

The view of "the self-defeating poor" emphasizes pathology and does not recognize strengths upon which to build.[12] It leads to a heavy emphasis upon individual rehabilitation rather than social change as a source of improvement. If the new working class is as unrelievedly badly off as these portrayals claim, then individual rehabilitation certainly is needed and extraordinarily difficult to achieve. The emphasis on pathology fails to explain what appear to be spontaneous positive developments of self-help and social action in low-income communities.

The view of the poor as incompetents leads to an emphasis upon training and retraining (for jobs and for social living) rather than upon opening up the job structure, providing basic services, and the like. Undoubtedly, some of the new working class are self-defeating, and individual counseling and personality probing may be necessary for some. But we do not share the easy assumption that most suffer from "inadequate personality," a phrase of dubious descriptive powers, or that a major source of poverty is the poor themselves.

Clark has well stated the possibilities of change among the poor:

> ... individuals and groups modify their behavior only to the degree and in the direction demanded by the external situation as it is perceived.

The internal determinants of behavioral changes are themselves the product of past external effects and are subject to modification by the continuous interaction of the organism in the situation. While to bring about a specified desired change in behavior within a given period of time may require a concern with the internal effects of past influences, the habituation of the verbalized attitudes, and just patterns of behavior, these factors do not operate as a permanent block to future changes but rather determine the strength and duration of the external pressures which are required to effect them. When these are determined and applied, appropriate relearning . . . occurs and is internalized and reinforced in the same way as the previously learned behavior.[13]

The Victimized Poor

The poor are the results of the ineffective or pernicious working of society, long-time discrimination, economic change destroying economic livelihood, the preying of unscrupulous landlords and businessmen in the slums,[14] inadequately remunerated work, and the neglect of government in providing adequate income and services to the poor.[15]

In this view, improving the conditions of the poor largely depends upon a commitment to all the poor, not just those likely to improve with little help. What is required is institutional change to provide more and better paid jobs, to widen and deepen the social-security and assistance schemes, to improve the educational systems, employment services, and other governmental activities. While some of the poor may need counseling, guidance, and social-work help to be able to take advantage of opportunity, the stress is on providing opportunity, rather than on preparing individuals to seize opportunity which may not exist. Social change rather than individual rehabilitation is the reference point.

The Culture of Poverty

All of these subgroups and others can be found among the poor. The question is, however, what are the major emphases and tendencies among the poor which might be a basis for policy? It is not just that many views of the poor have been undiscriminating, ignoring the wide variations which exist. The most popular view of a culture of poverty must be questioned. This view incorporates elements of the self-defeated perspective but is broader.

The "culture-of-poverty" thesis has three sources. As discussed above, Allison Davis and his coworkers have argued that the lower classes are less able to defer gratification. This inability to delay action in order to reap future rewards constrains against school and occupational success.[16] A second dimension of the thesis was added in the middle and late fifties, building from an analysis of delinquency. It was contended that a delinquent subculture developed because of the inability of low-income youth to find legitimate channels to achieve success in American society. Seeing that they "couldn't make it," they repudiated legitimated routes,[17] and followed, instead, less legitimate modes. (Other analyses of delinquency, however, argued that the values of the poor were not contra-cultural; they did not arise out of opposition to middle-class society, but, rather, out of the history and experiences of the poor themselves.[18] The poor do not reject the larger society but they possess a subculture centered around a different set of values.)

A third strand developed at the end of the decade with Oscar Lewis' intensive case studies of Mexican families in poverty.[19] In verbatim excerpts from fascinating, evocative interviews Lewis portrayed what he described as a "culture of poverty." This pattern of culture cut across societies, merging many of the world's poor into a life of apathy, failure, discontent, and anguish. Michael Harrington used this perspective in his important book, *The Other America:* "If a group has a will—if it has aspiration—it may live in dilapidated housing, it may eat an inadequate diet, and it may suffer poverty, but it is not impoverished. Even when there are programs designed to help the other Americans, the poor are held back by their own pessimism."[20]

These threads have been woven into a group tapestry of a monotonic, resistant-to-change, ineffective poor. There is obvious value in seeing the poor not as individual distillates but as influenced by interaction with other poor as well as with the rest of society. But we do find the tapestry insufficiently realistic.

In general, the new working classes have been seen to repeat this culture of poverty. Proponents of the vulgarized version of the "culture-of-poverty" position have failed to grasp Lewis' point: that he is talking about a slice of the poor, not all. The surge of Negroes in the so-called Negro revolution came as a surprise because low-income

Negroes were regarded, by and large, as living in the culture of poverty, incapable of self-action. While incapacitating elements do appear among the poor, significant non-destructive and non-debilitating features coexist.

If the culture of poverty is more than an interesting metaphor, it implies an inter-generational transmission of values and practices which inhibit constructive action. To some extent this does take place. But one should not neglect the number of times a family attempts to improve its conditions only to fail and finally to give up the struggle. "Apathy" is frequently a protective coating against repeated failure rather than the barrier to effort. As we understand the situation, contemporary experiences and difficulties, rather than inter-generational residues, are frequently more crucial in determining behavior.

A century ago it was argued that to provide the British poor with better housing would result in their putting coal in the bathtubs. They would not know how to use the new homes. This kind of inability to take advantage of new opportunity may exist, but it usually falls away rapidly for most of the poor. For example, Jaffe reports that birth-control methods are accepted with surprising rapidity by the poor who were supposed to be highly resistant to this kind of family planning.[21] Thus, the culture of poverty theme underestimates the changeability of many of the poor in new circumstances.

An Alternative View

Our assessment of the new working class—which, it should be said, is not widely accepted—is as follows:

1. Great variation occurs within the new working class.

2. There are important differences from many middle-class patterns. Many of the middle-class values, like success, are of less importance or have a different character and priority. "Getting by" is more important than "getting ahead" for most. Unemployment is not so stigmatizing an experience among the low-income population as among those better off. The former are in economically vulnerable positions and recognize unemployment as a recurring possibility mostly out of their control.

3. While many of these patterns and orientations are carried from

generation to generation, contemporary influences are decisive in maintaining them.

4. Many positive elements of strength, of coping, exist.

5. Many of the poor are open to change, to taking advantage of new possibilities. But in offering new possibilities, their experiences, orientations, and traditions must be considered.

While this assessment is less succinct and less pessimistically glamorous than the culture-of-poverty thesis, we feel that it is a more reasonable basis for the development of policy and action and change.

The Positives of the Poor

Many of the community antipoverty programs initiated by the Office of Economic Opportunity aim at helping the poor through encouraging their action on their own behalf. To be successful, these programs must consider the positives of the poor or else face an enormous contradiction in their thesis.

Initially the antipoverty crusade in its search for financial support found it useful to accent the ravages of poverty rather than the strengths of the poor. But that section of the poverty movement which calls for community organization by the poor in its own behalf is faced by a major dilemma if it simply stresses the plight of the poor. Because if the have-nots have nothing—no culture, no strength, no anger, no organization, no cooperativeness, no inventiveness, no vitality—if they are only depressed, apathetic, fatalistic, and pathological, then where is the force for the social action and self-help to come from?

Of course, if we believe that help for the poor is to come only from the outside, from above, to be patronizingly doled out, then we can stress only the great needs of the poor and request money to meet these needs. One wonders, however, whether there will be a sufficiently propelling force to win the enormous programs required, if the poor themselves are not deeply involved in generating these demands.

We do not mean to suggest that the poor spontaneously and without alignment with other groups and forces in the society are going to pull themselves up by their own bootstraps and produce Negro "revolutions," poverty movements, and revolutions in education and social service. These "revolutions" are a possibility and in some measure are in progress because of a combination of forces and groups. But without pressure from segments of the underclass these "revolutions" may, as is threatened in the civil-rights movement, remain watered down and unfulfilled.

Poverty has dialectic, uneven effects. In part, it produces apathy and pathology. In part, it produces strengths, some of which are glamorized and idealized by anti-middle-class proponents of the noble-savage myth. The strengths themselves are complex; often they are the reverse side of weaknesses. Thus the positive features found in the peer culture and the greater sibling interaction may arise from the limited time that the parents can spend with their children in large families; the greater freedom from intellectualization may stem from less access to intellectual occupations; the less prestige-centered, competitive, individualistic ethos may be derived from removal from the more individualistic professional occupations and preparatory educational structures; the proclivity for independence and self-education and the maturity of the children may be related to the fact that the poor are less educated by parents and teachers and hence forced to develop their own resources at an early age; the greater receptivity to therapeutic techniques based on suggestion and authority is probably the other side of their more authoritarian training and traditionalistic world view.

Comparison with the middle classes is dangerous because the new working classes and the middle classes face different problems. A middle-class yardstick generally should not be employed in appraising the characteristics of the disadvantaged. But in analyzing the origins of the strengths of the poor it is necessary to recognize that one of the sources is removal from some of the more harmful conditions of the life of the "haves." This argument becomes spurious only if one then attempts an over-all comparison of the classes and concludes that the "spiritualness" of poverty offsets the costs of deprivation.

The strengths of the new working classes arise out of their efforts at coping with an essentially negative environment. These efforts may in some cases lead to new difficulties, but it is important to view the behavior in terms of what the disadvantaged are trying to do rather than to place one-sided emphasis on their failures and pathology. Nor should these efforts be compared to standard middle-class behavior as though the latter were an available alternative.

For example, let us re-examine the so-called "broken" family or, more accurately, the female-based extended family structure, that presumably produces child neglect, disorganization, lack of male identification figures for the boys, and so forth. If we look at the situation carefully we see that economic and related historical factors have produced a condition in which job stability and security have been far less available for the Negro male than for the female. This threatens the traditional patriarchal family pattern. If nothing were done in face of this threat, disorganization, anarchy, and the disintegration of family life would eventuate. But among the Negro poor a new family pattern evolved, namely, the female-based, extended family structure where the mother, grandmother, aunts, and other members of the larger family frequently evidence considerable interdependence, organization, and stability. But it also has many constant strains and pressures, and sometimes these pressures produce "pathology" (drug addiction, violence, delinquency, and the like). Most likely this pathology erupts when the coping efforts embodied in the normative family pattern are not operative—when the family is really smashed.

The extended matriarchal or matrifocal family represents an important asset of the Negro poor. This is not to say that this is a "good" family pattern, one to be striven for in the long development of history. Quite the contrary: as poverty disappears this family form will undoubtedly be replaced by more patriarchal and equalitarian structures. But this should not prevent us from seeing that under special undesirable environmental conditions, the female-led, extended family is a powerful device for dealing with the problems of the poor.

Conceptualizations developed in the field of psychiatry also have important bearing on this issue of strengths and weaknesses. For example, it has come to be recognized that mental health and mental illness can coexist in the same individual. A person may have considerable pathology and at the same time have considerable strength. One is not the inverse of the other. In other words, it is not accurate to assume that because an individual has more pathology, that he has less strength or health. Health and pathology are both continuous and overlap each other. This conceptualization has enormous implications for social action because it draws attention to the need for concentrating on the health-producing aspects of an organism or group.

But the positives of the poor are not to be viewed in an abstract, idealistic fashion as though they represented some ultimate qualities to be aspired to by man. To repeat, frequently their strengths are partial, interwoven with weaknesses, transitory reflections of the situation of the poor.

There are a number of other sources for the strength of the poor:

1. The minority poor (Negro, Puerto Rican, Mexican) often preserve their ethnic traditions more fully than their richer brethren, who often shed their old cultural ways as they adapt to American middle-class life. Thus whatever strengths there are in the ethnic tradition probably remain with the poor.

2. Quite apart from any coping efforts or removal from middle-class conditions, the actual life of the poor results in many positive features of personality, style, and custom. A particular creative potential of the poor, namely, the physical, visual pattern, is probably related to their work-life and child-rearing experiences.

3. Traditions of various groups of the new working class often contain elements contributing to their strength. Negro history is important in this context as is Puerto Rican and Mexican tradition. Rural traditions might also be looked at in other ways than as non-preparation for urban life.

There are a great many positive dimensions of the culture and style of the poor: the cooperativeness and mutual aid that mark the extended family; the avoidance of the strain accompanying competitiveness and individualism; the equalitarianism, informality, and humor; the freedom from self-blame and parental overprotection; the children's enjoyment of each other's company and lessened sibling rivalry; the security found in the extended family and a traditional outlook; the enjoyment of music, games, sports, and cards; the ability to express anger; the freedom from being word-bound; and finally the physical style involved in learning.

Hardheaded and Complex-Minded

What we have said about the positives of the new working class may subject us to great criticism and some misunderstanding, for invariably when the strengths of the poor are mentioned, an immediate image springs to mind. The image is that of the "noble savage"—uninhibited, enjoying nature, unfettered by the responsibilities of middle-class life. People respond to this image in what appear to be two diametrically opposed ways, both of which are harmful to serious understanding. On the one hand are the romantic supporters of the supposedly impulse-free poor. Their view is typically contaminated by pervasive anti-middle-class sentiments and invidious class comparisons to enhance the qualities of the have-nots. This admiration of the poor is rooted, not in the struggles of the disadvantaged themselves, but rather in their removal from the disagreeable elements of middle-class life—whether these be inhibitions, competitiveness, disloyalty, pretentiousness, or boredom.

Those who oppose this view ridicule the "positives of the poor" and can see no meaning in the concept other than the "noble-savage" interpretation. Recognizing that the poor are not uninhibited, do experience serious strains, and want no part of poverty, this view holds that an emphasis on the strengths of the poor is sentimental drivel and naïvely anti-middle class.

Both of these viewpoints painfully miss the point. The "noble-savage" frame of reference is misleading and harmful to the poor and actually represents a misplaced argument about the pros and cons of middle-class life rather than a central concern for the deprived.

We are neither making an over-all assessment of middle-class life nor exalting poverty. Neither praise nor condemnation is the issue. Rather, we assert that efforts to improve the material conditions of the new working class have to be built on what is positive among the poor. The critics of this view like to pride themselves on being hard-headed in their analyses, unmoved by emotion and ideology in interpreting events. In many cases, their hardheadedness becomes a simple-mindedness, equating the press of environment with what happens to people and asserting that all dissenters from their analysis of the needs of the poor are naïve romantics. We think a more complex view is needed than this simple "tough-minded" approach.

The views that we expound have frequently been linked by critics to the notions of those who espouse poverty as a way of life which is preferable to the rat race. That is not our view. Nor would we want to make decisions for poor people as to what kind of life they want to live. We want to maximize the range of choice, not narrow it.

In our perspective, the possibilities and positives of the poor have to be considered in selecting, developing, and conducting programs. Increasingly, the poor will be demanding—and should have a legal right —to affect policy decisions which affect them. To utilize the present outlook of the poor is not to be bound by it. But to ignore it leads to irrelevance and likely failure.

In the current stress on the inadequacies and weaknesses of the poor, we are in danger of moving from the position of hereditary defects as the source of poverty to cultural inadequacies. Having successfully overcome the dangers of a biological approach, we are now facing the dangers of a cultural approach that stresses the defects of the poor and does not focus on the possibilities of change.

For example, it has been said that the poor are "unreachable," that they will not "utilize" services offered to them. Cultural explanations of these limitations are offered. As a result, for a period there was diminished effort to expand services in many low-income communities. The experiences of the antipoverty programs are revealing here: in most communities where there has been an effort to deliver services in the neighborhoods of poverty, there has been an enormous run on these services. This has been true among the "hard-to-reach" Puerto Ricans and Negroes of the South Bronx who have flocked to the Lincoln Hospital Neighborhood Service Centers, and among the "too proud" Appalachian whites who overloaded the facilities of a rural service center in the poorest county of West Virginia. The problem of "inadequate utilization" has inhered more in the absence, the irrelevancy, or the inhospitality of the service than in the reluctance of the poor.

But we are not arguing that just providing needed services will solve all the problems of the poor. Nor do we believe that employment or services will completely do the job. We ourselves are divided as to whether high-level employment and adequate income would solve most of the problems of 80 per cent or 50 per cent of the poor today.[22] But we are convinced that the way jobs and services are offered must consider the traditions, style, and positives of the poor. Emphasizing the positives of the outlook and behavior of the poor is part of a strategy for getting more effective changes.

Broad economic programs will solve most of the problems of many or most of the poor, but not all of the problems of all of the poor. There is much to be done outside of economic change, particularly if we wish to strengthen the social-service, educational, and political components of well-being. An emphasis on pathology and inertia can be a stubborn "crackpot realism," confusing monocular sight with a telescope.

NOTES

1. Richard Titmuss in the foreword to A. F. Philip and Noel Timms, *The Problems of the Problem Family* (London: Family Service Units, 1957).

2. Cecil Woodham-Smith, *The Great Hunger* (New York: Harper and Row, 1962).

3. Thomas Gladwin, "An Anthropologist Looks at Poverty," *Social Welfare Forum* (New York: Columbia University Press, 1963).

4. The median age of aged persons receiving OAA is 76.4; the median age of children receiving AFDC is 8.6, and more than three-quarters of all children are under the age of thirteen.

5. "1956 Amendments to the Social Security Act: After the New Look—the First Thought," *Journal of Public Law*, VI (1957), 123.

6. Rowntree, in his conceptualization of poverty, referred to "secondary poverty" as arising not from inadequate incomes, but because "some portion (of income) is absorbed by other expenditures, either useful or wasted." See Rowntree, *Poverty and Progress* (London: Longmans, Green, 1941), pp. 101–103.

7. See Louis Schneider and Sverre Lysgaard, "The Deferred Gratification Pattern: A Preliminary Study," *American Sociological Review*, XVIII (April 1953), 142–149. Sverre Lysgaard, "Social Stratification and the Deferred Pattern," *Proceedings*, World Congress of Sociology, Liege, International Sociological Association, 1953, p. 142. Allison Davis, *Social Class Influences upon Learning* (Cambridge: Harvard University Press, 1949).

8. We shall not discuss the social value of the DGP and the possible individual and social prices exacted by them. Paul Goodman has questioned the gain in impulse renunciation. Indeed, some of those who pioneered the concept of deferred gratification, such as Allison Davis, were extremely critical of the price the middle classes paid for their impulse renunciation, but felt that it would be well for the less affluent to pay this price in order to advance.

9. The literature on this subject is analyzed in S. M. Miller, Arthur Seagull, and Frank Riessman, "The Deferred Gratification Pattern: A Critical Appraisal," in Louis Ferman, Joyce Kornbluh, and Alan Haber, eds., *Poverty in America* (Ann Arbor: University of Michigan Press, 1965).

10. For changes in child-rearing practices in the middle classes, see Urie Bronfenbrenner, "Socialization and Social Class through Time and Space," in Eleanor E. Maccoby, Theodore M. Newcomb, and Eugene L. Hartley, eds., *Readings in Social Psychology* (New York: Henry Holt, 1958).

11. S. M. Miller and Frank Riessman, "The Working-Class Subculture: A New View," *Social Problems*, IX, No. 1 (1961), and Miller, Riessman, and Seagull, *op. cit.*

12. Our perspective has long been to raise the question of discovering strengths as a basis for promoting change. See Frank Riessman, *The Culturally Deprived Child* (New York: Harper and Row, 1962).

13. Kenneth Clark, "De-Segregation: An Appraisal of the Evidence," *The Journal of Social Issues*, IX, No. 4 (1953), 76.

14. David Caplovitz, *The Poor Pay More* (New York: The Free Press of Glencoe, 1963), portrays sharp business practices which fleece the poor.

15. Patricia Sexton has described the comparative disadvantages of educational facilities in low-income areas. *Education and Income* (New York: Viking Press, 1961).

16. Allison Davis has espoused this position in a number of papers: Allison Davis, "Child Rearing in the Class Structure of American Society," in *The Family in a Democratic Society*, Anniversary Papers of the Community Service Society of New York (New York: Columbia University Press, 1949); Ruth Cavan, *The American Family* (New York: Thomas Y. Crowell, 1953), pp. 182–183; Allison Davis, "Socialization and Adolescent Personality," in Swanson, Newcomb, and Hartley, *op. cit.*

17. Albert K. Cohen, *Delinquent Boys: The Culture of the Gang* (Glencoe: The Free Press, 1955).

18. Walter Miller, "Lower Class Culture as a Generating Milieu of Gang Delinquency," *Journal of Social Issues*, XIV (April 1959).

19. Oscar Lewis, *The Children of Sanchez* (New York: Random House, 1961); and *Five Families: Mexican Case Studies in the Culture of Poverty* (New York: Basic Books, 1959). He continued this mode of analysis in *La Vida: A Puerto Rican Family in the Culture of Poverty* (New York: Random House, 1966).

20. Michael Harrington, *The Other America: Poverty in the United States* (New York: The Macmillan Company, 1962), pp. 10, 161.

21. Fred Jaffe, "Family Planning, Public Policy and Intervention Strategy," 1965, unpublished.

22. Leon Keyserling argues: "During World War II, we reduced unemployment to less than one million. Now we have full-time unemployment of more than four million. It would be dangerous nonsense to think that the number of shiftless or otherwise unfit people have multiplied four times in the intervening years" (p. 14). "The number of people whose personal characteristics render them ineligible to participate in this process (of increased employment openings with on-the-job training) if given the opportunity is relatively small; our wartime experience and other periods of full employment and rapid economic growth proved this to the hilt" (p. 36). Leon H. Keyserling, *Progress or Poverty* (Washington Conference on Economic Progress, 1964).

III

Education

5

THE CREDENTIALS TRAP

Education is now the major route to social mobility in the United States. Failure in the educational system means limited economic opportunities and, to a considerable extent, political and social exclusion. Schools, consequently, bear heavy burdens today. Willy-nilly, their practices and successes and failures are so important that educators cannot have a narrow perspective on their work. Improving the long-view prospects of the poor and especially of Negroes, Mexican Americans, and other minority groups requires increasing the capacities of schools to do an effective job with the not so easy to teach. We devote the succeeding chapters of this section to the issues of school improvement.

In this chapter, however, we deal with the excessive reliance on education as the door to opportunity. Using schools as social-mobility corridors frequently distorts education.

Education, which once probably served as a great means of ascendancy for the poor, now is becoming a bar to the new working class's efforts to change their conditions. The hope of one generation becomes the barrier of the next.

Education served to free society to a considerable degree from the rule of nepotism and arbitrariness. Educational qualifications rather than connections alone became important. Standards which applied to (almost) everyone meant that the rewards of privilege were not so

This chapter was written with Pamela A. Roby.

great as before. Thus, education was a contributor to the democratiz-
ing of society.

But note the use of "was." For the insistence on education as a
prerequisite for jobs is becoming a barrier to the occupational ascendancy of today's disprivileged.

We have become a credential society, where one's educational level
is more important than what he can do. People cannot obtain jobs that
they could well fill because they lack education qualifications. Negroes
who dropped out of the educational steeplechase before a high-school
diploma cannot get jobs. Employers and the better off do not feel that
there is discrimination; rather the low-educated are "not qualified."

The assumption is that we have a very well-organized economy with
a rational purpose and methodology. Jobs are organized in the most
rational forms possible; the persons who can best perform these jobs
are in them. The excluded are excluded because they lack the requisite
ability. Merit is recognized and rewarded. In one version of this
portrait we have a meritocracy where talent gets its just reward.

But any probing of this rational surface reveals the confusion and
ambiguity which prevail. Industry seeks to employ the most qualified
workers, yet Ivar Berg has discovered that at every occupational level
the high-educated have a poorer record than the low-educated: more
absenteeism, turnover, dissatisfaction, and probably lower productivity.
Perhaps most striking in Professor Berg's study is that few companies
even know the connections between the educational level of their
employees and their performance. They have not bothered to probe
their records to find out if their beliefs accord with the results of their
practice.

We focus on the exclusion of the low-educated, but the processes
that we are concerned about build Chinese walls of exclusion around
an increasing number of occupations. We have a new guild system of
credentials, licenses, certificates—largely built on the base of education
—which keeps people out of many occupational channels. There is
increasingly for many occupations only one route in—that to be taken
when young. Failing to take that route bars one forever from the
possibilities of that occupation.

Presumably these credentialing procedures assure a better product—
those who receive the credentials can do much better in the occupation
than those who do not; those who successfully go through the steps
needed to gain the credentials are better fitted for the occupation than

those who are not interested to go through these steps or fail to succeed in the prescribed educational climb.

The evidence to test these two assumptions is lacking. To some extent they are undoubtedly untrue. But, if we take a broader assumption, that those who do not go through credentialing activities are unfitted for the demands of the occupation, then that is clearly inaccurate. All of us know of individuals who cannot get jobs that they would be able to perform well because they lack the appropriate credentials—whether it is a high-school diploma or a Ph.D. Recently when we spoke on this issue more than two dozen people came up afterward to give personal witness of how they had been barred from activities, which they were confident they could do well, because they lacked some required credential.

Schools today are not a humanizing or an educational force so much as a credentialing agency, sorting people out who do not fit into the regular channels of educational development. Schools function to certify that someone is not harmful rather than to develop the potential of all. Many of the poverty and job-training programs serve the same function.

One does not have to accept our sweeping condemnation of credentialism in American society as a threat to social mobility of the discriminated and poor and as a bar to full utilization of every citizen's abilities to be disturbed by its galloping growth.

Why is credentialism growing? One reason is that we like to assume that our world is rational and scientific. We invest confidence in the present structuring of occupations as optimal; then the question becomes how best to fit people into these wisely constructed occupations.

Then we presume that we know enough to sort out "potential" and "ability" from their opponents. Consequently, we repose an enormous misplaced confidence in testing and educational achievement—that is, getting by in schools—even when we have quivers of doubt about their "real meaning." But the latent gain of resting on objective measures is that it seems to take away notions of irrationality and discrimination in favor of universally applied, objective rules. Where there has been oversupply of labor and talent, then processes of exclusion on some basis will occur. But when shortages occur as now in many professions, maintenance of exclusions as the core process is obviously peculiar. Such peculiarity is undoubtedly based on some fear—a fear of having to make choices and exercise judgment.

This fear is related to the third reason for the spreading tide of credentialism. More and more results and achievements are difficult to measure in a service-growing society. Norms of production output are difficult to use in the professions or in government service. Ambiguity of purpose further compounds the measurement problems. If 70 per cent of patients seeing a physician have no ascertainable medical reason for being there, how does one measure the achievement and productivity of the physician? Our uncertainty about what is the product and how to measure effectiveness throws us back to the input —that is, what is the training of the occupational incumbent?

A fourth reason for emphasizing exclusion is the "marshal's baton" syndrome. Napoleon asserted that his military prowess was based not only on his kitchens but on his promotion outlook—every soldier carried a marshal's baton in his knapsack, ready to jump into a command position. In many occupations and organizations, the notion, at least for men, is frequently to employ only "topnotchers" who can move to the peak of the pyramid. Yet the possibilities of moving to the top are slim indeed. In many organizations there is enormous turnover; only very few stay very long, and yet the notion is of "long-distance promotabiliy." Furthermore, as Robert K. Merton has pointed out, there is no possible definition of "topnotchers" nor an adequate number of them, so that organizations and professions are doomed to feel that they are being shortchanged in their share of "topnotchers." The important thing in this context is that the "marshal's baton" syndrome serves to make it appear wise to exclude many, even when talent and ability are in short supply. And certainly it caters to the yearning for prestige to be able to say that the profession or organization has only top-qualified people.

A fifth reason for credentialism is the importance of social appearance. As organizations and professions not only become more uncertain about criteria of performance, but require more intricate "teamwork," getting along with others, appearing "mature," and more acceptable to the public to be serviced, the desirability of insisting on educational credentials grows. For the credentials certify not educational achievement but personal serviceability—that one knows how to get by, conform, manage. The educational failures—at whatever level—are social failures, bad risks.

Does this attack on credentialism imply that there should be no standards of training, no qualifications for entrance into occupations? (Note, as has William Goode,[1] that we seldom raise the question whether individuals perform well enough to be permitted to stay in an occupation.) We do not think that these are the implications, although our impatience with exclusion processes at a time when we need inclusion processes may lead us to border on an across-the-board disclaimer against credentials in any form. But that is not our reasoned view.

The following policy implications flow from this analysis:

1. There should be a general downgrading of the importance of education as the major credential. Experience and performance should gain greater importance than they now have. Many people are not seriously considered for a job because they lack educational credentials; prospective employers will not even pause to investigate whether the low-educated can perform well. The absence of the certificates results in automatic exclusion. Individuals should be judged on what they can do rather than where and how long they have gone to school.

If we treated experience and performance seriously, civil-service regulations would be changed so that low education was not an automatic bar to many positions. Testing would be downgraded in favor of trying people in jobs and then assessing their performance. In many situations, such as that of school principals, we get many people who are good at taking tests but are poor performers on the job.

Since much of job training today is not relevant to work, there should be a strong movement toward "jobs first, training later." The absence of this practice means that many minority group members are now serving lifetime sentences of low income and unemployment for their educational delinquencies.

2. "Dropout" is a label assigned at sixteen; it persists through a lifetime. The consequence is that individuals who may have outgrown the issues which propelled them out of school or who now have demonstrated and developed considerable skill are still economically disenfranchised because of their youthful educational difficulties. Once a dropout, always a dropout. As in many other aspects of American life, we need a delabeling procedure which takes the curse off individuals who once ran afoul of conventional styles and were labeled and cast aside—whether the label is "dropout," "delinquent," or "mental patient."

3. We need deepened awareness of and respect for the abilities of those who have educational difficulties. We should not believe that our educational hurdles infallibly pick those who should be successes and unerringly cast aside those who should be failures. Nor that employment testing services are much better.

As we increasingly face the manpower problems of scarce talent, the great hope will be in the cultivation of talents among those who are now disadvantaged.

We do not wish to imply that every poor individual deserves and can use a marshal's baton. But many can. The failure is in cultivating these talents. We have much to learn here that we will not learn if we persist in the new fashion of denouncing poverty families for their deficiencies as educational environments. We then excuse the schools for their failures to learn how to adapt to and develop different varieties of students.

The first step of liberation from the shibboleths of invincible ignorance is to recognize the educational and occupational potential of many who have difficulty with educational systems as they are presently conducted.

In this connection the youth we interviewed in Syracuse—dropouts who were denoted as "unemployable," "hard core"—provide hope. At the beginning of the interviews they were laconic, uncommunicative, inarticulate, unintelligent. When we succeeded in involving them in the interview and they responded to us, they became expressive, near-poets, with a fine touch for the exact feeling or analysis.[2]

4. The need is for new channels of credentialing and new points at which credentials can be expanded. While we are eager to see reduced emphasis on educational credentials, we are realistic enough to know that this kind of change is slow. Consequently, it must be easier for individuals to obtain educational credentials.

Today, if one does not get twelve or sixteen or eighteen or twenty years of education in the orthodox way of continuous immersion without a break in the apparatus of formal education, one has much reduced chances of gaining credentials. We should more effectively develop school programs and procedures so that once out does not mean permanently lost.

To some extent the poverty programs are new credentialing systems in our society. Experience in the Job Corps or in the Neighborhood Youth Corps or in Manpower Development and Training Act programs may not be primarily important in terms of providing skills. Rather, employers may be more willing to hire youth who have gone through one of these self-selection and molding systems. Neighborhood Youth Corps experience may be a new way of getting a credential which employers will accredit and accept.

By multiplying the number of credential channels, we make it easier for individuals to gain them. Those defeated by our educational system at age sixteen might be able to get needed credentials at age eighteen, twenty-two, or thirty. One should have second, third, fourth chances and ways of getting credentials. The more the number of different ways of getting credentials, the less the number of people who would fail to get some of the brownie points needed for acceptance into the main economy.

What is needed is the idea of a second-chance university which permits "dropout" adults to get further and more useful opportunities to get credentials. (The second-chance university is discussed in greater detail in Chapter 7.) Experience should be given educational credit; courses should be more relevant to activities—liberal-arts education need not be taught in traditional ways in order to reach traditional ends. While there is need for a formal structure to facilitate re-entry into the educational atmosphere, there is also need to recharge that educational atmosphere so that it is more hospitable and useful to those who have found the established educational practices less than useful or stimulating.

5. Every credential system should have an escape clause which permits the unusual person to be admitted to the realm of the elect. As professions "tighten" up their qualifications, there is usually a "grandfather clause" which exempts old-timers from meeting the new qualifications. A similar idea is involved here of exemptions from usual practices. At least 5 per cent of each year's entrants into a profession or other highly credentialed occupation should be individuals who have "qualified" in non-usual ways—taking tests without the traditional educational prerequisites, getting credit for enriched experiences, etc. Some collective-bargaining contracts have a similar provision: the company is allowed to hire back after a cutback up to 10 per cent of the labor force without paying attention to seniority; the other 90 per cent of the labor force must be rehired according to seniority. The company is permitted some margin of choice and selectivity to meet its production needs.

Without a minimum percentage, it is unlikely that there would be in practice unusual entrance into the field of what might turn out to be a "creative minority." Arbitrariness and favoritism could be avoided by a blue-ribbon panel of decision makers.

The need here, as in so many other parts of our society, is for making pluralism possible in a complex, variegated, but pseudo-rationalized society. We need a variety of social inventions to provide the structure and the reality of pluralism.

6. We should not assume that the present structuring of occupations is optimum. There are many jobs—e.g., school superintendent or policy-oriented social theorists like us, that are impossible; too many different kinds of skills are needed and too many time-consuming tasks that should be broken down into finer tasks for many hands. On the other hand, many jobs should be enlarged to absorb greater responsibility.

With the tightening up of educational qualifications, it will be increasingly difficult to turn out an adequate number of professionals. As a consequence, the role of professionals should increasingly be that of making it possible for less trained people to do effective work. (See chapters 9 and 14 for a discussion of non-professional roles.)

Professionals are increasingly becoming the gatekeepers of the welfare state, deciding on "professional" grounds who receives what kind of services and who is allowed to perform various services. The pivotal importance of professional and organizational services has led many of the New Left students to focus on the professionals as the "enemy." While the assault is overdone and frequently misguided, there is something to the view that professions are hardening into barriers rather than aids. The guild-like features of professional occupations frequently are more visible than their commitment to broad social concerns, although there does seem to be important growth here. The emphasis on "competence" and "quality" frequently means a lack of attention to the poor or to those who do not easily fit into professional activities.

Business also deserves criticism in its reluctance to rethink its job structuring. Private enterprise could probably get needed labor (and at high-productivity levels) if it restructured more jobs so that the less trained could perform at least part of them. The credentials problem is an issue vital to both the private and public sectors. The national interest of gaining decent employment for the low-educated and the poor could be joined with the private interest of profit.

We live in a pseudo meritocracy where individuals are presumed to be selected for talent and placed into appropriate squares. Education becomes the major route to social mobility as the historic alternative routes are shut off. As social mobility becomes more important in our national policies, we narrow down the routes to it.

We have raised some issues about credentialism and professionalism chiefly in terms of the poor and discriminated. But as in so many other realms of our existence, the needs of the poor focus issues that are important to many others. For example, if we had discussed the problem of credentialism in terms of that permanent category of the near Ph.D.—the individual with graduate training and much rich experience who is never going to get a Ph.D. and is therefore barred from many posts—many more would see the poignancy of the issue of credentialism. (Incidentally, our social invention here would be to give a Ph.D. to individuals of training and worthwhile experience who have passed the age of thirty-five.)

The general issue which the plight of the poor and discriminated raise is that of a hardening and narrowing of society into fewer and fewer acceptable routes to economic improvement. That is a problem which all of us should be concerned about, for it also is involved in the issues of the general climate of our society.

Slowly and rather hazily Americans are re-examining core values and practices. Our contention is that we avoid our anxieties by relying on the processes of schools to resolve our value choices. The patina of rationality is preferred to the search for equality and purpose. Credentials substitute for judgment; "educational qualifications" become the lever of de-facto discrimination.

The future of individuals has been placed to a large extent in the hands of school authorities. In this chapter we have argued for diminishing the importance of education in economic ascent; in succeeding chapters we discuss how to improve schools so that the students of the new working class have a better chance at educational success.

NOTES

1. William J. Goode, "The Protection of the Inept," *American Sociological Review*, XXXII. No. 1 (February 1967), 5–19.

2. S. M. Miller and Ira Harrison, "Types of Dropouts—'The Unemployables,'" in Arthur B. Shostak and William Gomberg, eds., *Blue-Collar World: Studies of the American Worker* (Englewood Cliffs, N.J.: Prentice-Hall, 1964).

6

❀ ❀ ❀

SCHOOL DROPOUTS
AND AMERICAN SOCIETY

Dropouts—those who do not obtain high-school certificates by completing twelve years of education—are receiving great attention in the United States. From preschool to college new programs are advanced to reduce the dropout rate. Yet, the percentage of dropouts in the United States is declining. The reason for this quickened interest in a smaller percentage is produced by the growing disadvantage of not having a high-school (and college) certificate. The development of new technology demanding new skills, the decline of industries requiring high labor inputs, the lack of growth of unskilled jobs, and the increased demand for high educational credentials regardless of actual need have led to the concern about dropouts. Unemployment is greatest among the unskilled and the low-educated.

The issue of dropouts also gains great attention because it intersects the problems of the rising Negro population in the United States. One characteristic response to growing Negro demands for "progress—now" is that Negroes can obtain it only through education which will open new higher-paying jobs to them. (That higher income does not automatically open up housing is ignored in this contention.) The Negro rate of dropouts from schools is high for a variety of reasons, and some of the campaign to do something about dropouts is primarily aimed at Negroes.

The "dropout problem" is part of basic economic and political as well as social issues in the United States. It is frequently seen, however, as a technical or communications problem of convincing youth to stay in school. Discussions are consequently inadequate and frequently misleading.

Discussions about dropouts are too broad and too narrow. They are too broad because they seem to assume that the category of dropouts is a homogeneous one and that little variation exists within the category. The discussions are too narrow because they do not adequately look upon the problems of dropouts as economic and political issues, but mainly as educational ones. It is the purpose of this chapter to redress the balance.

Types of Dropouts

Adequate information on school dropouts is lacking. The best available estimate is that presently one-third of all youths will never finish high school. This rate varies considerably from region to region, by degree of urbanization, by character of community, and the like. New York City is not America; nor is Muncie. Conditions vary tremendously from community to community and have marked effects on dropout rates. Rates for one community cannot be extrapolated to produce national trends. The preconditions and later experience of dropouts are not the same in different communities.

Contrary to some popular beliefs, dropouts are not exclusively from working-class and lower-class or low-income families. Our studies in Syracuse, New York, revealed that 30 per cent of the parents of dropouts were in white-collar occupations.[1] Similarly the ecological distribution of Syracuse male dropouts shows that at least a fifth came from "fair" or "good" neighborhoods.[2]

Schools within a city vary markedly in dropout rates. A crucial factor, of course, is the socioeconomic and ethnic character of the area. The dropout rate can vary from 70 per cent in one low-income district to less than 10 per cent in others. Some schools in low socioeconomic areas have much lower rates than others, depending on the nature of the school climate promoted by the school authorities or the traditions of the ethnic group in the area.

A reanalysis of data collected by the Bureau of Census suggests that

70 per cent of all dropouts come from families whose income is below $5,000 a year. While this under $5,000 group is, of course, over-represented among dropouts, the surprising result is the large percentage of dropouts who do not come from the poorest families.

Another way of analyzing the data is to study the percentages of stay-ins. Of low-income youth (under $5,000 family income) perhaps 60 per cent do graduate from high school. Thus, not all dropouts are from low-income families nor do all low-income youth become dropouts.

These data strongly underline the heterogeneity of those called dropouts. Instead of discussing "the dropout," it is necessary to analyze the etiology and experience of different types of dropout. Different strategies may be required for each type.

The New Working Class

We would suggest four types of dropouts whose families are in the new working class: (1) school-inadequate; (2) school-rejecting; (3) school-perplexed; (4) school-irrelevant.

The school-inadequate category refers to those who may have difficulty in completing school because of low intellectual or disturbing emotional functioning. This category is probably much smaller than generally assumed. The data on IQ show considerable overlap between working class and middle class. Siller's study demonstrates that if a few extreme cases of low IQ performance are disregarded, the class differences are small.

The second type of low-income dropout is propelled by a push away from school. Not a few find school as presently conducted confining, unuseful, ego destructive. They want to get away from this negative, boring experience, and in many cases the school would like them to get away. In a group of boys who have dropped out and were unable to get a job, most of them, we found, claimed that they did not voluntarily withdraw from school—they asserted that they were pushed out and frequently in a fairly direct way.

We doubt if most low-income dropouts leave school because of a pure dislike of it. Three conditions indicate the likelihood that the push from school is not omnipotent among low-income dropouts. First, most dropouts do not leave school as soon as they are legally eligible. Second, many dropouts, as pointed out earlier, withdraw in the senior year. Third, in Syracuse, so-called "unemployable" dropouts, who should be likely candidates for the post of school critics, had a generally favorable attitude toward school: they asserted that they had a positive feeling about at least some teachers; they thought teachers were generally fair, and they missed school because of its social aspects—such as meeting friends during the school day. This attitude may be a nostalgic glow for a past which appears in retrospect more attractive than a difficult present, but the absence of a deep, pervasive antipathy toward school is surprising in a group which had problems of "adjustment" in school and conducted itself or was conducted out of it. We would guess that neither of these two categories is large.

School-Perplexed Dropout

The school-perplexed dropout has been largely ignored in the emphasis on cultural values operating as barriers to school achievement among those of low income. It is widely assumed that all or most low-income families and youth have very little interest in school or in high-level occupational achievement. A variety of studies show, however, that this is not the case, at least for low-income Negroes. At the same income levels, Negroes voice much more interest and concern about education than whites. Many Negroes see education, as Patricia Sexton has pointed out, in power and prestige terms, giving them a standing and protection in a discriminatory world. But it is not Negroes alone who are concerned about education. The Reiss-Rhodes study in Nashville reports that less well-off youth are much more likely to say that education had overwhelming importance than are youth from better-off families. When it is pointed out that Negroes have very high educational and occupational aspirations, that, indeed, study after study shows an extraordinary belief in education among Negroes, the reply invariably is that these aspirations are "unrealistic," that Negroes are jumping from "porters to neurosurgeons." When we declare that this criticism of lack of realism may be true, but that it is different from the complaint that there is no interest in education, we are greeted by puzzled silence. Although some youth may have unrealistic aspirations, Lockwood's study in Baltimore reports for high-school seniors (of all classes) that only 5 per cent overestimate their occupational potential while more than 35 per cent underestimate it! But this contention is a far cry from the previous assertion that aspirations were too low. If aspirations are very low, then we are told cultural barriers inhibit educational achievement; if aspirations are high, then we are informed that they are unrealistic.

We think that what is being said is that we do not know how to deal with the kinds of educational concerns and problems many low-income families and youth have. For many low-income youth and families, a complete and unrelieved rejection of school does not exist. Many come to school with some personal or family concern about education but become perplexed, lost, and sometimes reactive against the school experience, ending up as dropouts. Many low-income families are unable to translate their interest in education into effective school assistance to their children.

School personnel should learn how to capitalize on this interest in education. Frequently, they have been unwilling to reset their procedures so that they work with what exists. Often, what is the problem to be dealt with, namely, that parents do not know how to help their children in school, is used as an explanation of why school personnel fail to do an adequate job.

The School-Irrelevant Dropout

Many prospective dropouts never have expected to graduate—they have a job level in mind which does not require much education. Since they see education instrumentally, they are not interested in school as such and the school's inability to interest them compounds the problem. They may be described as having "low aspirations." But do high aspirations provide a desirable goal and the likelihood of achievement? Does graduating from high school really provide entry into higher-level jobs?

Let us examine the latter question. The long-term data on education and income indicate that the general rise in the level of education has not reduced the importance of education; it has shifted upward the breaking point where education leads to high or low income.

It is certainly better to be a high-school graduate than a dropout, but it is much better to be a college graduate. As Vance Packard has pointed out, the "diploma elite" is clearly advantaged. The differences in annual income between high-school graduate and high-school dropout are less than those between the high-school graduate and the college graduate, and the gap between those with a high-school diploma and those with a college diploma is increasing.

Nor are occupational differences between high-school graduates and dropouts starkly in favor of the graduate, as is commonly believed. While one of six graduates does distinctively better than dropouts, the advantage is not overwhelming. Putting the data differently reveals that there is great occupational overlap for the majority of dropouts and graduates, so that the advantage of graduating from high school is not immediately obvious.

Comparisons of the occupational experiences of dropouts and graduates do not attempt to hold social class constant. Many non-college-going high-school graduates are from middle-class homes; their occupational achievement may be influenced by this social-class variable rather than by the graduation variable. It is our guess that social class does make a big difference among high-school graduates. The higher the social-class level of the graduate's family, the more likely it is that he will obtain a high-level job. Graduates from working-class and lower-class families are not at all as likely to do well. We suspect that if we could remove the impact of family status in estimating the relation of graduation to occupation, we would find that graduation does not make a great difference for the boys from the new working classes; it is the linkage of graduation with prior middle-class status that makes the difference in the over-all results of the relation of high-school diplomas to occupations.

We do not have good evidence to support this hunch. We have made some very rough computations by manipulating census data. These calculations suggest that at least one-quarter of high-school graduating non-college-going working-class sons end up in low-level, low-income, low jobs. This is the picture soon after graduation; it undoubtedly improves in later years. Less than 10 per cent end up in fairly high-level jobs soon after graduation. High-school graduation helps working-class and lower-class boys but the aid may not be great or immediately apparent.

We suggest that at some level many lower and working-class boys, especially Negroes, have some awareness of the facts about them. Consequently, they are not particularly interested in doing something about school—to say that they are "culturally deprived" or "unmotivated" is choosing the wrong target. It is not clear what they should be motivated to, if the chances of getting a good job are not great. To say that getting a 10 per cent or 15 per cent or 20 per cent advantage by graduating from high school is still a distinct improvement ignores the fact that by the same token for perhaps eight of ten working-class boys graduation is not going to produce much.

Improving economic prospects may not have an immediate effect or an all-powerful effect in reducing dropouts. But without such an improvement in prospect, various tactics for encouraging dropouts to stay in school are not likely to be effective.

"Unemployable" Dropouts Speak

In Syracuse, New York, Ira Harrison interviewed fifty "unemployable" male dropouts (thirty-seven white, thirteen Negro) concerning their attitudes toward school and their job expectations. The boys were under the age of eighteen, had had difficulty in obtaining or keeping jobs, had gone to the New York State Employment Service for placement help, and had been classified by the office as "presently unemployable" in the Syracuse labor market. These were boys who had decidedly more economic and social difficulties than the average Syracuse dropout. Although one-quarter of those in our census of 1959–1960 dropouts were known to have been apprehended by police, at least two-thirds of the sample which we interviewed had police records, and many had been in penal institutions. Several of the boys had been brought up in foster homes. Mothers supported one-quarter of all the families. We call these youth "unemployable" dropouts to distinguish them from other types of dropouts.

In response to a series of questions about their attitudes toward school, about half of our dropouts declared that they did not drop out of school but were asked or forced to leave. They would have stayed, most contended, if this pressure had not been exerted on them. They defined themselves as "pushouts" rather than "dropouts." Obviously, such reporting cannot be taken at face value, and undoubtedly many acted so as to incite action to expel them from school, whether they intended that result or not. Most had been suspended from at least two schools.

The pattern showed generally a great deal of residential mobility, so that many had attended eight different schools before leaving school in the tenth grade. In school they met their friends and acquaintances; frequently, as the youth reported it, these friends and others "wised around," and sometimes it was admitted that they themselves had done this as well. "Wise around" could include talking out loud, laughing, throwing paper, hitting students, drinking whisky. This action frequently ended in trouble—reprimands by the teacher, being grabbed or shoved by the teacher, having to stay after school, stand in a corner, or being sent to the principal's or counselor's office.

Two factors were frequently reported:

1. The boys were aggrieved by school: they frequently contended that they were not immediately involved in the event for which they had been kicked out and the teacher's misinterpretation of what had occurred led to their getting involved in the event which led to their school dismissal. They saw the school personnel as "bugging" them, constantly keeping after them, until they finally turned to defend themselves.

2. The boys, to our initial surprise, were not negative about school. School represented a convenient place to meet their friends and for this reason they frequently missed it. In reply to a question about the "fairness" of teachers, most indicated that they felt that teachers were fair. Further, many volunteered that some particular teacher had been particularly fair or interested in them. Yet, as one boy expressed it, "School and I just aren't friends."

What struck us was that in a dropout population that had been particularly afflicted with school problems there was not a pronounced rejection of school. The youth were perplexed by school because it placed great constraints on their behavior, was not intrinsically interesting, and did not have visible connection with the actual content of jobs on the outside. A touching story of his travails was told by a boy whose father was in a mental hospital:

I quit. I went to school in September 1962 this year. I started in September. I guess it was just about the end of the month, I quit. And then . . . the reason why I quit was that my mother wanted me to help her out. So I went to work and I lost a job. I was laid off. So then I couldn't find another job. My mother asked me to go back to school so she could get welfare assistance for me. So I went back to school. And then when I went back to school, I just completely lost interest in it, you know, didn't care too much about it. After that I didn't feel like doing my work or anything. I wanted to go to work.

Getting youth to stay in school is difficult if courses do not have any clear connection with their occupational future or do not otherwise enrich their lives but are merely ways of accumulating credit for a credential. Going to school is not seen as a way of learning something which is of value later for a job or for enjoyment of living, but a mode of getting a high-school diploma. It is the diploma, not the content that it presumably sums up, that is seen as opening up the possibilities of a greater range of jobs and higher pay. And in truth it is the diploma as such, not the courses, which provides the opening wedge into the educationally cleavaged upper levels of the occupational pyramid.

We suspect that this situation makes it more difficult to "put up" with school than would be the case if courses were providing something useful for later activities. If high-school graduation does not advantage or does not seem to advantage youth they know (a likely occurrence where racial discrimination is involved and in our kind of economy where layoffs are likely with recurring recessions and an extending wave of declining industries) they are not likely to think of investing further time in school.

The formal organization of schools may be an obstacle. One dropout was absorbed by drawing. When he could not continue his art classes because he was doing poorly in all his other classes, he left school. School personnel are perplexed by what they see as school antagonism on the part of youth, but the latter do not reject school out of hand. Teachers and difficult students have not learned how to become "friends," but there is more of a potential for this on the dropouts' side than has been realized.

Ninety per cent of our dropouts liked the following school subjects, math, science, physical education, art, and shop. English and social studies were courses our dropouts had the most difficulties with; they were dull and uninteresting. The potential of these generally disliked courses is revealed by a Negro dropout whose social-studies teacher had the class "act out" historical events. He relates: "You might think it was crazy, but you actually felt that you were there, at the Boston massacre. Now, why can't other teachers do that?"

The great interest in science fields among our male dropouts and the "culturally deprived" generally has not been developed. Martin Mayer has pointed out that it is regrettable that the innovational programs in science teaching have been mostly beamed at the elite schools, public and private, rather than at the slum schools, where they might capture the imagination of youth who find many school subjects uninteresting but not those in science. The constant reporting that many dropouts are too poor in mathematics to be able to benefit from advanced vocational and technical training underlines the inadequacy of math teaching.

Orientations to Problems

We were concerned to see to what extent this group of "unemployable" dropouts identified their problems as products of their behavior or as essentially arising from external causes over which they had little control. We classified as "impunitive" responses those that indicated self-deprecatoriness, tendency to blame self for outcomes, and the like, and as "extra-punitive" responses in which others are blamed, causes are seen as external, or problems are not perceived. (The distribution had to be divided into two such omnibus categories because of the small number of cases.) We estimated that 55 per cent of the boys were impunitive and 45 per cent extra-punitive. Since many, if not most, of these boys generally would have been classified as "acting out," these results raise further questions about that overworked and overstretched category. Similarly, the findings of our interviews raise questions about the category of "sociopathic personality" and the like, which presumes a lack of concern for social values that did not seem to be exhibited by these boys.

Our Negro dropouts showed a higher incidence of extra-punitiveness than did the white dropouts. Although 40 per cent of whites are extra-punitive, 55 per cent of the Negroes were so classified. The Negro dropouts may have a point here in identifying outside pressures as causing difficulties. Negroes who have been in the work-training program have had greater difficulties getting jobs than the white participants. The training program does not primarily provide any skills; it has been mainly aimed at developing a more positive orientation toward work. Improving the outlook of whites seems to enhance their chances of getting low-level interstitial jobs, but not those of Negroes. The latter seem to know this and are less willing to take low-level jobs, in the hope of being able to move up. White boys have this hope; Negro boys see the first job as the terminus, not as the gateway station to further occupational advance. Similarly, many white dropouts are willing to become policemen, but almost no Negro is—it is a dirty job in their experience, as they have seen what they consider to be prejudiced behavior against them.

The "Now" and the "If" Worlds

As we pointed out above, the question of occupational and educational aspirations and expectations has become very cloudy in contemporary analysis. In response to questions in our interview which implied that the respondents should not consider immediate limitations, the youth often indicated quite high aspirations and hopes. If they had had their choice, white dropouts would have become factory owners, majors in the army or air force, mechanics, truck drivers, and factory workers. Negro dropouts, if they had had their choice, would have become doctors, lawyers, scientists, majors in the army, and garbage collectors. On questions that dealt with what they are expecting to do in some immediate time span, they were very rooted in reality. Forty-eight per cent of the dropouts had a specific job aspiration (mechanic and so forth); 8 per cent of our dropouts had a very specific job, place, and time in mind (for example, a forester in New York State); 6 per cent of our dropouts stated a broad area of work (skilled, semiskilled, for example, construction work, and so forth); 8 per cent of our dropouts were inconsistent (one time mentioning one job and later another, for example, lawyer, then construction worker); 10 per cent were diffuse with respect to type of job (no specific ideas at all); and for the remaining 20 per cent, future job expectations were either not obtained or impossible to classify. Dropouts frequently indicated the routes by which they expected to get to these occupations. Job expectations were realistic and related to their experiences.

All but 10 per cent of the boys felt that a high-school education was all that was necessary for them. They seemed to tailor their occupational (and consequently their educational) expectations to what they could reasonably get.

Once they were out of school and had experienced the difficulties of the labor market, the majority of the boys wished they had not left school, although many did not see on what basis they could have remained in that environment. It may be that, once boys in eighth grade or later have begun to move onto the school-leaving track, little will keep them in school. Perhaps it is after they have entered the labor market and have tested its possibilities and pitfalls that they then offer the greatest potential for satisfactory school performance.[3]

Structural Change

School systems generally have not developed the qualities of flexibility and adaptiveness necessary for the problems of today. The great expansion of education in this century and the unevenness of its quality have led quite naturally to regulations and procedures aimed at maintaining standards and insuring common practices over a large educational enterprise. At this stage—at least of large city schools—flexibility and experimentation become important.

One strategy is to have the schools operate as do some modern mental hospitals which, once a person has been a patient in them, feel a recurring responsibility to him. He can live in the hospital at night and work in the community; he can utilize the facilities of the hospital during the day and live in the community at night. He can sign himself into and out of the hospital at will—his stays can be short or long. The social-service department will provide aid in the community to former patients and their families. The hospital attitude is to help provide what is needed to aid the individual at different points in his life. The general aim is to facilitate the individual's functioning in the larger community by using the hospital in a variety of ways.

The dropout is not a mental patient. But his needs, his recognition of them, his ability and preparedness to do something about them, differ at various points (as do the needs of mental patients and all of us). Schools should be willing, for example, to readmit at any time a youth who has left school rather than insisting that September and February are the entry points. Extending counseling and guidance to dropouts until perhaps these activities might be the continuing responsibility of schools might be important; with the diversification of services and agencies one problem can become "multi-problems," as many agencies become involved. Courses in the early years of high school might be those which particularly interest nonverbally oriented students, and some of the required courses (e.g., English and history) might be concentrated in the later years when motivation or understanding is higher.

These suggestions are illustrative of structural changes in schools which could have ramifying effects. These types of changes have to go hand in hand with the general improvement in teaching youth of low-economic families. The current emphasis seems to be much more on pedagogic innovation and upgrading than on structural innovation. The latter, we feel, has considerable importance.

Large-city school systems have in some ways more possibility of structural flexibility than smaller systems. Because of the great school population, there is likely to be a sizable number of youth who have common needs at a particular time; consequently, the per-capita cost of a program can be less than when only a few youth need "adaptive school arrangements" at a moment of time.

Economic Issues

THE LABOR MARKET AND ECONOMIC GROWTH

The concern for dropouts is great because of the confluence of five factors: (1) an anarchic, unorganized, inefficient labor market prevails; (2) technological change is occurring at a rapid clip; (3) the push from the rural and agricultural areas is leading new migrants to the large cities; (4) employers are reluctant to hire the unskilled, especially if they are young Negroes, and train them for their needs; and (5) economic growth has not been great enough to propel us to full employment.

The impact of technological change would not be so dangerous if the other four factors were not also operative. Similarly, the anarchic labor market would not have ill effects if economic growth were taking place. From the point of view of change and public policy, it is obvious that we are not going to attempt to slow up the processes of technological change and urbanization involved in (2) or (3). The labor market and economic growth—(1) and (5)—become fundamental axes of public policy.

In former years, with the operation of apprenticeship systems, there was orderly progression through the job structure. Today, this is not true. Indeed, Harold Wilensky has gone so far as to argue that for many blue-collar people it is erroneous to talk of "occupational career" since there is no progression or clarity to occupational movement.

It would be helpful if there were a rational labor market in which job opportunities were chartable, the roads to them clear and accessible, and the movement into the niches serviceable. There is no clearly optimal way of obtaining jobs today because a rational procedure for making jobs available does not exist. The academic world is a familiar and a horrible example of irrational and nonrational ways of sorting people and jobs. What is needed, among other things, is an adequate sorting device in terms of employment exchanges.

Needed are new substitutes for apprenticeships; "workerships" have been suggested by Kohler and Friedman—some orderly, regular system by which one is inducted into a job and progresses to higher-level occupations. Probably much on-the-job training would be involved.

Considering the nasty things that are said about education, high-school diplomas do not magically transmute their holders into intellectual giants. To a large extent, social attitudes toward dropouts and the excess labor supply rather than dropouts' actual incapacities are the important limiting factors for dropouts. (We shall discuss this further in Chapter 7.)

An anarchic labor market creates problems at any time. When it coexists with economic growth processes that only slowly benefit the low status and the discriminated, difficulties are compounded. We are attempting makeshift poverty-reduction devices because of an ineffective economic steering mechanism in this country. Very high and selective economic growth would probably eliminate all but the thorniest of our dropout problems.

Selective Mobility

Gans has referred to "guided individual mobility" and Turner to "sponsored" mobility. What seems to be happening with the increased emphasis on education is that we are coopting people for "success" if they perform in certain socially acceptable ways. High-level intelligence may forge its own way, but for the more ordinary ascendant, a certain social cast is required—for educational advance and then occupational admission. Much can be said about this mold and its effects, and we want to point up some neglected and perplexing (social) issues and consequences.

In emphasizing efforts to encourage students to graduate from high school and in making special efforts to locate talented youth and encouraging them to move ahead, some important considerations may have been ignored. An emphasis on such programs as Project Talent can be a way of attempting to go around the problem of educational discrimination rather than breaking through it. For it is obviously possible to make strenuous efforts to locate potential graduates without breaking down existing practices of discrimination in terms of de facto segregation and the distribution of educational resources. Helping the talented few is not solving problems of discrimination and avoids direct confrontation with a basic issue of contemporary American education.

It may well be that our efforts at guided individual mobility may result in providing enough mobility to enough people so that pressure for real, basic, pervasive social change will not take place. We could be providing sops rather than solutions.

Parallel to this possibility is the lack of concern for those who will not be "making" it. What about those left behind by the educationally mobile? They will be filling a variety of low-paying, low-skill jobs. There should be considerable effort to improve the conditions of these jobs in terms of pay, rationalization so as to reduce layoffs, working conditions, and the like. Legislation (a minimum wage that provides a floor which makes sense in terms of today's cost of living), more effective union organization, and concentrated local planning may be necessary to decasualize the labor force and improve conditions. These aims are minimal and a necessary prelude to any effort to provide the kind of job meaning with which Paul Goodman has rightly been concerned.

In picking a boy for the mobility route, whatever the reason for his choice or the nature of the route, what happens to the community from which he comes? If we become more concerned with those left behind, we have to consider questions such as these: Is it possible to have guided individual mobility that improves the chances for improvement of those who do not move ahead? Should an effort be made to encourage those who have moved ahead to attempt to help those who do not—that going up does not mean opting out of the plights of one's former mates? Does social mobility necessarily mean that potential leaders are lost to the group which fathered them?

Do we want to change the conditions of a lot of people a little or greatly change the conditions of a small number of people? In medical care, with its present state of economic organization, the general purpose is to improve a lot the condition of a few. Certainly this is true of the orientation of private psychiatry and even community mental-health programs supported by tax funds, as the late Paul Hoch, New York State Commission of Mental Health, pointed out. Whenever a shortage of professional talent occurs, the emphasis is upon upgrading professional talent to provide really high-level personnel and thereby restricting the supply, rather than trying to see how the tasks can be subdivided so that more adequate service can be given to a greater number of persons. (We shall discuss this issue in Chapter 14.)

Programs of social action which are oriented to facilitating the upward mobility of individuals as individuals (i.e., not through collective action or through improved conditions of the group as a group) are likely devoted to the principle of greatly changing the conditions of a few. Is this our overriding social value?

Every decision is a death; a choice means that we cannot pursue other possibilities. The price of every act is the loss of alternative opportunities; the economist knows this well and talks of opportunity costs: What other utilities are foregone in achieving a particular gain? Have we adequately assayed the opportunity costs of our present-day efforts?

We do not intend these questions as rhetorical ones, for we are not sure of the answers, but they seem to reflect important issues that are not currently discussed. Should we concern ourselves only with individual change and not primarily with social change? In the attempt to do something about dropouts, should our efforts be as directed toward the end of discrimination and the achievement of full employment as toward publicity aimed at encouraging youth to stay in school?

Conclusion

Our emphasis on economic factors is a result of the feeling that attitudinal factors have been overstressed. It may be that a great surge in educational attainments of the low-income might lead to a great demand for economic expansion, leading to the production of more jobs. We rather doubt this. A great educational surge is more likely to lead to unrest, unemployment, underemployment. How that unrest would become crystallized is unclear. It could be a dangerous road—made less threatening by the likelihood that the campaigns to stay in school will not succeed.

The varied campaigns to get youth to stay in school can only be successful if they are unsuccessful. For if everyone were to graduate from high school (and many went on to college), there would not be enough appropriate jobs available. It is dangerous to raise aspirations if we cannot be sure of a payoff for the additional effort involved. We doubt if these campaigns will gain many new recruits for high-school diplomas; those who see school as irrelevant to their lives—because of its inability to deliver occupationally or esthetically, as Friedenberg and Goodman contend—are unlikely to find the propaganda of a campaign an irresistible siren song. It should be noted, too, as Maurice Connery has pointed out, that the campaigns may have some boomerang in lowering the self-esteem and enterprising efforts of dropouts by convincing them that they have no occupational chances at all.

A second possibility is that there would be some increase in opportunities; this increase would be followed by a large increase in educational achievement and expectations; then we would again have the problem of whether opportunities match the supply of labor.

Other possibilities abound. But what is worrisome in the situation is not the lack of aspirations and desires but the likely absence of opportunity. Aspirations may lag beyond opportunity, but that is usually a short-run phenomenon.

In American life, it has been customary to offer "education" as the panacea for all problems, whether those of racial prejudice, sexual happiness, or economic conflict. To the problems of discrimination, inadequate economic functioning, and poverty, we are again offering the reply of "education." In doing so we are essentially making it a bootstrap operation, telling those who have the most strikes against them that they have to do the most work to improve the situation.

But decreasing the number of dropouts is only one way of dealing with the growing problem of youth and employment—and it may be a very inadequate one if decent jobs are not available in sufficient numbers for high-school graduates. In this century many community problems have been thrust upon the schools; it may be important for school personnel to point out constantly the responsibility of the polity generally for the functioning of the economy and for its impact upon youth. Schools cannot solve the problems of uneven economic growth, anarchic labor markets, and the like. They can serve to improve, to some extent, the quality of labor, but the demand for labor would still be a prime problem. The efforts of American schools to improve the prospects of low-income youth can only be one mode of attack on the problems. In each community, schools may have to play the important role of pointing out the varied and extensive programs and actions that are needed.

These remarks are not to say that all kinds of educational programs and experiments to improve schooling and its attractiveness are not of the first order of activity. They certainly are, and in the following chapters we offer suggestions for improving educational policies and practice. Nor do they argue that subjective attitudes play little role. What we are questioning is how effective this emphasis alone would be for the school-irrelevant dropout and in the attack on the overdetermined *social* problem of youth, unemployment, discrimination, and poverty.

NOTES

1. The middle-class dropout has not been analyzed as such. The likelihood is that there is considerable variation among middle-class dropouts; three types seem to emerge: (1) the dropout with school-related emotional difficulties; (2) the emotionally disturbed dropout whose difficulties are not directly related to school; and (3) the dropout from a family which is economically or educationally marginal to the middle class. The latter type, we would guess, make up the bulk of the middle-class dropouts. It might prove worth while to expend research effort on the middle-class dropout. Probably more important would be studies of the working-class and lower-class high-school graduate. For seeing the factors that lead many to stay, we may be better able to depict ways of helping others.

2. The Syracuse data indicate that not all recent dropouts are having job problems. Perhaps 40 per cent of white males have been able to obtain fairly good jobs (white-collar and skilled manual) two years after dropping out. See S. M. Miller, Carolyn Comings, and Betty Saleem, *The School Dropout Problem,* New York State Division of Youth (1963).

3. But in very few cities is there the flexibility which permits readmission any time during the year and provides special programs for returnees. The Federal programs of Job Corps, Work Experience, Neighborhood Youth Corps, and Manpower Development and Training Act programs are new devices to build an accessible tier of education and training that is largely outside of the regular school channels. The need for them indicates the inflexibility of the traditional school in continuing an interest in those who have floundered in the usual school programs.

7

✿ ✿ ✿

THE SEARCH FOR AN
EDUCATIONAL REVOLUTION

Breakthroughs and Breakdowns

A revolutionary vision has emerged in American education. This vision is to educate the "disadvantaged," for education today is central to security and status. The issue today is how to promote this vision into deep-seated change and effective practice. We need to move from an image of what we wish to its realization in practice.

Each year a new major educational breakthrough is heralded. One year it is programmed instruction. Another year it is team teaching. Later, prekindergartens for the "culturally deprived" became the answer. (We discuss this solution in the next chapter.) Educators and citizens hunger for a one-shot, magic potion.

We vacillate between two reactions to these claims and efforts. On one hand, we feel that little is known about how to do an effective job of educating the new working-class youth. On the other hand, we feel that if what we know were implemented we would be much further along the line. In either case, we really cannot talk about programs unless we have assurance that we have an educational structure and citizen and professional pressure to implement them. We are not utilizing what we know, as Alvin Eurich has contended about the neglect of educational television. Demonstration and pilot projects often do not grow into national practice, even when they prove out.

Despite the "breakthroughs," the vaunted "educational revolutions," we are disturbed about what is going on. We feel that we are not advancing very rapidly toward the goal of effective education for low-income groups in the United States.

Despite all the hoopla about higher horizons, educational saturations, change agents, we are not really achieving much. The breakthroughs rapidly break down. True, there has been considerable change in some schools and some low-income youth have benefited, but the change is not very great nor does it tend to be continuing.

Some Dangers in the New Education Trend

It would be surprising indeed, if, in the context of past discrimination, patronization, and ignoring of the poor, the new positive shift toward interest in the education of the new working class were to appear uncontaminated by the negative history of the issue. Hence, there are a great variety of potential regressions as well as new dangers to be guarded against:

1. The danger of overemphasizing vocational, nonacademic education for children of low-income background, because of their physical style. The intellectually relevant aspects of the physical style are ignored and misunderstood in this approach, and the physical style is seen simply as preparatory for physical occupations.

2. The danger of aiming for no more than bringing disadvantaged youngsters up to grade level, as though this were some lofty aim. Overlooked here is the positive style and creative potential of the low-income child.

3. The danger, currently quite prevalent, of stressing the deficits, the weaknesses in the background of the low-income child. If the deficits are seen in the context of the strengths of low-income culture and style, then a full-scale attack on the weaknesses (lack of school know-how, test-taking ability, anti-intellectualism) will be beneficial; but divorced from this framework there is a strong likelihood that the low-income youngster may develop a negative self-image because of the constant accent on his deficiencies.

4. The danger involved in proposals for new separate tracks for the previously segregated and deprived Negro children, who, it is argued, will be damaged by the demands of the integrated classroom

and pace of the white middle-class pupils. Unspoken, or less frequently mentioned, is the fear that the disadvantaged child will retard the middle-class child. Again, this view is rooted in the one-sided stress on the deficiences of the low-income child and the unwillingness of the school to adopt to the styles and needs of non-middle-class children.

5. The danger involved in stressing one-way communication from the school to the parents of the disadvantaged, in order to stimulate the parents to encourage their children to have a more interested, less estranged orientation toward the school. Actually, it is through two-way communication, in which the parents can genuinely influence the school (actually participating in vital policy decisions), that the alienation and estrangement will be broken down.

6. The danger involved in searching for gimmicks, cure-all tech-niques for teaching low-income youngsters, rather than focusing on teacher abilities and the imparting of knowledge regarding the cultures and style of low-income groups. In the context of teaching know-how and changed attitudes, new techniques can be very useful, especially in aiming toward far-reaching intellectual growth of low-income pupils; however, by themselves, techniques and gimmicks will probably have limited effectiveness and can easily serve to obscure serious issues. For example, role playing degenerated into just another gimmick where it was applied without awareness of why and how it can be the basis for a completely new approach to teaching the low-income child.

7. The danger of relying upon team-teaching devices and teaching machines to solve teaching problems in connection with low-income children. Many applications of team teaching with "slow" children actually watered down the subject matter, lowered standards, and made negative assumptions about the slow child to the effect that he is less capable of understanding intellectual material, and therefore requires more "practical" subject matter. In one high school where Russian history is taught on a team-teacher basis, the "slow" group spent more time on Russian cooking and the like, while the other students did much more intellectually relevant research.

Teaching machines also are no panacea. While the low-income child likes the game dimensions and the physical dimensions of the teaching machine, he is quickly disillusioned as he comes to realize that this is "just another reader," and reading is not the best medium through which to appeal to the low-income person's style.

8. The danger arising from oversimplified, mechanical efforts at

correcting traditional errors, such as the early efforts at revising the white middle-class oriented Dick and Jane readers. Initially, the old readers with Dick and Jane in a lovely suburban home were modified by simply blackening the faces of some of the families. The old themes, setting, and language remained, but the faces were now black. (Bank Street College has now developed urban readers with new and broader themes.)

9. The danger of assuming that in order to educate a low-income youngster it is going to be necessary to middle-classize him—to give him middle-class values. Part of this error lies in failing to understand that low-income groups, and Negroes in particular, have very positive attitudes toward education (although they may have highly critical attitudes toward the school), and they do not have to be middle-classized in order to appreciate and desire education. An important deterrent to this trend would be the recognition of the positive elements in the mental styles of low-income people, and the inclusion of these styles in a modified school culture—rather than one-sidedly attempting to change the children to fit the traditional middle-class school culture.

10. A most crucial danger that must be guarded against is the possibility that the current wave of interest in the poor may simply become a fad without impact. Many people who never evidenced much serious interest in the problems of poverty have suddenly jumped on the bandwagon; what will happen when some other issue becomes au courant? It should be noted that programs such as Higher Horizons and Headstart, despite all their excellent intentions, contain the risk that they are rooted too much in short-run zeal and special extra effort that cannot easily be maintained for long periods of time.

Unfortunately, the failure to achieve great educational advance in the face of the new vision of the mission of the schools is leading to scapegoating of low-income children. Frequently, the struggle to aid children who do not easily fit into the school situation is given up. For example, we do not find the concept of "cultural deprivation" a useful one. It leads people into confusing ways of beginning to analyze the problem. People are different—but the obligation of the school system is to learn how to deal with people who are quite different in terms of their ways of dealing with the learning situation.

The emphasis should not be upon people measuring up to a standard before we deal effectively with them, but rather upon professionals' learning to deal effectively with people who are quite different in out-looks, experiences, and capacities. The obligation is not in the people who are different. Rather it is in the professional to learn to deal with a wide variety of students. If a physician's patient is not successfully treated with penicillin, he moves to sulpha or to another form of treatment. The medical model is that the obligation is the physician's to do something about the problem. We submit that this obligation attaches to all professionals. Professionals have to avoid the stance that problems rest fundamentally with clientele. Patients or clientele do not fail; only practitioners do. The use of a term such as "cultural deprivation" leads us away from looking at ourselves as practitioners. We begin to scapegoat those with whom we are having difficulty.

We fear that we are beginning to move toward the possibility of a do-nothing policy in regard to making sweeping changes in the school. For example, as we pointed out in Chapter 6, the present emphasis upon prekindergarten education as basically necessary for the advance of low-income children is terribly exaggerated. Obviously, there is an important role for it, but we should not act as though it is a panacea that obviates other changes.[1]

We do not think that this view is valid. This ideology bars schools from moving in more flexible, adaptive directions. The escape from failure, the fear of defeat, is leading to a search for gimmicks, for movement without change. We are trying to avoid upsetting the old ways as we paste on some new ways. At its worst, we are subjected to a series of public-relations maneuvers masquerading as educational programs. We need less public-relations announcements and more internal reorganization of the schools.

We are basically looking for a technology to solve our problems with the disadvantaged. Technological changes such as prekindergarten programs, team teaching, or reading machines and the like will be an important part of any educational revolution. But we doubt very much that they will be the most important part of the revolution today. And we emphasize today. Different times, different problems, different procedures. Today, something else is needed in addition to new technologies. Just as we may have false gods, so may we have false revolutions.

Although many issues spur an educational revolution, this chapter emphasizes the currently neglected role of administration: the need for adaptability and flexibility and for an effective school climate.

The Nature of the Educational Revolution

Everybody knows why Rome fell—the Goths came down from the north and took over the city. Many explanations stress the external forces that subjugated the mighty Roman Empire. However, Vladimir Simkhovitch, economic historian and author of *The Fall of Rome,* had another approach: Rome fell because of the declining marginal productivity of the land. Rome was no longer able to support itself agriculturally; this weakened the population. The tensions which existed within Rome emerged out of its economic plight. The important element in the demise of Rome's imperial grandeur was not the coming of the Goths, but its internal stresses. The questions were: What was happening within Rome to weaken it? What were the kinds of tensions, the schisms, that were taking place, making it possible for an outside group to be victorious?

We think this mode of analysis is appropriate to education. What are the problems within educational institutions today? We have to look increasingly toward the internal structure and operation of education. This is particularly important now, for many of the new technologies and new programs require a new kind of administrative structure which permits and facilitates these programs.

The administration of a school impregnates every nook and cranny of the school. Frequently, after a half-hour stay in school, one can describe what the chief administrator is like without ever meeting him. Walk along the halls, look into classrooms, and the style of the institution is clear. It has an atmosphere and climate, a way of operating, which affects everything that takes place. The superintendent or principal sets this style.

Many programs of innovation succeed because they really are changes in school administration, and sometimes school administrators, rather than because of the specific content of the program changes. For example, we suspect that a core element of the positive phase of progressive education was that its supporters devotedly provided an effective climate for the teachers and found school administrators who made it possible for teachers to be flexible and imaginative. To some extent, at its beginning, progressive education was a revolution in educational administration, permitting teachers to be experimental and adaptive.

In the absence of an appropriate organizational base, innovational programs fail. For example, in the summer of 1963, President Kennedy provided funds for the U.S. Office of Education to encourage school dropouts to return to school. In the month of August, counselors went out into some communities to talk to dropouts; and a sizable number of youth did return to school. From what one can learn, many, if not most, of those who returned to school dropped out shortly afterward. This gung-ho campaign did not accompany any change in schools. Dropouts went back to the same kind of situation they were in before. They were returning exiles. Shortly, they again became expellees and refugees from the school—the displaced persons of the affluent society.

Many innovations require an atmosphere, an organization, a structure, which permits them to take root. For example, many schools in low-income areas are now emphasizing school-community relations, getting parents more involved in the educational outlook of their children and closer to their schools. In one school, this increased contact backfired. The low-income parents grew more alienated from the school than ever before. Through greater intimacy with the school, they learned how the school operated and how their children were treated by teachers and administrators. And they did not like what they regarded as the punitive behaviors of school personnel. Increased parent contact with the schools, if it is to be effective, may be more important in changing the attitude and behavior of school personnel than those of parents!

New technology and procedures are needed, but they will tend to have limited effects without organizational change. New technologies will rapidly become calcified without organizational change. Fortunately, the new technology can be a leverage for organizational change.

Administrative Imperatives

What are the ingredients of the needed changes in educational administration?

Today we need administrators and teachers who have an authentic commitment to low-income youth. The commitment has to be clear, honest, dedicated, and implemented. It has to include sizable amounts of new money for schools, especially those in low-income areas. Parents and the community have to share in policy decisions. Against these fundamentals, we should examine school outlook, organization, and climate.

First, the schools have to adapt to the variations in students. No one method works with everybody. Variability and flexibility of programs and approaches are central if we are right in our theme about the variety of perspectives and needs among the "new" working class.

Second, schools have to provide satisfactions to students. If schools operate as or are perceived as prisoner-of-war camps, then we think Edgar Friedenberg and Paul Goodman are correct in their defense of the dropout. The honorable course for a prisoner of war is to break out of camp. School climate and effective school programs are obviously crucial here in building satisfactions in the school.

Third, more effective teachers are needed. We have routinized and overorganized schools, making it very difficult for teachers to be effective. Sometimes the basic perspective in administering schools appears to be that the task is to make it possible for morons to teach idiots. This view can be a self-fulfilling prophecy. The teacher's role has been overly circumscribed and tightly determined from on top. Standardization, routinization, and accountability have been positive steps in the development of schools, as they have been in industrial practice. But the present situation calls increasingly for flexibility and individualization within the school. This is a general problem of large-scale organization.

Flexibility and Adaptability

What is involved in moving toward more organizational flexibility and adaptability?

ASSUMPTION A: EDUCATION TODAY IS NOT A CONTINUOUS PROCESS BUT A DISCONTINUOUS ONE

Increasingly, the educational process is going to be discontinuous. People will be dropping out of public schools and returning; college students will drop out and return—this is already exceedingly common.

With changing occupational demands, people are going to have to be retrained—"redeveloped," in a sense—at different points of their lives. Education and training are not one-time, one-shot activities. Leaving and returning to education and training at different points of one's life will be the typical practice. We need many entry and re-entry points to the school system and training. This is especially true of those who have difficulty in making the educational grade. We need programs which fit the unique development and experience of individuals at the time they re-enter school. The tenth grader who has dropped out and worked for a couple of years and returned to school differs from the tenth grader who never did. We need new bridges and linkages between school and the outside. It is not enough to open a few re-entry doors; the returning student has to be provided an experience which is individually useful.

ASSUMPTION B: PEOPLE VARY

There is tremendous difference among youth today, whatever the social class level. In any given socioeconomic level there are many different kinds of youths. Upper middle-class progeny are both hippies and Reaganites. Some school dropouts are able to get decent jobs, while others are candidates for permanent economic dependence. Variations in experience and outlook mean that different people need different things at various points in their lives. No one method works equally effectively with everybody. This is our experience with teaching reading. Adherents of some educational practices are members of religious cults, vying in protestations about which cult has the revealed truth. The unfortunate truth is that everyone has the revealed truth, but only a small part of it. Certain methods work very well with certain groups, but they do not work very effectively with others.

We cannot be bound to method. To some extent, arguments about methods are controversies about different ends. Obviously, different ends may require different means. The more frequent situation is that we do not recognize that there may be many different routes to the same end. We have become bound up in the means. The teaching of reading, for example, should be based on a set of empirically based generalizations. What procedures work with whom? If a procedure does not work with some, then we have to learn ways that are more effective with them. The teaching of reading today is ideologically rather than scientifically based.

One of the central issues in achieving effective differentiation is how to avoid stigma. The less "normal," less "typical" tracks tend to become stigmatized. In turn, stigma leads to degradation and low-quality education. Those recruited to do the low-prestige teaching jobs tend to be of lower quality; they frequently do not have much pride in what they are doing. Many youth who are receiving special attention in school or out are stigmatized because of this attention. Consequently, the help they receive from the new programs is very slight indeed.

The need in our society is for differentiation without stigma. Historically, though, perceived differences are attached to a scale of values, and honor and stigma are parceled out accordingly. We need differentiation in society—we certainly would not want everyone to be like us—but the criteria of the present distribution of honor and stigma are certainly questionable. Perhaps, too, the intensity of feeling about honor or stigma might well be reduced.

These are large issues. For the school administrator, their immediate mandate is to treat as a major task the achievement of individualization and differentiation without producing stigma.

ASSUMPTION C: GOOD TEACHERS EMERGE WHEN THEY HAVE ENOUGH INDEPENDENCE AND SCOPE TO PERMIT PERSONAL STYLE TO FLOURISH

There is no one best type of teacher, or one all-purpose teaching approach. Teachers have to be permitted more independence, more scope, and more initiative. A perplexing difficulty here is how to build teachers' accountability for performance at the same time that individual teacher variations are encouraged. In order to attain teacher accountability, school systems have determined what the teacher puts into the system: the boundaries of the syllabus, the class plan, and so on. When, for example, class plans are stressed, then inputs are central and individual initiative curbed. The end product, the output in terms of students' achievements, is often given less attention than the input. This occurs because of disagreements about goals and the means of measuring movement toward them, and the fears of a clear-cut evaluation. If outputs are emphasized as the mark of success, then teachers can have wider latitude and still be held accountable for their behavior. New administrative outlooks are necessary.

ASSUMPTION D: NO PERMANENT SOLUTIONS EXIST

Too much of the feeling persists that following a particular policy or procedure would solve our problems for all time. Different times, different places, different issues require different policies. Change and adaptability, assessment and appropriateness are the continuing imperatives. No one-time change will safeguard us forevermore. We constantly have to adapt to new circumstances. As our political climate changes, as our economy moves in new directions, as education becomes the prime route to social mobility in America, as we develop a new poor, we have new demands upon education. Educational systems have to move. All organizations, including educational systems, have to adapt or become anachronistic. There is no necessarily enduring value in any particular strategy or procedure.

The orientation to change runs the danger of falling into novelty and fadism for change's sake. The question is can we become adaptive and flexible without becoming fadists and novelty hunters, thrill seekers of the new?

Organizational Climate

What ingredients are required for innovational programs to succeed? The climate of the school is of great importance. It affects—as well as is a product of—the behavior of students and teachers. In consequence, it is paramountly the administrators' responsibility to improve it.

In analyzing the important ingredients of a "positive" school climate, personal biases are inevitable, since values determine to a large extent the definition of what is positive. We need a pluralism in our quest for desirable ends. What is the best way depends upon particular circumstances. What is positive in some group or situation may not be positive for others. Nor do we know enough to be definitive about what builds the different types of effective climates. It is important to recognize many different kinds of positive school climates and the diverse roads to each.

One of the basic ingredients in a positive school climate is *respect*.

Students have to be respected. Teachers have to be respected, particularly by school administrators who frequently implicitly denigrate their staff by such devices as time clocks.

Our impression of many programs aimed at low-income youth is that school personnel not only have meager understanding of these youth, but that they really do not like them. We doubt that you can go very far with a youth whom you do not like. Thus, the attitude of the school toward disadvantaged youth—who are disturbing to the more affluent in part because they are disadvantaged—is essential to effective programs.

Learning and knowledge have to be respected, which is not always true in our schools. We are sometimes more respectful of particular teaching methods than we are of knowledge itself. There are many different kinds of positive school climates, many different ways of achieving this condition. Respect has many different doors.

A second important theme of a positive school climate is *authenticity*. The faculty and administration have to stand on what they say. Edgar Z. Friedenberg in his *The Vanishing Adolescent* and elsewhere has been trying to show us the inauthenticity in the relationship between schools, school personnel, and students. Frequently, school administrators are phonies. Youth recognize that they do not say what they mean. Little is going to work as long as inauthentic relationships prevail. If a school changes, its people have to believe in what they are doing. The changes cannot be for public-relations effectiveness alone. There has to be a real commitment to the changes.

The third theme of a positive school climate is the fostering of *competence*. The school has to be able to do the job it sets out to do. Youth generally, and low-income youth particularly, do not respect authority figures who are incompetent, who make promises which they cannot achieve, who have goals which have little relationship to the outside world. The school situation has to be built on competence.

The fourth need is for *consistency* and *predictability* in a school. Many schools do not have predictability. The prison experience is interesting. Prison riots usually occur when the practiced, predictable rules, the formal and informal procedures, are broken by the warden. In most prisons the inmates have taken over a good deal of the functioning of the prison. This is known by the warden and it is permitted. It is an easier way to run a prison. In fact, it is difficult to run it any other way. When the warden is forced to change procedures because of a break or the insistence of the board of overseers, he begins to get tough, to put the screws on, to break up the informal groups; the informal loci of power are prevented from operating as they did before. Then a food riot or strike may occur. The predictable modes of behavior have been supplanted and prevented from operating in their usual way. We do not want to liken schools to prisons, although highly controlled institutions have many similar characteristics.[2]

Predictability and consistency are essential to any positive school climate. Consistency is perhaps the most important element in the personality or outlook of those who are effective with low-income youth. A wide diversity of personality types, not just the hearty athlete or the "one of the boys" types, can do well. We think of a dandified, pedantic little Frenchman whom few would predict could be effective with tough New York City boys. Yet—he showed respect for them even when he forced them to take off their hats; his behavior was always predictable and consistent. And he was effective.

Fifth, the school has to have purpose and direction. It has to believe in something. It has to have a *mission*. A school is unlikely to have a positive climate without a mission. If the theme is just that everyone love everyone else and there is no tie beyond that, the love won't last very long. A good deal of the positive impact of programs aimed at low-income youth depends on the Hawthorne effect on school personnel. They believe in what they are doing; they are consulted and involved in the new programs. Morale is high in the pursuit of a common goal.

Finally, school programs have to be *relevant* to low-income youth. They have to see that what the school is doing has some relationship to their own lives.

Important developments are occurring in the United States. We are learning important things. But we are not sufficiently implanting them. We are moving toward a more positive school situation for center-city youth, despite hesitations and obstacles. The greatest lag is in the area of internal school organization.

Implementation

New technology may produce revolutionary changes in the schools, introducing new dynamics. This result is more likely when the technology forces changes in the relationships among administrators, teachers, and students who are involved through the technology. We think this is the crucial point to understand. New technology is necessary to work more adequately with low-income youth, but this technology will be inadequate unless facilitating administrative change occurs.

How is the kind of educational revolution that we need going to be produced? Pressure from within the educational establishment and from without are both necessary. The needed external pressure for change is more apparent than the internal drive for transforming schools. The Negro revolution and the war on poverty have focused attention on schools, asking how well they are doing the job of educating low-income students. Many changes have resulted from these pressures. We expect them to continue and to be sharpened in their specificity and sophistication. But are we doing enough?

The recent availability of funds for education of the "culturally deprived" is leading many who have had no interest in disadvantaged youth to begin to manifest a concern so that they can drink at the new financial trough. With the smell of poverty money, many are running to the youth they have long neglected. Our initial response to this phenomenon, we must confess, had been a moralistic one: Repugnance at the new-found "mission" that money can now buy but social responsibility did not. But more reflective friends have convinced us that the achievement of change requires giving people a reward, a material interest, in moving in new directions; altruism cannot be depended on. Poverty money is providing school systems, schools of education, and affluent professors, with a stake in doing new things about the poor. Sometimes the interest in low-income youth comes out of unloving things such as developing good public relations, or obtaining money to do other things under the guise of helping the poor, or striving to reduce politically important pressures. But the most important result is that more attention is being given to low-income youth. Nevertheless, these activities have to be policed —held accountable—to see that they actually benefit those to whom we dedicate ourselves in the preambles to our projects.

External pressure is thus leading to increased attention to low-income youth, although not without difficulties. But have teachers done all they could to bring about change? Teachers' organizations—both the unions and the professional organizations—have paid inadequate attention to the reorganization and rededication of schools so that they can deal more effectively with low-income pupils. It is important that teachers and their organizations take the responsibility of initiating and demanding action for the improvement of schools, especially those in low-income areas. Teachers' initiatives in securing modifications in the schools are of grave importance.

One of the frequent complaints of fledgling teachers is that they cannot implement their good ideas because the school authorities resist them. Schools of education are caught in the bind of preparing students for what is desirable practice, which may lead to strain in the actual teaching situation, or to reduce their goals to what is acceptable practice to many school officials. This is a widespread problem in American life, having many different faces.

The encrustations of professionalization and the rigidities of bureaucratic organizations force dedicated professionals to be in tension with the organizations in which they work. *They have to subvert as well as live with their bureaucracies.* Every large organization has a bureaucratic underground, a group resistant to the existing practices of the organization. Much of what we learn about American foreign policy is leaked out by dissident groups within the State Department. Some of us will have to be provocative, raising questions and following policies which are not fully acceptable to the organizations in which we work, if we are to fulfill our responsibilities to our students and to our society. We need courageous, creative discontent.

Increasingly, as we live in bureaucracies, we shall have to face the Eichmann question: What is our individual responsibility for what our organization does? To what extent does organizational loyalty supersede personal morality and require us to ignore or protect incompetence and irresponsibility? Should not teachers, singly and in association, publicly and privately, criticize what their schools are doing when youth are victimized?

Obviously, such pressure is insufficient to swing the battle to the rapid improvement of conditions for low-income youth. But it is one of the things that can be done.

We have stressed that respect for students and competence are important elements in successful teaching of low-income youth. Does this imply that teachers have to have "mature" personalities or exceptional intellect; that we can succeed only if we have more restricted criteria of admission to teaching, thereby aggravating the teacher shortage? No one, of course, can argue against the desirability of getting more feeling teachers into the system; this may happen as salaries and the status of the profession increase. But this is unlikely in the short run. Nor will we be getting the intellectual giants who made lycées and gymnasiums the superior schools they have been; the special factors leading learned persons into lower levels of education do not exist in our society. What are our possibilities of getting better teachers in the immediate situation?

Few of us can consistently rise above our surroundings. In a fascinating study of physicians, it has been shown that those with the high-level training do not do well in poor medical settings. More important than the training of a physician is whether or not he is in a hospital situation which permits and pushes him into quality medical practice. Similarly, for teachers, the community and organizational setting of a school affect whether or not teachers can have authentic relationships with their students. If a community does not have commitment to low-income youth, few authentic responses can occur. Authenticity occurs not only because of personality and value characteristics of the teachers, but from the situation as well. Some people can triumph over adverse conditions and demonstrate devotion and respect. But for most of us, if the situation indicts authenticity or does not encourage it, then authenticity will be a rarity.

Teacher Training

Nonetheless, much more can be done to promote teachers' positive feelings about low-income youth. The emphasis, we have asserted, is that teacher training should lead to the development of each individual's style rather than to the emulation of one grand style of teaching. People have different ways of developing and of expressing their style. Many teachers have to become more aware of how they can more effectively use themselves in the teaching situation. We do not mean that they need psychotherapy, but that they lack adequate mirrors in their training so that they can learn their strengths and weaknesses. They are not aided in discovering useful leads to develop teaching approaches with which they are creative. Much of this can be learned. And we think that teachers and prospective teachers can be provided experiences and knowledge about low-income youth that will build positive feelings and respect.

We have to shed the strait jacket of thought about the process of teaching teaching and the overemphasis on formal credentials, a mark of our uncertainty about what is effective performance. Research has to be conducted in a serious way. Studies of school dropouts fill us with oceanic despair; many are almost criminally incompetent.

The cookbook approach to pedagogy, research, and administration prevents teachers and administrators from learning how to think imaginatively about their problems. Underlying much of the teaching in schools of education is an absence of respect for the students and their potential. Lacking, frequently, is a sense of vitality and enthusiasm about teaching itself.

Schools of education—like medical schools—have a tremendous impact on practice. A mission to work with the disadvantaged is needed—and a willingness to forego comforting clichés, to face the anxiety and adventure of discovering how to deal effectively with low-income youth and to build school institutions which attract rather than repel.

Conclusion

If we agree "that loyalty to petrified opinions never yet broke a chain nor freed a human soul," then we must beware of the persistent danger of traveling on old roads and triumphing on old fields, lacking the courage to take off from where we are. We hope for great breakthroughs in pedagogy. Perhaps they will soon come; probably not. In either case, the educational revolution largely depends on the outlook and behavior of the educational establishment.

NOTES

1. We are not discussing Martin Deutsch's useful programs, but the way in which an ideology is being built around a useful idea. See Alvin W. Gouldner's discussion of this process in "The Metaphysical Pathos of Bureaucracy," *American Political Science Review* (1953).

2. This is reflected in René Clair's great movie, *A Nous la Liberté*, the predecessor of Charlie Chaplin's *Modern Times,* which has a fascinating sequence where the camera moves between a factory's mass-production line and a prison, showing the similarity between the pace and control of the prison and the production line.

8

ⵓⵓ   ⵓⵓ   ⵓⵓ

THE NEW PRESCHOOL
MYTHOLOGY

A powerful new educational mythology has appeared in America. To deal with the school problems of low-income youth, the new "radicals" propose to catch the child early and educate him before he arrives at the school. In essence, preschool programs such as Operation Headstart attempt to prepare children for the presently inadequate educational system. The emphasis is not on changing educational institutions but rather on changing the youngsters to fit into existing structures.

Proponents of this view, such as the able *Fortune* editor Charles Silberman, have defined it as "radical." Presumably, it is radical because it gets to the child early, before he has been too damaged by the school system. (There is considerable evidence that the disadvantaged child's measured IQ declines as he "progresses" or regresses through school.)

This chronological radicalism is in sharp contrast to a radicalism which espouses institutional or structural change as the fundamental approach to improved education. Child-centered radicalism sees the world transformed through the changing of children. Sociological radicalism denies that the world changes in this fashion and rather proposes that adult institutions must change first, and that child development may then reflect these basic institutional changes.

One is reminded of the simplistic application of psychoanalysis in the forties and fifties which envisioned a changed world arising from altered child-rearing practices. This absurdly innocent view never left the oral (optimist) stage. Parents with hostile, antihuman values and relations to society had difficulty bringing up their children in the presumably healthy child-rearing fashion. Those parents who partially succeeded found that their early positive efforts were rapidly vitiated when the child moved into the other institutions surrounding him. One of these institutions, of course, was the school.

The great hopes for preschool education were smashed within two years after the excitement and high optimism that heralded Operation Headstart, the Office of Economic Opportunity's preschool program mainly for children of the poor. The exaggerated expectations could have been avoided, for they overlooked the fact that most improvements or gains that are easily achieved in preschool programs evaporate when children enter traditional school programs.

We argued at the beginning of Headstart that age six was not the crucial year for evaluation but age sixteen. It turns out that age seven is —the gains of attention in the preschool program wash out by then! Martin Deutsch, a leading proponent of preschool activity, observed this in children in his program and early warned about the dangers. In Ypsilanti, Michigan, David Weikart produced sharp rises in the average IQ's of deprived children through special preschool experimental programs, but when these children entered the traditional kindergarten, their scores declined.[1] In Oakland, California, J. M. Regal followed up children who had and who had not been in a Headstart program; the non-Headstarters had a greater absolute gain in the second year than did the Headstarters! (Although the gain was not great enough to reduce all of the initial advantage of Headstart.) Max Wolff's New York City study of the decline in gains of Headstart children stimulated the Office of Economic Opportunity to trump its Operation Headstart with an Operation Follow-up.[2]

What are the difficulties of the preschool approach?

First, the entire preschool thesis is essentially a compensatory one: it emphasizes deficits rather than strengths. It has already been shown to be a considerable failure, at least judging from the Ford Foundation program in the Fourteen Great Cities, which utilized this approach with an admitted lack of success.

Second, the emphasis upon getting "low-income youth early" carries with it the implication that not much more than remedial work can be done with these youngsters in the school proper. It is another way in which the school can shirk responsibility, but instead of passing it on to parents as hitherto had been the fashion, the kindergarten and nursery school are the new dumping grounds. A much more relevant approach would seem to first emphasize positives and then build the child's basic confidence through utilizing his strengths to overcome weaknesses and deficits.

Third, contrary to the popular stereotype, numerous reports indicate that disadvantaged youngsters come to the first grade with considerable curiosity, enthusiasm, and freshness—presumably good omens for learning.[3] Unfortunately, these characteristics do not appear to be capitalized on by the school, and before long the child retreats from the school both attitudinally and educationally.

Fourth, the preschool strategy postpones delivery of significant results for thirteen or fourteen years—that is, until the child is an adolescent or an adult. Since we believe that significant developments in our society are now on the national agenda, we do not feel like waiting for these present-day four-year-olds to make a major contribution fourteen years from now. We prefer that we educate people throughout the school system, with particular attention to junior high-school and high-school youngsters. New programmed learning methods indicate that it may be possible to teach the entire academic program from grade school through high school in less than eighteen months. In other words, we can now think of basic approaches that are habilitative at all ages rather than rehabilitative and remedial.

Fifth, the preschool thesis is predicated on the assumption that deprivation in the early life of the disadvantaged child produces a basic retardation which is essentially impossible to reverse or overcome later in life. Special educational efforts, it is argued, must be introduced while the child is still very young, or all is lost. A number of current studies indicate, however, that illiterate youngsters and adults at all ages have been able to learn reading and other subjects quite rapidly. One reason is that we now have available excellent new techniques, such as the Initial Teaching Alphabet which demonstrated high effectiveness with illiterate candidates for the army in England.

In addition, we underestimate growth possibilities. Howard University's Community Apprentice Program showed that functionally illiterate, delinquent dropouts, through a program that provided jobs with training built in, could be rapidly trained as research aides, recreation aides, and preschool aides.[4] This program not only enabled the youngsters to learn to read but also to do mathematics and even statistics.

Preschool programs should not be used as a substitute for interventions at later stages of the school life cycle. The best guess today is that *interventions at the later stages can be effective without interventions at the early, but that interventions at the early stages without interventions at the later will have a very limited payoff.*

Sixth, the common assumption that "cultural deprivation" destroys intellectual potential is open to attack. Initial results of an IQ test, developed by Dr. Leon Rosenberg of Johns Hopkins University to eliminate cultural advantages in measuring intelligence, indicate that there is no difference between the intelligence of Negro slum children and that of white middle-class children. Most of the standard IQ tests that are used on disadvantaged children are "verbally loaded" with middle-class words and concepts, Dr. Rosenberg says, and even those that are nonverbal depend heavily on experiences not usually had by these children. His test, relying on matching random forms, yielded results that differed drastically from scores on standard IQ tests for a group of Negro slum children. The scores of white middle-class children on the test correlated closely with their standard IQ test scores.

Seventh, the preschool Headstart strategy was based on a loose overgeneralization of various animal experiments and special human (or inhuman) experiments on sensory deprivation. Implications of these studies were projected to disadvantaged children on the presumed ground that the deprivations these children experience are really similar to the severe deprivations endured by experimental subjects. This entire thesis overlooks the significance of a "levels" approach (Novikoff's Theory of Integrative Levels); that is, it oversimplifies by mechanically extrapolating from one level (e.g., animal level) to another (human level). It also ignores the tremendous stimulation of television for all children—not just the advantaged.

Eighth, the Headstart program suffered an ambiguity and vacillation of goals. It was initially a program that talked about preparing youth for school. Then it was described as a program whose major contribution was in identifying health defects, in the hope that communities might feel compelled to do something about these problems. In many communities, however, this does not seem actually to have taken place, although over the long run the highlighting of the illnesses and defects of youth may lead to more effective programs. The identification of need does not always spur action. The movement from an educational program to a stress upon health is actually a regression of objectives. Programs which do not succeed on their primary mission often offer secondary gains as substitutes. Obviously, secondary gains have much to offer, but they are not the same as the gains of the primary mission. Health gains are not substitutes for educational gains.

Ninth, the preschool emphasis is basically conservative. It takes the heat off schools at a time when public temperatures are rising over school inadequacies. Schools can present themselves as moving to aid low-income youth through preschool programs when they are actually attempting to adapt youth to poor educational systems. The obvious attraction of preschool programs to school authorities is that such programs emphasize changing children to be more easily adaptive to school needs, demands, and abilities. The confidence with which many supported it suggests that they believe that very little other change is required for much improved school performance. This belief is unwarranted and dangerous—lengthening the school cycle may become a substitute for improving it.

When there are great lacks and inadequacies in basic services, it is difficult to criticize or even assess a program which does provide some gain. And Headstart did have substantial gains: it captured the imagination of many who had not been concerned about disadvantaged children; it began to acquaint teachers who became interested in the Headstart program with new approaches to disadvantaged youngsters; it partially filled a need to relieve mothers from continued child care; it established a model for the employment of nonprofessionals as preschool aides and, indeed, these nonprofessionals were perhaps the most effective part of the program; it introduced health checkups; it is improving the general quality and aims of preschool programs in the United States; the Child Development Group of Mississippi, a Headstart program, is of great significance in affecting the situation of Negroes in that state; many Negro parents are becoming politically concerned because of the many difficulties faced by Headstart programs.

But if one is to argue that any gain is better than no gain, then we have no basis for choosing among the alternative programs and strategies that are possible. Merely to stress that a particular program does yield improvements is insufficient, especially when a program is as expensive as a full year-round Headstart would be, adding at least 10 per cent to public school budgets. The question is whether the resources are utilized in the most effective way at that particular moment.

The absence of gain at the third-grade level of children who have had preschool experiences indicates that schools must change if the early improvement is to be maintained and built upon. The original Headstart preschool approach had few mechanisms for pressuring for school change. Indeed, most Headstart programs had no direct connection to the local school system.

We have stressed an alternative strategy from the beginning of the preschool talk. Obviously, preschool programs have value even though they do not solve the educational problems facing low-income youth. Since these programs are very attractive to both money givers—which is a question of feasibility—and to schools—which is a question of acceptability—they should be utilized as a way of inducing change within schools. Preschool funds such as Headstart should be given to schools that will make effective changes in the later school years. Those schools that move achievement levels up the most should be rewarded with additional funds. The relatively vast funds now being used primarily to take schools off the hook would be better used as incentive for change throughout the school years.

Simply spending more money is not enough to improve the quality of educational output. As it is now, we are probably not getting as much return per dollar of expenditure in schools in low-income neighborhoods as in high-income areas. Effectively changing the schools, not just supporting them, is needed.

What is suggested here is that preschool programs not be looked upon as revolutionary panaceas; they are neither revolutionary nor panaceas. They are ineffective if schools do not follow up the gains which a good program might provide. Their most useful role is as a strategy of innovation within the school rather than as an adjuster of low-income youth to inadequate schools.

There is no question that preschool programs have a place in a total school strategy. At issue is giving them a central place in this strategy, thus directing us away from an emphasis on the school itself. Particularly naïve is the notion that the preschool strategy is some fundamental or revolutionary approach. As a major strategy, it can be highly regressive and distractive from major institutional changes.

What is suggested here is using preschool programs as a strategy of change in the school rather than providing school services which are useful but insufficient to improve the caliber of education. The new Follow Through program belatedly aims in this direction. Preschool education must have magnified impact through affecting the nature of the large-scale institutions which primarily distribute the main resources—education. And schools, as we argue in the next chapter, can do a much better job than they are now doing.

NOTES

1. See Bernard Asbell, "Six Years Is Too Late," *Redbook*, CXXV, No. 5 (September 1965).

2. It could be argued that these disturbing results are due to low-caliber crash programs. The organizational difficulties in getting Headstart under way were comparable to the astounding logistics of D-Day. But what assurances are there that the needed high-quality programs are possible on a large scale?

3. Moreover, studies indicate that the parents of these youngsters have a very positive attitude toward education. These parents in overwhelming numbers state that "education is what they missed most in life that they would like their children to have." See Frank Riessman, *The Culturally Deprived Child* (New York: Harper and Row, 1962).

4. See Arthur Pearl and Frank Riessman, *New Careers for the Poor* (New York: Free Press, 1965), for a discussion of the Community Apprentice Program which provides a model for the proposed development of millions of non-professional jobs and careers for the poor. This may, indeed, be a radical proposal because it will allow poor people to become non-poor and should stimulate significant institutional changes in a variety of areas.

9

TEACHERS OF THE POOR:
BLUEPRINT FOR CHANGE

We have stressed in chapters 6, 7, and 8 the need for organizational change within the school. But we also believe that practitioners must have an effective technology for performing their tasks. In this chapter we address ourselves to the possible technology for a major breakthrough in the education of the disadvantaged.

Educational Failures

Despite encouraging reports, large-scale improvements in the learning of disadvantaged youngsters have not been achieved for at least three reasons:

First, the efforts have been piecemeal and unintegrated. One technique is used here and another there without any theoretically directed, integrated approach.

Second, the major emphasis has been on deficits and "compensatory" efforts directed toward overcoming them; there has been little understanding of how to use the strengths and positives of disadvantaged youngsters, if, indeed, it is recognized that these strengths exist at all.

Third, there has been no concerted effort to meet the felt needs of the teachers—for lower student-teacher ratios, techniques that work, a voice in decisions that affect them, etc. The classroom teacher has not typically been perceived as the strategic change agent for massive improvement in the learning of the poor.[1] (Instead, much stress has been placed on parents, preschools, teaching machines, psychological guidance, and special services.)

The present period combines strong demands of the civil-rights movement for quality education,[2] with increased financial support from the Federal government. In this climate it would seem that a revolutionary breakthrough in the education of the poor can now be planned, as a step in revitalizing public schools and winning back the middle classes who have fled to private schools. It is time to aim high and not accept improvement up to grade level. *We need the educational equivalent of a moon shot.* American society is not aiming high enough in improving the educational achievements of the poor.

What are the ingredients for revolutionary achievement in education? Should we combine all the various features that have worked in a kind of potpourri or should we, rather, selectively choose approaches based on an analysis which offers an explanation in a coherent fashion of why they have worked? The latter is not only theoretically more meaningful, but probably less expensive.[3]

The starting point is the need of teachers.

The New Manpower

Perhaps the major complaint in the schools today is the large classes that each teacher must manage. The ratio of students to teachers is frequently greater than thirty to one. New manpower to assist the badly overworked teacher is the paramount need of the day. Where can it be found?

The utilization of larger numbers of people drawn from the ranks of the poor themselves, so-called nonprofessionals, to serve as teacher assistants, teacher aides, parent-teacher coordinators, and the like may be the answer. Important steps have been taken but the nonprofessional role has not expanded as rapidly as it should.

Currently in the classroom there is but one designated role—teacher. Incorporated in that role are a great number of diverse functions—the teacher is an educator, but he is also clerk, custodian, and operator of audiovisual equipment. In many slum schools teachers act as though they were part lion tamer and part warehouseman. The latter roles must be eliminated, while many of the others can be assumed by less qualified personnel.

This new kind of nonprofessional manpower serves a number of positive functions: [4]

1. It frees teachers from the many nonprofessional tasks they now perform, e.g., taking attendance, helping children on with their boots, tying children's shoelaces, running moving-picture projectors, taking youngsters on trips, etc. The new teacher aides would take over many of these tasks, freeing teachers for their basic professional assignment—teaching and teaching creatively.

2. Nonprofessionals, especially males, drawn from the ranks of the poor, serve as excellent role models for disadvantaged youngsters in the schools; the youngsters would see that it is possible that people like themselves, from their own neighborhood, can "make it" in the system.

3. The trained nonprofessional and the disadvantaged youngster could probably communicate effectively because the neighborhood nonprofessional speaks the language of the poor and understands his social class peers. Many of the advantages of peer learning or learning from people at the same level would be utilized.

4. The atmosphere of the school would be different. Many of the management problems expected in the urban, newly integrated or completely segregated schools might be reduced. [5]

The use of aides should not be imposed upon teachers. In fact, teachers' associations and unions should actively participate in planning for the use of nonprofessionals. Probably the best way to introduce nonprofessionals into the system is to ask teachers to volunteer to accept an aide to assist them. The teachers who thus select themselves can then define the tasks on which they would like nonprofessional assistance. (They may also receive consultation on this from the program planners.) Teachers would have to be trained and assisted in utilizing nonprofessionals.

If the aides are really helpful, the program will stimulate other teachers to request nonprofessional assistants for their classrooms. In this way the idea could be institutionalized with the full cooperation of the professional staff and the new professional-nonprofessional team could be built on a solid foundation.

Techniques and Goals

Teachers not only need new manpower to assist them in the classroom; they need new approaches as well. Too often teachers are asked to act like psychologists (understand the underlying emotional conflicts of the child); like sociologists (appreciate the environment and culture of the deprived); like prison guards (keep order and prevent violence); like substitute parents (love the children); like ministers (impart the right values).

Teachers need to be allowed to concentrate on applying and developing the art of teaching. Teachers cannot be expected to become sociologists or psychologists and acquire an intensive understanding of the psychology and culture of the poor. While they must understand how the techniques they utilize are related to the style and strength of the poor, the emphasis must be on the techniques themselves. As teachers successfully employ these techniques, their confidence will improve and their motivation will be enhanced. Our stress, therefore, is on giving the teachers what they want, namely, know-how.

The techniques to be employed should be based fundamentally on the goals one is striving for with the disadvantaged. We do not have the goal of simply producing a carbon copy of the middle-class child.[6] To aim for this middle-class replica is not only inappropriate in principle but not easily achievable in practice. Many disadvantaged children will resist this objective and, to the extent that they acquiesce, will become poor editions of middle-class youngsters—faded carbon copies. Our objective, therefore, is to build on the strengths which are found in many inner-city children, not to deny them or suppress them, but rather to utilize them as the key to developing, for example, language. But our concern for building on the strengths of disadvantaged children is not simply to bring them more efficiently into the main stream of American life; rather we want also to help them blend into this main stream some of their characteristics: their style, pep, vitality; their demand that the school not be boring and dull; their rich feeling for metaphor and colorful language.[7]

In another area one group of disadvantaged people in America, the Negro, has made an enormous contribution to the main stream of American life through its articulate demands for desegregation and equality. A new morality centering on an attack against institutionalized and personal white racism is emerging. Similarly, in education, the main stream of American life can profit from what the various groups among the poor could bring to the school system, in their demands that the system be peppier, livelier, more vital, more down to earth. This style will enable the school to become less bookish and a better utilizer of a great variety of styles—an action style, a physical style, a visual style—far more than the overemphasized reading-lecture patterns in vogue.

The techniques that we discuss are uniquely related to these goals and to the belief that there is a positive style among many of the disadvantaged which can be utilized to the great benefit of all social classes. Even if this contention is not accepted, the techniques can still be utilized with varying degrees of effectiveness.

The Dialect Game

The best way to illustrate the relationship of the teaching technology we advocate to our educational goals is to look at a very simple technique which we learned from a teacher who evolved it out of her own practice. We call it the dialect game.

One spring day a youngster turned to his teacher. "Do you hear that boid outside the window?"

And the teacher replied, "That's not a boid. It's a bird." Following the old joke, the youngster said, "He choips just like a boid."

All of which goes to show that teaching standard pronunciation in this way might not work. It might, in fact, confuse the student about the nature of the avowed objective.

But the teacher in our story decided that she might get positive results if she did not require students to reject their own speech—the slang, the "hip," and the other elements that make up the dialect acquired at home and in the neighborhood. So she decided to play a game. She took any word at random and asked the student how it would be said in his language and in standard language, the language of radio and TV. Now her students knew what was going on. They were learning new words and new ways of expression as they might a foreign language. They were discovering that their own language was perfectible, that it was even the best language available in the right place—home, on the street, at the ball park. But in more formal circumstances another language would get better results, and this was the language being taught in school.

The students began to learn something else, too. They became interested in language itself. In their discussion of "cool," for example, it was decided that fairly good synonyms for it were the standard words "calm" and "collected" and the more formal "nonchalant." But these were not true equivalents. "Cool" had connotations that could not be conveyed by other words.

These students were acquiring a feel for words, an appreciation for the nuances of language, even one of the basic skills of style—the ability to choose among words according to their appropriateness for the occasion.

Once this kind of learning occurs, there is every reason to expect that it will grow. Enjoyment of words leads to love of words; it can lead even to the reading of poetry and dictionaries—prime sources for those who like word play.

But most important of all, perhaps, at least for those students who bring "nonstandard" dialects or a foreign language to school, is learning that one's own language is not to be denied. One's own language is in basic ways one's own self; by denying and suppressing the student's language we are truly denying and suppressing him. But when it is shown that the student's language is a positive asset, it is not hard to teach him respect for it—and thereby for himself. For every dialect there are times and places for which it is appropriate, and there are intended meanings for which it provides the best word equivalents. In fact, this is one of the ways all natural languages grow and become richer. New human conditions require words with new nuances. And for our human condition today, colorful and richly metaphorical words such as "jazz" and "hip" and "cooling it" have nuances that no other words can convey. It would be impossible to describe modern urban life adequately without them.

If we approach the language of disadvantaged students in this positive way, we can build on it the layers of standard English; by adding rather than subtracting, we can bring the strengths and interests of the so-called deprived into the main stream of American life.

This dialect game can be adapted in many simple ways. In tutoring a disadvantaged high-school student in English, we employed a *hip*-tionary[8] in a systematic and formal fashion. The first and rather immediate result was that the student learned a great many new English word definitions for the "hip" words with which she was long familiar:

Hip Word	Definition
bug	to disturb, bother, annoy
cop out	to avoid conflict by running away, not considered admirable or honorably accepted
cool it	to be quiet, peaceful, tranquil
far out	not comprehensible
weak	inadequate, inappropriate

Words such as "tranquil" and "inappropriate" were not known by this youngster, but through use of the hip "word game" she quickly became familiar with them and derived great pleasure from a new-found use of various "big" words.

It should be clear that we are not suggesting that teachers employ "hip" language in normal conversation with the underprivileged youngster; it is not intended as a device for attempting to be friendly with the child by imitating his culture. This would indeed be patronizing and dangerous. Rather, the use of hip material in a formal lesson plan can become an excellent avenue to the style and interests of the disadvantaged and contribute to the development of their verbalization.

Another interesting illustration is furnished by the problem of teaching English to Puerto Rican and Mexican children entering our school system in New York, California, and other parts of the country. The typical tendency is to force these youngsters not to speak any Spanish, their mother tongue, insisting that they speak only English, on the supposition that this would be the best way of their acquiring the English language. While this may be a useful way of teaching a language to an adult in certain contexts, when it is associated in the child with rejection of his minority culture (something he experiences quite frequently), he is not likely to be an apt pupil in the new language. Furthermore, he is constantly in the inferior position of having to acquire this language while the remainder of the youngsters in the class already know it.

The dialect game can be utilized beautifully to reverse the whole procedure. Instead of emphasizing the need for Spanish children to learn English, the situation can be reversed for part of the day, and the Spanish children can be instructed to teach Spanish to the American children. In other words, both languages become important in the class. The English children have an opportunity to learn a foreign language, presumably a positive benefit when that language is French or Latin, and the Spanish-speaking children can be placed temporarily in the position of some superiority through helping others. In addition, for the Puerto Rican or Mexican-American youngster to teach Spanish to English-speaking children, he must be able to communicate to some extent in English. Thus, in the very process of teaching the foreign language, he must acquire more English in order to communicate (unless he arbitrarily insists that only Spanish be spoken when he is instructing!).

Thus the dialect game which can be utilized by anyone as a gimmick or an auxiliary technique in teaching takes on considerable depth when seen in the context of two cultures, two languages functioning along-side of each other, both respected, both affecting each other, with no condescension toward the minority culture.

The Helper Principle: Learning through Teaching

In Flint, Michigan, disadvantaged sixth-grade youngsters with reading difficulties helped fourth-grade children who had reading problems. The performance of both groups went up!

This experiment, which is being duplicated in various parts of the country, indicates that children benefit from playing the teacher role.

At the 1965 White House Conference on Education, Professor Jerrold Zaccharias proposed that students teach as a major avenue for improving their own learning; Montessorians have long utilized children to help other children learn in the classroom.

Schneider reports on a small study in which youngsters with varying levels of reading ability were asked to read an "easy" book as practice for reading to younger children. She observes:

> For the child who could read well, this was a good experience. For the child who could not read well, it was an even better experience. He was reading material on a level within his competence and he could read it with pleasure. Ordinary books on his level of interest were too difficult for him to read easily and so he did not read books for pleasure. Reading for him was hard, hard work; often it left him feeling stupid and help-less. This time it was different . . . he would be a giver; he would share his gift with little children just as a parent or teacher does.[9]

Mobilization for Youth's experience with homework helpers showed that the greatest academic advance was not among those tutored but among the tutors who were high-school youngsters.

As any teacher can report, there is nothing like learning through teaching. Explaining to someone else focuses attention and accentuates clarity.

In the new situations in the schools, where (hopefully) integration will be taking place, youngsters coming from segregated backgrounds will need help in catching up in reading skills and the like. It is generally argued that the white middle-class children who do not need this extra assistance will suffer. Their parents want these youngsters to be in a class with advanced pupils and not to be "held back" by youngsters who are behind.

The helper principle suggests that more advanced youngsters can benefit in new ways from playing a teaching role. Not all fast, bright youngsters like to be in a class with similar children. We have been led to believe that if one is fast and bright he will want to be with others who are fast and bright and this will act as a stimulus to his growth. It does for some people, but for others it most certainly does not. Some people find they do better in a group in which there is a great range of ability, in which they can stand out more, and finally—and this is the point of the helper principle—in situations in which they can help other youngsters in the classroom. In short, some children develop not by being challenged by someone ahead of them, but by helping somebody behind them, by being tutors or helpers.

The helper principle may be especially valuable for disadvantaged youngsters because in their formal, out-of-school learning they tend to learn much more from each other, from their brothers and sisters, than from their parents reading them a book or answering their questions.

Capturing the Action Style through Role Playing

Role playing is the flexible acting out (doing) of various types of situations in a permissive group atmosphere. Most role playing is usually done in groups where a few children act out a situation and the group discusses it. Since it is free of the tensions of an actual problem situation, role playing stimulates children to try out new alternatives and solutions in lifelike situations without the consequences which in reality may be punishing. Role playing thus increases the participant's role flexibility in an atmosphere where he can safely take a chance with different kinds of behavior.

Role playing can be used, as Professor Lawrence Senesch observes, to teach arithmetic and economics (by "playing" store); to teach history by acting out, for example, George Washington signing the Constitution; even language can be taught by acting out words (in fact, the game "In the Manner of the Adverb" consists of "doing" the adverb—e.g., walking quickly, writing quickly, etc.).

Role playing has long been popular with disadvantaged youngsters. The technique is very congenial with the style of many low-income people: physical (action oriented, doing rather than only talking); down to earth, concrete, problem directed; externally oriented rather than introspective; group centered; game-like rather than test oriented; easy, informal in tempo. Many disadvantaged youngsters tend to work out mental problems best when they can do things physically (whether it be through role playing, dance, taking a trip, etc.).

A Route to Verbalization

In many role-playing sessions the verbal performance of deprived children is markedly improved in the discussion period following the session. Deprived children are apparently able to verbalize much more fully when talking about some action they have seen. Typically, they do not verbalize well in response to words alone. They express themselves more readily when reacting to things they can see and do. Words as stimuli are not sufficient for them as a rule. Ask a youngster who comes from a disadvantaged background what he does not like about school or the teacher and you will get an abbreviated, inarticulate reply. But if a group of these youngsters act out a school scene in which someone plays the teacher, a stream of verbal consciousness that is almost impossible to shut off frequently occurs.[10]

Pluralism in Teaching Strategies

We have seen how varied dropouts are. We should not be thinking of *the* dropout but of different kinds of poor students, needing different environments and aid at various times. Obviously, then, various kinds and types of teachers are needed.

Unfortunately, an implicit model of an ideal teacher frequently prevails. Teachers are expected to, or believe that they should, fashion themselves after this model. The existence of many different kinds of successful teachers has been inadequately recognized. In observing schools we have been struck by the great variety of successful teachers, some of whom have quite antithetical styles. An enormous range of styles seem to be effective with low-income youngsters. A model, even implicit, of the ideal teacher pushes teachers into a mold.

The emphasis rather should be on each teacher developing a style which fits with her interests, personality, and orientation as they relate to the particular students she has at a particular time. Teachers of new working-class children need a variety of concrete teaching tactics. They need to be able to adapt so they can build on their own abilities and inclinations. The orientation should not be toward specific techniques which are thought to have all-powerful consequences, but upon the uniqueness of teachers and their differentiated abilities. It is important for teachers and training programs to accept the diversity of teachers and to try to develop the kinds of strategy that would be most effective for a teacher, given her personality, interests, and aptitudes (although these can be developed and channeled).

In this connection, inadequate attention has been devoted to effective teachers. In every school, no matter what its general character, some teachers are successful with children. We need better understanding of what these effective teachers do. An important research project could be developed around close observation of and interviews with such teachers so that it would be possible to develop inductively a scheme of effective teaching processes. We are not referring to the use of clip books or other tactics that may be employed by an effective teacher, but to the underlying and frequently implicit strategy that is involved. Frequently, the tactics of effective teachers are picked up and distributed to a wider group of teachers, but the teaching strategies which give rise to or utilize these techniques are ignored. The job of research is to sift through tactics, seeing which have transfer value of themselves, and to uncover the basic strategies which could be adapted in many ways by other teachers.

Teacher Institutes

Without detailing the methods whereby teachers receive the training for these approaches, some general principles can be outlined: [11]

1. Where possible teachers themselves (master teachers, consulting teachers) should do the teaching or group leading. It may be necessary first to hold "master" institutes where teachers, who would later train other teachers, would be exposed to the techniques discussed above. At a later point these master teachers would be supervised as they translated the program for their local schools. The master institute could call on all kinds of specialists, including sociologists, psychologists, artists, Montessori specialists, role-playing leaders, etc. The institutes could be introduced as special courses in preservice training (in regular sessions or summer sessions) as well as for in-service programs.

2. Training that is provided close to the operations in which it will be utilized will be most effective. Teachers, for example, should be worked with around their specific school and classroom problems and the "trainers" should visit the classrooms, observe the teachers closely, and discuss problems and suggestions with them in considerable detail.

3. A group or team approach should be a central feature in the training, with a strong emphasis on building esprit de corps in the groups. The group experience would be examined itself and utilized for the development of concepts, understanding of group process, etc. (T group approach.)

4. Full participation of the trainees should be intensively solicited. They should be encouraged to formulate their needs, to identify their problems, and to suggest ways of meeting these problems. Hence, small teacher meetings should be organized to discuss (and role play) ways of meeting classroom difficulties, teaching techniques, and approaches, etc. In this context the trainers would offer for discussion techniques that have evolved elsewhere.

5. In order to have training become a part of the "neuromuscular" make-up of the trainees, a variety of techniques should be instituted: supervisory conferences, role playing, films, demonstrations, quizzes, intensive brief reading, small-group discussions, lectures, debates, and the writing of a paper. This methodology is based on two principles: (a) People learn through a variety of styles—some learn best from doing, others from lectures, others from films, etc. (b) In order to internalize material taught over a relatively short period of time, it is necessary to provide as much active practice and involvement as possible, along with corrective feedback from the supervisory staff; thus the emphasis on role playing and "supervisors' " sessions. In addition, having the

learner teach the material to other trainees appears to be an excellent device for the development of deep learning.

Blueprint for a Revolution

Piecemeal approaches to the improvement of the education of the poor have provided many exciting experiments and some definite gains in learning. The time is now ripe for an all-out attack, integrating our best knowledge to produce truly large, enduring improvements in the learning of disadvantaged youngsters at all ages. A national program rather than a pilot, small-scale project requires leadership, new techniques, and new manpower.

A four-stage educational design is needed. The first stage stresses the contact curriculum of Fantini and Weinstein which is oriented toward connecting the specific subject matter with the specific interests and styles of the child. The second phase is directed toward students' learning how to learn. The third stage is concerned with developing skills and knowledges on an individualized basis, with particular emphasis on the use of programmed learning monitored in part by nonprofessionals. The fourth stage is concerned with developing concepts, ideas, structure, understanding.

For this attack the following are proposed:

1. An emphasis on the strengths of the children rather than a compensatory, deficit-oriented approach.

2. Young teachers who would be trained in the use of teaching techniques (e.g., the dialect game, the helper principle, role playing, etc.) attuned to the styles and *strengths* of disadvantaged children. The positives must come first and around these positives we can begin to correct the limitations of the child in relation to reading, school know-how, language skills, etc. *If the teacher expects more, he will get more* if his positive expectations are built on an understanding of why he is using the exciting new technologies.

3. Nonprofessional teacher aides, recruited from among the poor themselves, to assist so that they can more fully play their professional roles as teachers.

4. In-service teacher institutes using trained master teachers to introduce knowledge and techniques related to immediate classroom problems. An attempt should be made to have teachers use techniques that

fit not only the style of the children, but their own style and interests as well (style match). These efforts should be part of a powerful stress on the training and retraining of all school personnel, especially administrators.

5. New urban readers and other appropriate curriculum materials and especially the new teaching machines (programmed learning). Readers that have been developed in Detroit by Follett Publishing Company and in New York by Bank Street College, and published by Macmillan, should be included in the program. These readers incorporate disadvantaged people and themes in a more representative view of urban life. Research in Detroit indicates that all youngsters read better with these readers, not only disadvantaged children—that they laugh more and feel that the stories are more interesting and lively.

The new literacy techniques, *Words in Color,* published by the Encyclopaedia Britannica and Woolman's Progressive Accelerated Technique, are achieving dramatic rapid results with low-literate adults and we would suggest that they become integrated in the proposed program.

6. New administrative arrangements such as team teaching, multiple periods, nongraded classes, educational parks, intensive extra school programs (during summers, weekends, and after school hours). These extra school programs can introduce specialists into the school, such as artists, dancers, musicians, to develop the artistic talents of the youngsters. Tutors could be brought in here also and special uses of programmed learning and educational TV could be planned.

7. Special parent-teacher groups, led by nonprofessional parent-education coordinators, directed toward developing full, genuine two-way communication between the parents and the schools. Parents could be involved as important supportive elements in the program. They should be used to back up the role of a school that really wants to teach the child and they should be listened to attentively by the school and by the nonprofessional parent-education coordinators who mediate between them and the school. They should not be asked, however, to read to the children or to do homework with them or any tasks which they find essentially uncongenial. They can check on homework, as Samuel Sheppard had them do in St. Louis, and work in a unified way with the school, encouraging the child to learn, to attend punctually, to do his homework, etc.

8. An approach to guidance which emphasizes the utilization of the

student's learning style, rather than the usual emphasis on emotional conflict, personality problems, family difficulties.

9. An intensive after-school program directed toward rapid assistance for youngsters who need to catch up in their school learning. This program would use high-school students as homework helpers (as in the Mobilization for Youth model), not only to assist the learner but to aid the tutor to become a better learner through teaching.

10. The use of approaches directed toward increasing the school confidence and positive self-image of the students. (As learning improves, self-confidence will expand, as well as vice versa.)

11. In order to insure that the program does not diffuse its efforts, reading and language arts should be the major concentration, especially at the beginning. All features of the program should key on these areas; thus techniques such as role playing should emphasize acting out words; games such as the hip word game, "Playing It Cool in English," should be related to the development of English as a second language; a battery of the new reading improvement techniques should be introduced; Jensen's techniques for developing verbal mediators in problem solving might be experimented with; prizes should be offered for class improvement in reading and language skills; the after-school program should concentrate on reading and language development; films of teachers who effectively teach language and reading might be utilized; parents should be informed of this over-all emphasis and asked to encourage it.

12. These gains can probably be made most effectively in the context of the educational park, which we discuss in the following chapter.

13. The context of school change should be community gain. While the schools of a locality are being upgraded, general community conditions should also be improved—greater employment opportunities, decentralized and adequate neighborhood-based services, stability, and cohesion. Interrelated sets of changes have a good chance of occurring if the "model-cities" programs move from planning to implementation, from piecemeal actions to profound changes. (In section V we discuss some of the strategies for more effective politicalization of issues and delivery of results in community-action programs.)

14. Finally, what is needed are exciting, committed educational leaders. This type of leader will "expect more" and he will get more. He must be flexible enough to permit and encourage innovative class-

room arrangements. System change and administrative flexibility must be tied to drive and competence.

Whether the existing systems of developing and selecting school leaders are adequate for the task of producing numbers of effective leaders is very doubtful. Traditional credentialing procedures should be expanded so that outstanding people of diverse experiences could be drawn into school administration.

This blueprint is directed toward the teacher and what he wants and needs—assistance in the classroom. He will get this from non-professional manpower and from techniques that work. Through his improved functioning, from success, will come the heightening of motivation. The teacher is the key to the disadvantaged child and the revolution in education. The educational organization provides the setting in which teachers work. If teachers are developed for their new tasks and have appropriate work conditions, we can have a successful moon shot in education.

NOTES

1. The beginning efforts for a national teacher corps and the special teacher-training programs under the National Defense Education Act are in the right direction.

2. We discuss integrated education in Chapter 10.

3. The programs could be placed within the framework of the developing educational parks or educational complexes which would allow for economic utilization of a great variety of new techniques and facilities (educational TV, programmed learning, team teaching, etc.) under one roof, but is not necessary for our moon shot. The educational park idea is discussed in Chapter 10.

4. The nonprofessional role in mental health, poverty, and social-service fields is discussed in chapters 12 and 14.

5. The shortage of school personnel predicted for the next decade might be drastically reduced through the employment of one million nonprofessionals in the schools. For a more detailed description of how nonprofessionals could serve the school, see *New Careers for the Poor*, by Arthur Pearl and Frank Riessman (New York: The Free Press of Glencoe, 1965), Chapter 4.

6. The real question for those who want to "middle-classize" the disadvantaged child relates to which middle class and which middle-class goals and values—the professional upper middle class; the anti-intellectual lower middle class; the new hip class that has adopted much of the speech and some of the manners of various disadvantaged subcultures; the progressive student left, etc. Furthermore, is it not likely that the disadvantaged youngster will selectively choose those middle-class characteristics that at least articulate with some of his own traditions and feelings?

7. We do not believe that all center-city children have these characteristics but that many do. Their special character is lost by the schools.

8. The words in this list were taken from a *hip*-tionary entitled, "The Other Language" developed by Anthony Romeo at Mobilization for Youth, January 1962, unpublished.

9. Gussie Albert Schneider, "Reading of the Children, by the Children, for the Children." Unpublished manuscript, 1964 (mimeographed).

10. Role playing has been utilized to some extent in schools but there has been little awareness of its special potential for connecting with the style of the disadvantaged and as a crucial avenue for developing their verbalization. Its use may serve a very different function for middle-class children; it may force them to be more concrete and reduce some of their intellectualizing tendencies. Teachers should be aware of these different potential uses of role playing.

11. There are other techniques and approaches that might be utilized in a program of education for the poor. Any of the following might be important "extras" to be added, depending upon the style, interests, and abilities of the teachers involved in the program:

a. The "organics" approach of Sylvia Ashton-Warner, presented in her book, *Teacher* (New York, Simon and Schuster, 1963). This should be especially valuable in utilizing the interests and strengths of the youngsters, and guarding against their being "acted upon" (which is the current trend in many of the "compensatory" programs designed for the supposedly "deficit"-ridden disadvantaged).

b. A "modified" curriculum, developed by Gail Donovan in Boston, which stimulated vastly increased interest in literature among poor youngsters.

c. Use of the dance as a method for developing concepts and language, as developed by Claire Schmais in Washington, D. C.

d. Jensen's techniques for developing "verbal mediators" (silent speech, so to speak) in problem solving.

I0

❀ ❀ ❀

THE CASE FOR
INTEGRATED EDUCATION

Five or even ten years ago a chapter with this title would have been entirely commonplace. Today, however, because of the strange alliance of white conservatives and Negro militants, there is an underestimation of what desegregated education has achieved and what an integrated approach could achieve if properly mounted. Moreover, there is a naïve overestimation regarding the possibilities of so-called quality separatist education.

The separatist education goal—once discarded by white liberals and Negro activists—is being readopted with little examination. Many whites are relieved by the separatist educational slogan. It eases their conscience and their fears.

This retreat within the Negro community is masked to some extent by highly militant nationalist posturing about black power, going it alone, not wanting integration in the first place, and strong anti-white feeling. Frequently, it is accompanied by an attack on "the establishment," "the power structure," on the assumption that this group really wants segregation and discrimination.

Actually the new goal represents a highly defensive reaction on parts of the Negro community while simultaneously feeding the backlash of the white community.

We will attempt to demonstrate why it is unlikely that separatist education will approach anything like quality levels for Negroes on a national scale. In fact, the Negro-white educational differential may actually increase nationally, although in isolated demonstrations some Negro gains may be won.

We will endeavor to show that the achievements (especially some of the indirect ones) of the integrated education movement have been overlooked. Moreover, we believe that a great deal more can be done in the integrated context if educational policy is reorganized to take into account previous mistakes.

The purpose of this chapter, then, is to reanalyze the case for integrated education in the context of the more recent moves toward separatist policies. But first how has the retreat from integration occurred? What are its roots and what can be learned from the errors of the past?

Recent History

The civil-rights movement's selection of education as a major arena in which to fight for integration was originally rejected by many social scientists, liberals and progressives. The latter asserted that an integration drive in this area would fail because education simply reflected housing and economic conditions. But civil-rights leaders saw that the education system was fluid and provided a significant opening to highlight the demand for integration in the society. They were right. Initially, important victories were won: great attention centered on education; significant laws were passed; and an important forum emerged for the discussion of integration on a wide scale. Moreover, this drive in the education area led to increased funding for education of the poor and thus indirectly for the Negro.

A number of factors prevented the integration movement from winning major victories in the educational sphere. Most important, is the fact that the inner city itself is residentially segregated to a great extent, and is increasingly so. This condition made it difficult to develop rapidly integrated schooling. School zoning patterns reinforced segregation, making it difficult to produce integration without changing school-district boundaries, even where it was geographically possible. These circumstances provided a difficult context and allowed for easy development of backlash among conservative white middle-class and working-class groups who vigorously and often openly opposed integration. Many if not most white liberals who supported integration in principle had moved out of the inner city or retreated to private schools on the grounds that education was so deficient in the public schools that they could not endanger their children's educational future.

Political support for education was weak and vacillating. Federal and local governments responded to pressure by equivocating in their support of the civil-rights position. School boards acted slowly; school redistricting was rare; minimum demands such as open enrollment were occasionally permitted, but deep, thoroughgoing reorganization was not supported with conviction or funds. Thus, educational parks which might have provided a most significant structure for developing integrated quality education have not been attempted in any significant number. Where they have been planned, their construction has been delayed. The paired-schools approach has lacked outstanding support from the local boards of education where it has been adopted. Reorganization of school levels with the new middle school playing an important role in abetting integration has not developed speedily. Most new schools in urban complexes are being built in segregated areas, sometimes in response to the demands of the citizens of these areas.

Highly significant, too, was the failure of the White House to support former Education Commissioner Francis Keppel when he threatened to cut off Federal funds to the city of Chicago unless it developed a faster pace in its integration plans. This was the outstanding defeat in the development of integrated schools in the North.

Perhaps even more significant was the educational failure itself. Integrating schools were not given sufficient support by the Federal government and the local school system. For the most part human-relations workshops were established to discuss the human-relations issues involved in integration, but essentially no large-scale economic support was provided for educational programming for the integrated school. Teachers, poorly prepared for the new situation of integration and functioning in inadequate school structures in the first place, did not greet the new situation with hope, even when ideologically they were supportive. Teachers were not assisted in how to develop effective groupings within the heterogeneous classroom. Instead, they were given ideas and courses about human relations and the value of integration; they were not aided in mastering teaching logic that would be more effective in the new situation.

Our contention is that *for integrated education to succeed it is necessary to build the most advanced educational system within the integrated network.* Integrated schools have to be the best schools in order to draw and hold reluctant parents. Parents would not mind bussing their children to the most excellent schools in the society—they do this all the time with special nurseries, art schools, music and dance schools. The sacrifice of bussing is mainly an issue to white middle-class parents when they are not sure what there is at the end of the bus ride.

The need to provide the highest quality schools in the integrated sector was not understood by school boards and superintendents, by governmental systems, or by the civil-rights movement as a whole. It is true that some civil-rights groups such as EQUAL supported the concept of the educational park as the most strategic instrument for an effective educational program. But in general the civil-rights movement tended to demand rapid integration and, more important, generally rejected involvement in developing or proposing educational programs. Instead they stated that this was the business of the school system. This position was most unfortunate. It left the job to people who had ambivalence about the goal. School authorities were themselves faced by a great variety of cross-pressures and frequently did not employ technicians or consultants who might have been most responsive to the needs of the integration movement. It would have been useful for the integration movement to involve intellectuals and program planners as consultants to help develop educational plans that could have been fought for by integration leaders.

Negro Forces

From the very beginning some groups within Negro communities were more concerned with quality education than with integration. They argued for the building of new schools within the ghetto, rather than for potential integration points. Then, too, various civil-rights organiza- at potential integration points. Then, too, various civil-rights organizations competed with one another to see who could provide the most militant stance. This contributed to a nonselective overuse of activist demonstration tactics and an inability to negotiate. To some extent the civil-rights movement has been caught in its own militancy. Currently, many of the formerly most outspoken advocates of immediate integration have moved toward a position of separatist education which they now present in militant garb.

Another contributing factor was the absence of simultaneous programs for integration in areas such as employment. Most of the emphasis on integration was in the consumption sector rather than in the production sector of the society. The stress was on integration in public accommodations, education, etc.; no large economic program was put forth by the civil-rights movement or by the government for the development of jobs and careers which could provide the base for integrated demands in consumption. New significant economic power would have been created via these jobs. Large numbers of Negroes would have obtained middle-income status, thus providing the basis for Negro-white integration on the same class level. This possibility contrasts with the current situation which typically involves the integration of poor Negroes with middle-class whites, stirring both class and race feelings.

The deficiency in national programming reflects, of course, the Federal government's lack of a cohesive plan for the development of integration in America. For the most part, Washington responded to pressure. It rarely initiated integration moves and frequently it attempted to provide token responses. For example, instead of developing integration in the school system itself, it was promoted in the pre-school system in Headstart. Nor were Federal, state, and local governments willing to spend major funds for the best educational programs in the integrated sector. Frequently, school administrators were exhorted and cajoled to fight for integrated programs, but special funds to achieve the most advanced educational programming and technology were not offered.

Essentially, people were asked to integrate as a matter of conscience and morality; they were not provided with opportunities for following their consciences without sacrifice. To be most effective, conscience, ideology, and morality must be combined with self-interest and visible benefits. The planners both inside the educational system and outside of it did not fully comprehend that conscience usually succumbs to interests.

The drive away from integration has been fed by and been joined to two other concerns in Negro communities. One is the increasing attention to poverty as the Negro problem; the other is the interest in self-image, dignity, self-respect, and political power.

The civil-rights movement has always been several movements.

Race themes compete with class issues. The race issue has revolved around the breaking of legal and de facto barriers to free entry and movement of Negroes into the larger society. The issues have ranged from bus and lunchroom seating and housing to job discrimination. In many if not most situations the issues have primarily involved better-off Negroes. Class themes center on the poorer Negroes and are concerned with improving the immediate economic and social conditions of the non-middle-class Negroes who are the overwhelming majority. The class issues supplanted the race issues with the passage of the civil-rights acts which attacked the legal basis of discrimination, and with the undertaking of a "war on poverty." For the Negro poor, the issue is seldom integration but immediate improvement of their economic and social conditions of life. This leads to an emphasis on what to do in the slums now rather than changing the long-run situation of Negroes.

At the same time that there has been a strong move from race to class issues, the concerns with "power" and self-image have emerged. Both of these issues have been defined as though only separate black institutions can provide power and positive self-image. The separatist urge infuses the concerns for power and dignity because these issues have arisen at the same time that Negroes have been increasingly concerned again with the class issue of poverty. The immediate problems of the poor are different from the usual issues of integration which have involved, as we have said, the better-off Negroes. Frequently, non-middle-class political forces in black life are connected to a separatist approach, as in the Garvey back-to-Africa movement. In our opinion, as we argue later, power and dignity can be achieved without separatism.

The Dangers of Quality-Segregated Education Efforts

The call for separatist education is strong, meeting as it does various strains within black and white communities. For a while, at least, it swept educational and political circles so rapidly that little thought was given to its chances of effectiveness. We are strongly pessimistic about the likelihood of separatist education becoming quality education in the United States.

To bring Negro children up to present white-grade levels is by no means quality education. Moreover, as new levels are likely to be achieved by white youngsters through the general improvement in educational activity, it is not enough for Negro youngsters to move up a little. The relative educational gap between whites and Negroes must be reduced if the latter are to have an effective chance in the job market later. The task of education is then very difficult—to reduce the gap between whites and blacks, not to achieve a particular fixed standard for Negroes.

In order to reduce the differential, large funds are needed for an educational "leap" or moon shot. Marginal investments in the ghetto are likely to bring only small gains for the Negro. What is needed is an educational program which will enable large numbers of Negroes to complete college, thus reducing significantly the black-white gap at this level.[1] It is only through a moon-shot approach along the lines of the preceding chapter that vast improvements will come for both Negroes and whites, tending to obliterate or smother the differential. New educational programs oriented toward a full utilization of the styles and potentials of both Negro and white groups will be expensive. But because both groups would benefit, there is a good political possibility that such funds may be forthcoming. It is highly unlikely that the major white groups will spend the huge monies necessary for quality separatist education for Negroes. They would only do this out of threat and fear, but fear money is generally fairly limited. It is much more likely that large funds will be spent where the education of all children is to be improved simultaneously; that is, through producing powerful new positive educational programs where both black and white children will benefit greatly.

This type of integrated program can be supported by all groups in the society because it is integration (the appeal to conscience) without sacrifice, and in fact with great benefits for all.

The old Negro-liberal alliance failed in its efforts to build large-scale integrated education because it failed to convert the moral imperative into practical education gains for all. Instead, it permitted desegregation to develop under adverse conditions, feeding the white fear that Negro benefits would come at the cost of white children.

Although the idea of quality separatist education began as long ago as Booker T. Washington, we have seen little if any achievement of quality levels. Segregated Negro schools in the United States almost uniformly trail white schools and schools that are desegregating. Whatever the faults and slowness of the desegregation process, Negro children have significantly benefited where it has occurred, as shown in the study by James Coleman for the Office of Education. It may be that the present social climate may produce a separatist education of higher quality than in the past, but some of the tactics of the separatist education advocates are undermining even this possibility.

If the quality separatist program is accompanied by a highly nationalistic orientation, there are a number of dangers. If anti-white feelings are ascendant, white teachers and administrators will become more fearful of serving in these schools, the cleavage between Negro youngsters and the teaching staff will sharpen, and the school could become the setting for acting out antagonisms between blacks and whites rather than an educational center.

All-black staffing is not necessarily an effective answer—for Negro communities to go it alone. There is no evidence that Negro teachers per se improve the educational performances of Negro children. For example, in the city of Washington, D. C., large numbers of Negro teachers teach youngsters in highly segregated schools with no improvement whatsoever in the performance of these youngsters. This may change where black pride is a stimulus but we have doubts that this will work if teacher competence is assigned a minor role.

In the separatist schools there will be an absence of Negro and white children educating one another. This peer function is extremely important in education, and the white youngsters have some specific things to contribute to their Negro peers and the black youngsters have some specific contributions to make to their white counterparts. Both will be missing this important dimension in separatist schools, no matter of what quality.

The Coleman Study's report is striking: Disadvantaged Negro pupils in schools with white youngsters with a strong educational background did better in educational improvement than Negro students in non-integrated settings.[2]

We are contending that unless the option (and goal) of integrated quality education is maintained, it is highly unlikely that much quality separatist education will be achieved. Whatever the difficulties in producing desegregation, these difficulties are likely to be at least as great as in attempting to achieve quality separatist education.

Even where quality separatist education is accepted as a temporary option, it is important to maintain from a strategy point of view the demands for integration. These demands have won even the small concessions of promises of funds for separatist education.

We do not question that separatist quality education can be attained in the abstract or under conditions in which a minority group is firmly accepted in society or has educational traditions, but in the United States, where the Negro group is a minority with a long history of discrimination and is possessed of little power vis-à-vis the 90 per cent majority group, it seems far more unlikely. What seems more probable is that some educational benefits will be provided for the ghetto, presumably aimed at the old fading grade norms, and in isolated cases (such as Dr. Samuel Sheppard's district in St. Louis) temporary gains will be achieved. But simultaneously the education of the white youngster will advance rapidly just because of the new educational technology (some of which may be developed and perfected in ghetto demonstrations!), and the Negro-white gap will either remain constant or actually increase nationally.

Countering the Immigrant Theory of History

One of the greatest dangers to the development of an integrated approach is the new rationale which is being provided for Negroes going it alone. This rationale proposes that Negroes first form their own institutions and build up their power so as to be able to function on a more equal basis later on. This theory arises from observing immigrant minority groups in American history, particularly the Jewish group. Thus it might be entitled "the immigrant theory of history." The theory overlooks some extremely powerful factors which will not be operating in the situation of Negroes.

1. The Irish, Jews, and Italians represented small segments of the population when they made big gains while the Negro group includes over 10 per cent of the population. Furthermore, Negroes are not newcomers to America, as were the older immigrants. While these immigrant groups were obtaining their equality via ethnic associations and the like, the Negro group was on the scene in America—always at the bottom of the pile. This has not changed.

2. To varying degrees Negroes have banded together in their own ghettos and sometimes have elected legislators without developing any serious impact on the economy and their own future. Frequently, the Negroes elected have not even represented a progressive cause.

3. If the Jewish group is used as a comparison, it is extremely im-

portant to recognize that the Jews have powerful education traditions as well as trading experiences in middle-class occupations which allowed them much more flexible adaptation to the educational and occupational scene.

4. The new rationale is far too concerned with the past rather than the future of America which lies much more in the development of new jobs for all rather than a situation where one group takes something away from another. It is very unclear who will permit the Negroes to take something away from them, hence it is especially important that there be an expansion of jobs, resources, and power rather than a zero sum game in which one group benefits at the expense of another group.[3]

The Gains of Integrated Education

We recognize that integrated education is difficult to achieve in some places, but to go completely down the separatist education route is to close off later options if we continue to discover that separatist education does not produce quality education. Once we locate new schools, it will be exceedingly difficult to change educational patterns.

We are frank to say that we favor the integrated-education route not only because we think quality separatist education will be unworkable but because we embrace integrated education as a social value. Further, we believe that integrated education situations have educational benefits by themselves. Our confidence in the attainability of integrated education rests on three planks—despite the weak efforts, the integrated-education movement has produced important if underestimated gains; integrated education can be made to work more effectively than it has and meet at the same time many of the objectives of Negro militants; and integrated education fits better into an effective over-all strategy of change.

Despite the vacillation on integration, U.S. Commissioner of Education Harold Howe reported there was as much progress (most of it in the South) on integration in 1966–1967 as in the previous twelve years since the historic Supreme Court decision in Brown.[4] This achievement is not great but it should not be ignored.

Moreover, the important gains of the integration movement have not been specifically in the integration area. What has happened is that the call for integrated education highlighted the deep inadequacies of the educational system and drew attention in a dramatic, undeniable fashion to the large numbers of people, particularly Negroes, who were not receiving an adequate education in our affluent society. The governmental response to this critique has been considerable. Enormous new funds have been directed toward the improvement of education in disadvantaged areas, through the Elementary and Secondary School Education Act, Operation Headstart, and the teacher-training programs under the National Defense Educational Act. A great, new educational concern has evolved and new funds have been appropriated to meet educational deficiencies, especially of the poor.

There have been pedagogic gains: the emergence of urban and multiracial readers for children; more useful curriculum materials; human-relations workshops for teachers and administrators; greater awareness of the school's responsibility for teaching rather than ignoring poor and Negro youth;[5] more involvement of the community in education. Moreover, desegregated education, while it has taken place only to a small degree, has definitely benefited Negro children.

Action for Integration

Integration in education is made difficult by segregation in housing. What can be done to increase educational integration during the next years when residential patterns will not have been changed very much? Obviously, the basic strategy is to increase Federal financial support and to change the neighborhood school as we have known it. The U.S. Office of Education has recommended three steps to promote integration—the educational park or plaza, the supplementary centers, and teacher-pupil exchanges.

The most important of these ideas is the educational park which represents an important development in producing high-quality education. The educational concept brings together the best in educational technology and facilities into a central area serving youngsters from all nearby areas.

The educational park in New York City, for example, could mean the reorganization and consolidation of the thirty school districts that now exist, with 30,000 students each, into ten educational plazas, each unit a model school. According to the model worked out by Nolan

Estes of the U.S. Office of Education each plaza would offer instruction to 90,000 students from different backgrounds. The Harlem school district, for instance, would be combined with two wealthier and whiter ones.[6]

The high educational quality in such programs could build great incentive among parents to utilize them despite transportation difficulties.

The educational plaza can improve quality and provide vastly increased educational efficiency and economy through the consolidation of resources and teaching personnel.

John Barden states the issue well:

> The neighborhood schools are inefficient and hopelessly expensive. Hundreds of schools located, neighborhood by neighborhood, over metropolises of hundreds of square miles, are incredibly wasteful. Precedent, too, affirms the advantages of consolidation. The consolidation of rural schools is almost complete, and great gains have been made thereby in instructional quality and impressive savings in money. Most junior and senior high schools in metropolitan regions are consolidated to a limited degree, with limited gains and savings.
>
> Consolidation will proceed because it pays and because the necessities of twentieth-century public schooling demand it.[7]

For the educational park concept to be successful Federal money must be available for school construction. In particular, the demonstration or model city projects of the Department of Housing and Urban Development should be expanded and more closely connected to educational expenditures, particularly those involving educational parks. This will allow for the development of new cities and broad recreational and sociocultural programs together with educational expansion and integration. The educational park concept should become an integral feature of urban redevelopment in the United States.

Supplementary centers would group high-quality model schools, specializing in certain subject matter or in certain teaching techniques or in both, in strategic locations for attracting a heterogeneous student body. For example, Mount Vernon, New York, a sharply divided city, proposed the establishment of a model "children's academy," offering the newest educational methods near the residential color line to promote school integration during part of the school day.

A third proposal calls for teacher-pupil exchanges. These would involve bussing students or teachers or both to different schools within a city or between city and suburb. In the fall of 1966, Hartford, Connecticut, transported a group of its deprived children to schools in five neighboring suburbs.

Efforts to change the physical structure of the schools requires more funding. This will have to come largely from the Federal government, for the cities where integration is an issue are desperately short of funds, fear to raise taxes, and need an incentive to integrate. The next major step in educational finances is to make available Federal funds for the construction of schools. Cities and their contiguous suburbs should be induced to work together. These funds should be available only to districts which locate schools in ways to reduce educational desegregation. If this demand is not always politically feasible, a less stringent provision would give sizable bonuses to schools that are located so as to produce greater educational desegregation. The carrot rather than the club may sometimes have to be used.

Site location has the greatest consequence for the future of desegregation and the demography of the city. Unless there is immediate action to direct efforts toward the possibilities of desegregation, crucial options in the future will be lost. If new school buildings are located exclusively in ghetto areas, the chances of later moving to integrated policies will be very dim indeed.

Inside the Schools

The physical setting for integration must be matched with effective programs within the school. In this chapter we select from our previous discussion of educational strategies those that are most immediately relevant to the integration situation.

Teachers should be prepared to function in the new settings. They must be assisted in working in new kinds of groupings, in using the "helper principle" and peer learning, in working effectively with the new nonprofessional aides and teaching machines which will assist in the individualized instruction that should enable the previously segregated children to catch up rapidly.

Teachers should not be forced to transfer into segregated or ghetto schools since teacher performance depends highly upon motivation. Rather, the teachers in these schools now should be provided special in-service training to improve the quality of their work.

Intensive and high-quality after-school programs should be developed not as a substitute but in addition to programs offered during the school day. The after-school programs should enable youngsters to catch up rapidly, and tutors and homework helpers should be brought into these programs. The strategy should be to lead from strength, building on the positive of the youngsters, rather than depending on a compensatory approach that emphasizes deficiencies, inadequacies, and the like.

Power and Model

Militant black-power groups have raised important demands in their drive for separatist quality education. They manifest a concern for African history and for the Negro's role in American history, a desire for more Negro teachers and principals and for more participation in decisions by Negro parents and the Negro community. While these demands can be distorted both in objective and tactic, they have much merit and can be met in integrated education settings.

Certainly Negro history should be taught in all schools, whether black, white, or mixed. The educational park idea may make it easier to have knowledgeable teachers present a positive appreciation of Negro history to many school levels.

Again, all schools should be actively recruiting Negro teachers and teaching aides. This would be especially important in integrated schools. A large number of teacher aide positions are being created throughout the nation; some 40,000 such positions have already been developed through Title I of the Elementary and Secondary Education Act. This program can not only change the character of the school but may provide an economic basis for integration in other areas of life.

Highly qualified Negro teachers should be recruited and given on-the-job training to become principals rather than relying on tests that have not always predicted accurately who would be an effective principal. Separate schools are not necessary in order to have Negro principals.

Parents and the community should be brought much more closely into relations with the schools. Exactly how much authority parents' groups and local school district councils should have is not easily settled. But the notion of more voice for parents does not rest neces-sarily on a separatist education situation. Nor does the demand for more parent involvement inevitably act against professional standards.

The stress on Negro history, Negro teachers and administrators, and Negro parents' involvement in schools has been coupled with the separatist approach. But these demands can and should be met in all educational settings.

It is very important, however, to recognize that these three demands —whether realized in a separatist or integrated school—do not add up to quality education. Changes must take place within the classroom itself for educational gains. Indeed, the great danger of these demands is that school authorities may make concessions on them without producing any genuine improvement in the educational performance of children.

It is important to have the right target; the present demands of the separatist education group concern means to a large extent. But the goal must be that children's achievements rise rapidly and that children learn how to learn.

The emphasis must be on achievement; strict accountability must be insisted upon. The progress of all children—Negro and white— must be readily and continually assessed. The constant concern for interested parents and groups must be the outcome—are children improving in their learning? Frequently, new programs and expenditures bear little fruit; intelligent and informed criticism is needed.

It is not enough in today's situation to indicate dissatisfaction with the schools' performance; we should have a program of action which could be effective. This program must be built around the learning situation inside the classroom. Unfortunately, demands for Negro history and teachers are more aimed at meeting other objectives than the immediate one of more effective schooling. This observation does not demean these demands; it indicates their inadequacy as a program to meet the educational needs of black youth today.

Interim Strategy

Although we criticize the prospects of separatist education, we are not naïve believers in the immediate prospects for integrated education. Obviously, in many neighborhoods it may be practically impossible to produce rapid integration. But it is extremely important not to surrender the integration goal and capitulate to the backlash, both white and black. The separatist goal, despite its appeal to widely different groups, may not be achievable. If we proceed as though its accomplishments were certain, we will be taking steps which may shut off for a long time to come any prospect of integration.

If separatist education is accepted as the policy in Central Harlem or elsewhere, it is crucial that this step be seen as temporary, as one to be phased out at a later point. There should be definite plans to move toward integration, and perhaps to work toward integration in at least a portion of the day. This could be done, for example, via the supplementary centers or via the development of integrated teams of students and teachers that go into schools and make specific contributions and presentations there. Alongside of temporary, hopefully quality, segregated education there should be a plan in the peripheral areas of Harlem for immediate phasing in our educational parks. Dr. Max Wolff suggests methods for doing this immediately—before new structures are constructed—by utilizing in a reorganized fashion existing buildings.

We are suggesting, then, that it is important not to make a virtue out of what appears to be a temporary necessity, or to make what is difficult impossible.

Taking the Cost out of Desegregation

The desegregation movement in education and housing has floundered because it has not had a payoff for whites. Marginal middle-class and working-class whites who have been the most vocal resisters to integration have been frightened by what they take to be a threat to their real-estate values and schools. They, rather than the elite groups who are attacked by black militants, are most personally challenged by desegregation. Since most elites have less and less need for segregation, the task is easier than it once was.[8]

The first line of strategy, then, is to shift the burdens of the cost of desegregation from marginal whites to the society at large. As it stands now, desegregation implies to the whites a zero-sum game in which Negroes benefit and they lose. The aim should be to make desegregation an all-win or no-lose game.

In housing, this would mean insurance to protect against loss of real-estate values in desegregating areas and increased public services to prevent deterioration in these areas. In education, it means better education in integrating schools than before. This aim requires spending more money on such schools and better programs along the lines that we indicated earlier.

By coupling an improvement in education with desegregation, whites would have a stake in integration. This joining of the two is more likely to engender increased outlays than is separatist education for Negroes. It is much more likely that large funds will be spent where the education of all children is to be improved simultaneously.

We must not only take the cost out of desegregation, we must make it profitable to desegregate in every possible respect, economically, educationally, and morally. Only the last has been emphasized thus far. It is not enough.

In order to achieve these new programs it will be necessary to forge a wide coalition. The coalition should include teachers and teachers' unions, parents, and the professionals who must assist in developing and evaluating the plans put forth. It must work toward designing educational programs which are beneficial to all groups in the society, white, Negro, middle class, and poor.

Conclusion

Unless historical perspective is maintained there is the great danger that frustration and anger will escalate the difficulties encountered in the development of desegregated education and turn back the timetable of integration a great many years. It is therefore crucial to recognize that despite what it has failed to achieve, the demand for integrated education in America has resulted in considerable progress in legislation and in concern for the education of the disadvantaged. New readers and curriculum materials have been produced; the community is much more involved in education; important new ideas have emerged, such as the educational park. Moreover, desegregated education, while it has taken place only to a small degree, has definitely benefited Negro children. These factors must be kept in mind as we develop advanced programs and approaches for a new level of integrated education which will provide immediate educational benefits for both Negro and white youngsters.

NOTES

1. Big investments in educational input are much more likely to produce a net relative gain for the Negro even though the educational levels of whites will be growing at the same time.

2. The Coleman Study should be widely publicized because it lends strong support to the development of integration by alleviating the fears of white middle-class parents. The study, directed by Dr. James Coleman, found that when disadvantaged Negro pupils were placed in schools with white youngsters with strong educational backgrounds the Negroes' educational achievement was likely to improve. But it also found that if a white pupil from a home that is strongly and effectively supporting education is put in a school where most pupils do not come from such homes, his achievement will be little different than if he were in a school composed of others like himself. This finding, in effect, refutes the argument that school integration must invariably harm the higher achieving white pupils. (*New York Times*, August 7, 1966, Review of the Week, p. E7.) The Committee on Civil Rights' study on recent isolation strongly supports the case for integrated education.

3. The new service economy requires that a significantly large number of new human-service jobs and careers of an integrated nature be produced, a benefit for all classes and groups. This is the path for absorbing the Negro into the economy without taking power or income away from anyone.

4. June Shagaloff, the educational director of the NAACP, reports that in the North greater gains in integration had taken place in the suburban and smaller cities. (See *New York Times*, Review of the Week, September 11, 1966, p. E11.) With the increasing significance of the suburbs in our society, it will be most important to observe how integration develops in these areas, where large numbers of Negroes will be migrating for jobs.

5. Obviously none of these measures is enough but they are important gains. Much more could have been accomplished, as we have argued, if the educational policies accompanying desegregation were more attuned to classroom needs.

6. *The Wall Street Journal*, August 12, 1966.

7. John Barden, "Community vs. Neighborhood—The Educational Park," *The Nation* (April 20, 1964), 389.

8. For example, *The Wall Street Journal*, an important voice of the business-men elite, has been a noteworthy advocate of integrated education.

I V

Mental Health

II

THE "UNDER-UTILIZATION" OF MENTAL-HEALTH SERVICES

Many studies and reports attest to the "under-utilization" of psychiatric resources by the old and new working classes.[1] While under-utilization has often been used to explain away inadequate, inaccessible, and irrevelant services, the seeming reluctance of low-income people to make as much use of mental-health services as do middle-class people is important.

At least seven factors have been suggested as contributing to the comparatively low rates of utilization:

1. Cost of services;
2. Availability of services;
3. Failure of the general practitioner to refer cases for psychiatric treatment;
4. Failure to define distress in psychologically relevant terms;
5. Attitudes toward mental illness;
6. Fear of institutionalization;
7. The middle-class character of the mental-health movement and the associated inappropriate nature of the services offered to low-income people.

We shall limit ourselves to a few observations about each of these explanations and devote more attention to the last point which seems to us to be crucial.

Cost and Availability

The cost of treatment by itself is probably not the most decisive factor deterring use by low-income people, although it is undoubtedly a contributing cause in most instances.[2]

Availability of help seems to be an additional relevant factor. Thus, in the Joint Commission on Mental Illness and Health's monograph, *Americans View Their Mental Health*, availability of resources seems to be clearly related to the decision to go for help:

> People who have more psychiatric facilities available to them are more likely to have had help, given the definition of a problem [as a mental-health problem], than people with fewer available resources: Less than half (46 per cent) of the group with the least facilities available to them have actually gone for help, as contrasted to 60 per cent or more of the groups with some facilities available. Thus, availability of resources seems to operate as a facilitating factor, serving to translate a psychological readiness to go for help into an actual decision to go.[3]

We must again note, however, that in union-sponsored and in health insurance plans, availability by itself was not sufficient to induce rapid utilization. Probably somewhat more important than either cost or availability are the attitudes held regarding mental illness.

Non-referral by Family Physician

Psychiatric referral by the general practitioner would seem a most promising avenue for increasing utilization of mental-health resources by low-income people who are notoriously low in self-referral. But unfortunately physicians often evidence considerable reluctance in this area. Avnet notes: "The average person's misgivings about mental illness and psychiatry find their counterpart in the attitudes of many doctors. The lack of empathy between psychiatrists and other physicians, frequently observed on an individual basis, seems to be partially substantiated by some of the project findings on referring and reporting customs."[4]

Failure to Define Problems Psychologically

Gurin and his associates stress the importance of attitudes toward mental illness and extent of knowledge about treatment facilities in determining whether or not "felt need" among various groups in the population becomes translated into "effective help." To paraphrase the authors: That lower-status groups get less psychiatric care would seem to represent a social problem. The problem seems to be twofold. First of all, these groups are less likely to define distress in psychologically relevant terms. But, secondly, even when distress is defined psychologically this need is less often translated into an actual use of help, particularly psychiatric resources.[5]

Attitudes toward Mental Illness

Surveys of public opinion about mental illness reveal that a large part of the population, and particularly lower socioeconomic groups, tend to equate mental illness with only the severest forms of disorder: those marked by loss of control, loss of reason, and inappropriate or violent behavior.[6] Individuals in these groups often delay efforts to secure treatment until the illness conforms to this concept.

The case studies presented by Myers and Roberts vividly illustrate class differences in attitudes toward medicine and psychiatry. They point out that, ". . . to the lower-class person [Class V in the study], mental illness was 'craziness,' or 'insanity,' or the like, not sickness. The only treatment for it that most knew of was involuntary hospitalization in a public mental institution, and they feared this so much that they avoided seeking help for themselves or their relatives even when it was obviously needed."[7] These attitudes were in contrast to those held by middle-class persons (Class III) who regarded mental illness as an "illness amenable to treatment," and one for which they were willing to seek professional assistance.[8]

The concept of mental illness held by worker and low-income groups often carries with it a rejection of the ill person and a defeatist, hopeless attitude about the possibility of the mentally ill patient's cure and future reinstatement into society. It is not surprising, therefore,

that Myers and Roberts found that in the homes of low-income patients "there was little support or encouragement . . . from their families and no acceptance of the psychiatric explanation of their illness.
In some cases, the patients did not even tell their families that they
were seeing psychiatrists lest their families conclude that they were
crazy or insane."[9]

The prevailing stigma against mental illness is also found in the industrial community. A recent study of employers' attitudes toward
former mental patients whom they had hired found that ". . . job tenure is shorter among ex-patients working for employers with unfavorable
attitudes toward the ex-patient status."[10] The effect of unfavorable
employee attitudes toward the ex-patient and his job tenure were not
directly studied, but other experiences show these also have an important effect on the job success or failure of the ex-patient. These
negative attitudes interfere with treatment and rehabilitation efforts
which require family and work-group cooperation (day treatment,
vocational rehabilitation programs, and the like). One concrete illustration of this is that trade-unions, characteristically alert to issues concerning their members' job and re-employment rights, are generally
not only unfamiliar with employers' criteria for determining the "fit-
ness" of formal mental patients to return to work, but also fail to take
positive steps to assist their formerly ill members in securing work
they can do.

Fear of Institutionalization

Pepper, in reporting on the ten-year follow-up of the New Haven
study of Hollingshead and Redlich, notes that of those of the lowest
income group who had been in the state hospital at the time of the
original study and who were alive, 93 per cent were still there.[11] The
inadequate treatment offered low-income people is probably the most
decisive factor accounting for the larger percentage of psychotics
found in this stratum. Redlich states: "We found, as far as the accumulation of schizophrenics in the lower classes is concerned, that although
not entirely, it is mostly due to the fact that the lower socioeconomic
groups get different treatment and have different opportunities for
rehabilitation."[12] Under these conditions it is not surprising that low-

income people have serious misgivings about psychiatry and the entire mental-health movement.

Our social and professional institutions and practices have not only failed to "re-educate" low-income groups about mental illness, but have, on the contrary, operated largely to create, confirm, and reinforce negative attitudes. The mentally ill of the poorer classes have indeed been rejected not just by kin and peer groups, but by the "best" social agencies and treatment organizations and a large part of the professional community. They have been considered incurable and stigmatized as permanent outcasts from society.

A vicious circle has been created in which life experiences have validated the lower socioeconomic group's "unscientific" attitude about mental illness. In turn, such attitudes have perpetuated the inadequate treatment and care accorded the mentally ill of these groups.

As we shall develop later, in this and the following chapter, we believe that breaking this circle requires an attack on both the experiential and attitudinal levels, with the primary emphasis on the former: the provision of experiences which can give rise to new concepts about psychological problems and their treatment.

The Middle-Class Mental-Health Movement

Kingsley Davis, in a classic article first published in 1938,[13] analyzed the social class bias in the basic conception of mental health held by practitioners and theorists in the mental-health field. The article abounds with evidence demonstrating the value bias of middle-class ideology in the assumed "scientific" description of mental-health characteristics. A later study by Gursslin *et al.*, using the Davis theme, provides a content analysis of more recent general readership mental-health literature aimed at describing in positive terms the characteristics of mental health.[14] This mental-health literature places great value on work; examples of this outlook are:

> Those who have a zest for working ... may be said to be mentally healthy. Satisfactions gained from work help to keep people healthy.[15]

While these work attitudes are consonant with middle-class values, ". . . work is perceived by lower-class persons as something which is necessary in order to obtain money to buy the essentials of life."[16]

The authors similarly analyze differences in the approach of middle-class and new working-class people to such things as problem solving, adjustment and conformity, control of emotions, planning ahead, and community participation.

McMahon notes the class bias in the personality traits used by a number of studies attempting to identify the type of patient most likely to survive the initial diagnostic interview. The following traits are often mentioned as positive indicators for excellent prognosis in psychotherapeutic endeavors:

> . . . psychological thinking rather than magical expectations; internalization of problems and the tendency to self-blame rather than acting out and projection; a wish actively to change one's environment instead of a passive fatalistic stance toward reality; self-control; a need to relate to people; a desire to talk with others about personal problems, etc. And the litany continues with "high motivation," "strong ego strength," and so on. In looking over these desired and prized personal characteristics in prospective patients, one becomes acutely aware that they are personality correlates of the middle class.[17]

Can practitioners with these perspectives work effectively with non-middle-class groups? We doubt it! The principal causes of the under-utilization of mental-health facilities by workers and low-income groups are the inadequate or inappropriate nature of the professional services offered them, and their own attitudes and fears about mental illness and its consequences. These are not, as we have seen, independent factors but are so closely interwoven that change in one area requires a movement toward change in the other.

The first move is the responsibility of mental-health professionals. We believe that they and public-health bodies have the primary obligation for introducing change in the present social organization and use of our psychiatric resources; as an adjunct, disseminating information to reduce fears and anxieties about psychological problems is crucial.

A Strategy for Professionals: Modification of Treatment Approaches

The greatest challenge confronting professionals is the development of new techniques of treatment.

Observations that traditional forms of psychotherapy have not effectively engaged the old and new working classes have led some to suggest confining psychotherapy entirely to middle- and higher-class strata.[18] It is claimed that the resistance of low-income groups to psychiatric treatment is fundamentally rooted in factors internal to these individuals: they are less introspective, tend to ". . . see the presenting problem as physical rather than emotional . . . desire . . . symptomatic relief only rather than over-all help, lack . . . understanding of the psychotherapeutic process."[19]

At one level the form of treatment is a value question since the different therapies are associated with different therapeutic goals, and the issues of what goals to select and who is to decide upon them lie in the realm of value. At another level, this is an empirical issue of whether other forms of treatment might not actually be more effective, rather than simply less costly and less demanding for certain groups of patients. Definitive empirical evidence does not yet exist to provide an answer to this question.

It is assumed that it is the psychiatrist who relatively completely controls the type of treatment given. It may be that patients search out psychiatrists who will give them their preferred type of treatment and reject nonpreferred treatments, both from private practitioners and within the clinics and hospitals. The selective process and pressures emanating from the patient cannot be ignored in a full account of the biased pattern of psychiatric treatment.

There is also a tendency to discuss the problem of therapy with old and new working-class persons in a way that implies that the therapist wishes to give the patient "more" than the patient wishes. For example, some practitioners assert that the therapist wants to help the patient come to his own decisions, but the patient only wants to be told what to do; the therapist wants to establish a long-term relationship with the patient, but the patient wants a quick remedy; the therapist wants deep and lasting changes, but the patient is satisfied with superficial and transient results. The alternatives may be multiplied beyond this, but what is important is that they seem to imply a rejection of the therapist and the therapeutic process by the patient.

We should like to suggest that quite the opposite may be happening. Rather than asking for "less" than he is offered, the new working-class patient may actually be asking for "more" in the sense that he wants a fuller, more extensive, and more permanent relationship than is possible either within the traditional definition of the therapeutic relationship or in terms of what the therapist wishes to enter into. In other words, it may be the therapist who drives the patient from treatment because he cannot handle the demands placed upon him, rather than the patient who drops treatment because its demands are too much for him.[20] With the knowledge we have of working-class and ethnic cultures it is difficult to subscribe without qualification to assertions that patients from these groups do not like to talk or have special difficulties entering into relationships. The basic questions are: What kind of relationships, with whom, and under what conditions?

The view that psychotherapy is not the treatment of choice for low-income people is rooted in a highly static concept of psychotherapy. It is based on the selective emphasis on certain categories, e.g., the low-income person's nonintrospective orientation, his desire for direction, etc. Ignored in the diagnosis are other qualities which may indicate a positive potential for psychotherapy. Perhaps most important is the low-income individual's tendency not to isolate or intellectualize. Indeed, this is an extremely important asset for treatment. Other dimensions of the low-income person's culture and style might especially prepare him for various forms of treatment such as role playing, group therapy, family therapy, hypnosis, hypnodrama, therapies that include physical aspects, play therapy, etc.

Diagnosis should not be selectively geared to those features of the low-income person's make-up that are unsuited for therapy. More attention should be directed toward those aspects that may be relevant for such treatment. If emotionally corrective experience rather than cognitive insight is the heart of modern psychotherapy, serving as the key to deep behavior modification, then the poor may be far better therapy risks than is generally realized.

Psychotherapy fails with low-income groups largely because of the insistence on a particular mode of treatment, namely, the psychodynamic, insight, reconstructive oriented approach. Basic revisions of psychotherapy appear to be needed in order for it to be maximally effective.

It is becoming increasingly clear that as treatment forms and approaches are modified in terms of the needs and style of life of low-income people, these people evidence a much greater acceptance of mental-health services. Reports on the walk-in clinic, for example, indicate high utilization by economically deprived individuals at Metropolitan Hospital serving East Harlem in New York City and the Benjamin Rush Center for Problems of Living in Los Angeles.[21] A surprisingly large number of their cases are self-referred. Walk-in clinics have demonstrated that "under-utilization" is a myth—new and appropriate forms of service have little difficulty attracting low-income people.

The basic issue, however, is to prevent unplanned treatment termination: the high frequency of dropout.[22] What is necessary here are more dramatic modifications of traditional insight-centered psychotherapy. When treatment technology is developed appropriate to the needs, style, and expectations of low-income groups, a much more accepting response takes place than is envisioned by those who portray the individuals as lacking in "psychological mindedness." An impressive number of new treatment approaches (on a small scale) appear to be quite effective in involving low-income clients. Some of these approaches are surveyed in the following chapter.

What steps can be taken to facilitate the development of new treatment methodologies and their dissemination? We do not know of any blueprint, but the first need clearly seems to be one of informing all the professions involved in treatment and rehabilitation of the factors contributing to lack of effective service to low-income groups. It is intriguing to note that at the present time sustained mental-health information and educational efforts are needed not only for the public at large but for mental-health planners and practitioners themselves who occupy the strategic role in determining the eventual outcome of bold, new plans. In such an effort each professional organization has its own indispensable part to play through its journals, professional meetings and conferences, training programs, and other channels. Public agencies as well as private and voluntary associations, and educational and clinical institutions can explore many avenues for stimulating review and reassessment and encouraging further experimentation.

We wish to make a special plea for evaluative studies of the effects of various forms of psychiatric treatment. There is a desperate shortage of systematic evidence in this area, and without such evidence our decisions regarding proper treatment tend to be determined by current fashions in psychiatry or by implicit social values and assumptions.

In the long run, we believe that lasting innovations will come about from those who are personally involved in programs serving the "new" working class and are directly confronted with the need for fresh thinking and practice. We would suggest, therefore, that public, professional, and labor and group health organizations develop a close collaboration to foster a variety of mental-health programs directly serving labor and low-income groups. These are needed to provide professionals with opportunities for learning about the circumstances and styles of life of working and low-income people, of the characteristics of their neighborhoods and communities, their organizations, their problems and resources. The validity of promoting such "special-interest" programs for special groups has been questioned. The counter-suggestion is for concentrating efforts in a "horizontal," all-inclusive community approach. This may be the ideal future plan. But we must first test out methods of working with the old and new working-class populations, now unfortunately little known to mental-health professionals outside of hospital walls. Basic changes are needed in the orientations and points of view of practitioners. These changes, which will be difficult and slow, need to be rooted in many experiences of numerous practitioners in order to have an impact on prevailing theory and practice.

NOTES

Note: Articles that were written with Sylvia Scribner and Elliot Mishler were drawn on for this chapter.

1. For a survey of the rather extensive literature see J. D. Frank et al., "Why Patients Leave Psychotherapy," A.M.A. Archives of Neurology and Psychiatry, LXXVII (March 1957), 283–299. See also Hugh Storrow, "Psychiatric Treatment and the Lower-class Neurotic Patient," Archives of General Psychiatry, VI (June 1962), 469–477.

2. Cost may also play a role, in that low-income families may believe that all treatment is expensive, or because it was expensive in the past, have become uninterested in it.

3. Gerald Gurin, Joseph Veroff, and Sheila Feld, Americans View Their Mental Health (New York: Basic Books, 1960), pp. 384–385.

4. Helen H. Avnet, Psychiatric Insurance (Group Health Insurance, Inc., 1962), pp. 36–87.

5. Gurin et al., op. cit., p. 403–404.

6. Shirley Star, "The Place of Psychiatry in Popular Thinking." Paper presented at the annual meeting of the American Association for Public Opinion Research, Washington, D.C., May 1957.

7. Jerome K. Myers and Bertram H. Roberts, Family and Class Dynamics in Mental Illness (New York: John Wiley and Sons, 1959), p. 204.

8. Ibid., p. 205.

9. Ibid., p. 210.

10. Charles D. Whatley, Jr., "Status, Role and Vocational Continuity of Discharged Mental Patients," Journal of Health and Human Behavior, IV (1963), 105.

11. Max P. Pepper, "Social Class and Mental Illness: A Ten Year Follow-up." Paper presented at American Public Health Association, Kansas City, Missouri, November 14, 1963.

12. Symposium on Preventive and Social Psychiatry, April 15–17, 1957. Walter Reed Army Institute of Research, Washington, D.C., USGOP, 1958, p. 139. Statement by Fredrick Redlich.

13. Kingsley Davis, "Mental Hygiene and the Class Structure," *Psychiatry*, I (1938), 55–56.

14. Orville R. Gursslin *et al.*, "Social Class and the Mental Health Movement," *Social Problems*, VII (Winter 1959–1960), 210–218.

15. *Ibid.*, 212.

16. *Ibid.*, 212.

17. James T. McMahon, "The Working Class Psychiatric Patient: A Clinical View," in Frank Riessman, Jerome Cohen, and Arthur Pearl, eds., *Mental Health of the Poor* (New York: The Free Press of Glencoe, 1964).

18. R. G. Hunt, "Social Class and Mental Illness: Some Implications for Clinical Theory and Practice," *American Journal of Psychiatry*, CXVI (1960), 1065.

19. Norman Q. Brill and Hugh A. Storrow, "Social Class and Psychiatric Treatment," *Archives of General Psychiatry*, III (1960), 343.

20. Some evidence exists that many patients of other classes may have similar sets of expectations and present similar problems to psychiatrists. In a by-product of the study under review it has been found that Class III and V patients exhibit strong resemblances in their expectations of therapy. Our hypothesis would be that it is the low-educated members of Class III who especially exhibit "non-psychiatric" attitudes. F. C. Redlich, A. B. Hollingshead, and E. Bellis, "Social Class Differences in Attitudes toward Psychiatry," *American Journal of Ortho-psychiatry*, XXVI (January 1955), 60–70.

21. William Norman *et al.*, "The Acceptance of the Psychiatric Walk-in Clinic in a Highly Deprived Community." Paper given at American Psychiatric Association, May 7, 1963; Martin Streckler *et al.*, "The Community-based Walk-in Center: A Promising New Resource for Groups Under-represented in Outpatient Treatment Facilities," *American Journal of Orthopsychiatry*, XXXIV (March 1964), 257.

22. J. D. Frank *et al.*, *op. cit.*

12

NEW APPROACHES TO MENTAL-HEALTH TREATMENT

As shown in the previous chapter, present-day institutional features of psychotherapy are primarily congenial to middle-class life styles. Middle-class patients are preferred by most treatment agents;[1] are seen as more treatable; psychotherapy is more frequently recommended as the treatment of choice;[2] and diagnoses are more helpful (with symptomatology held constant).[3] Conversely, treatment as presently organized is not congenial to low-income clients, is not congruent with their traditions and expectations, and is poorly understood by them. In essence, these clients are alienated from treatment.

We suggest that this situation calls for a twofold strategy: modify the traditional treatment approaches to accommodate the low-income client; educate and prepare the low-income client for the necessary aspects of treatment not suited to his expectations.

Our purpose will be to review the new treatment techniques which are evolving in work with low-income clients and to analyze some of the attitudes and approaches which we believe should characterize the treatment process.

In the aim of encouraging further experimentation, we have chosen to survey a wide spectrum of techniques appropriate to different types

This chapter was written with Robert Reiff.

of settings rather than to present one or two in complete detail and with fully-developed rationale.

The Treatment Process: Approaches and Techniques

NEW APPROACHES TO INTAKE AND DIAGNOSIS

There is increasing evidence that most of the clinician's diagnostic tools, whether in the cognitive sphere (for example, intelligence tests) or in the emotional sphere, are class linked and class biased.

Haase[4] found that essentially identical Rorschach records were interpreted quite differently depending upon the designated social-class origin of the patient. The protocols of individuals reported as "lower class" were diagnosed as more maladjusted with poorer prognosis than were their middle-class counterparts with essentially similar records who were used as controls. It is also interesting to note that "lower-class" records were more frequently categorized in terms of psychosis and character disorder while the essentially identical middle-class records were diagnosed as neurotic and normal.

Haase does not object to a class differential analysis per se, but rather to the fact that the analysis unwittingly, but consistently, concludes that the "lower class" is more maladjusted. Considering the lack of opportunity and difficult life conditions of the worker, a "lower-class" record which is identical with that of a middle-class person might be presumed to indicate greater health and better prognosis.

Apart from biases in interpretation, traditional diagnostic techniques which rely heavily on testing and interview procedures are not well suited to the low-income style which is far more oriented to physical forms of expression. For this reason we strongly urge the use of role playing and situational tests as diagnostic tools and the employment of more game-like devices in general.

The following are some general recommendations regarding intake and diagnosis:

1. Telescope the initial interview and intake (shorten, cut red tape).[5] Use group intake procedures. Start the therapeutic process at once. Permit fuller catharsis while gathering case history; be very open and flexible.

2. Utilize pictorial interview and diagnostic techniques.[6] Consider hypnosis, role playing, and dreams as diagnostic devices; use home interviews where possible; have problem-centered discussions.

3. Do not diagnose with middle-class standards and categories; do not presume inner conflict, "acting out," lack of values, lack of guilt, or lack of verbal facility.

4. Attempt to determine the style of the individual—work style, cognitive style, interpersonal style; learn to understand his individual language; note the idiom; client's humor, leisure pattern, interests, friendship pattern, extent of family relationships, identification models, defense mechanisms, role functioning.

5. Clarify the processes and goals of therapy; determine the life possibilities and specific direction of the particular patient.

The Development of Rapport in Initial Interviews

During the first series of interviews, every effort should be made to overcome the role distance and impersonality which contribute to the low-income client's alienation from the treatment agent.

As steps in this direction, we would suggest less stress on obtaining and recording objective (that is, nonsubjective) information about the client's problem, background, and situation, and less emphasis on defining the agency's role, functions, and mode of operation.

Instead of these emphases, the therapist might want to:

1. Encourage the client to talk about his problems and feelings subjectively, to express himself without regard to dates, places, details, and the like. Much useful information might be obtained in this way, but this would not be the emphasis nor the goal.

2. Talk about himself where relevant and possible. (E.g., "I had a problem like that once." "I come from a neighborhood [family] like yours." "I have trouble making both ends meet." Or, "A friend of mine has a situation a lot like yours.")

3. Record at the end of the meeting whatever minimum specific information is needed. The therapist or case worker could indicate that this recording of information was as unpleasant to him as to the client. He could share the low-income client's alienation toward impersonal bureaucratic procedure by indicating that "we have to do

this—let's get it over with as easily as we can" (so that we can go back to really coming to grips with your problems).

4. Provide whatever advice, service, or anticipation of improvement could be given at this stage.

In other words, "Stage One," beginning with the initial interview and proceeding through the first four or five meetings, could be cathartic, supportive, informal, and should provide immediate service and appropriate advice. The assumption here is that low-income clients can accept directive authority when it is combined with informal friendliness.

In addition to these modifications, another very different initial approach might be explored. Role playing can be introduced at the very beginning, not on a group basis at first, but simply on a one-to-one basis where the therapist and the client act out relevant situations (parent-child problems, marital difficulties, vocational-guidance problems of an interpersonal nature, etc.). Role playing of this kind is especially useful with young males (who are not receptive to "just talk") and in family counseling, and furnishes an excellent transition to group sessions. Role-playing sessions can be used diagnostically, while at the same time providing catharsis, support, problem objectification, problem sharing, and group solution.

Role-Playing Techniques

There are a number of reasons why this role-playing technology may be of special value in therapeutic work with lower socioeconomic groups:

1. It allows the practitioner (social worker, psychiatrist, educator) to reduce in an honest fashion the role distance between himself and the disadvantaged individual. It also permits the practitioner to learn more about the culture of the low-income person from the "inside" (through playing the latter's role in role reversal, for example).

2. It changes the setting and tone of what often appears to the low-income person as an office-ridden, institutional, bureaucratic, impersonal foreign world.

3. Low-income groups typically do not like the traditional test format and this limits diagnostic work with them. The requirements of

their style seem to be met better by game-like atmospheres and situational measures, both of which are found more readily in role-play technology.[7]

4. Low-income people are generally less introspective, less introverted, and less concerned with self. They respond more to the external, to the outside, to action. They are more likely to see the causes of their problems in external forces; they project more and tend to externalize their guilt.[8] Kohn notes that their child-rearing patterns center on conformity to external prescriptions—"in contrast to the self-direction focus of the middle class."[9] He relates this, in part, to "working-class" occupations requiring that one follow explicit rules set down by an authority, while middle-class positions permit more self-direction.[10]

Some cautions are in order, however. Role playing with low-income groups should assiduously avoid the theatrical aspects often connected with psychodrama.[11] Role playing seems to be more easily accepted by low-income persons when there are no stage or lighting effects, and when it is conducted very simply and directly. In work with homemakers and school aides from low-income groups, for example, it was found that they were able and willing to participate in role playing almost immediately, with practically no warm up or even preparatory discussions explaining the technique.

Indeed it sometimes appears that long preparation and discussion prior to role playing builds the resistance and fear of low-income people. In view of this, it is best to introduce role playing directly through a discussion centered around a specific problem (how to persuade a member of the family to come to the clinic). It can then easily be suggested that the group "do the problem" so that it can be dealt with more effectively.

It should also be pointed out that while low-income people readily accept the basic techniques, including role reversal, they are far less accepting of such features as "doubles," "soliloquies," and the like. More advanced technology of this nature seems to arouse feelings of inadequacy ("I'm not an actor," etc.). Although it is possible to utilize these techniques, they require considerably more preparation than is needed with middle-class audiences.

Finally, it is important, as Levit and Jennings warn,[12] to guard against the overuse of role playing and to keep in mind that it should be employed intermittently for well-defined purposes (as a stimulus for discussion, etc.).

The Use of Nonprofessionals

The use of indigenous personnel drawn from low-income communities can perhaps be a decisive factor in helping treatment agencies reorganize their approaches to low-income people. Neighborhood people functioning as nonprofessionals appear to be highly successful in developing rapport with low-income clients, including the most deprived and disadvantaged individuals in the community.[13] Their success seems to stem from the fact that they are similar to the clients in terms of background, style, language, ethnicity, and interests.

For this reason, and also because they serve as excellent role models, we would recommend that a great many more nonprofessionals be employed as aides in hospitals and social agencies in various capacities. One such capacity which we feel has an important potential but has thus far been little utilized is as an auxiliary in group treatment. Under the guidance of the professional therapist or group leader, the nonprofessional aide can participate in the group-therapy sessions and perform the valuable function of maintaining continuity of contact with the group participants by visiting each of them on a daily basis in between group sessions. Moreover, the integration of the aide's home-visiting and extra-session experiences with the patient could be integrated into the group sessions, thus enriching and enhancing their therapeutic value.[14]

The "Helper" Therapy Principle

An age-old therapeutic approach is the use of people with a problem to help other people who have the same problem in more severe form (e.g., Alcoholics Anonymous). But in the use of this now popular approach it may be that emphasis is on the wrong person. Currently attention centers on the individual receiving help. More attention might well be given the individual who needs the help less, that is, the person who is providing the assistance; frequently it is he who improves the most!

While it may be uncertain that people receiving help are always benefited, people giving help usually profit from their role. This appears to be the case in a wide variety of self-help "therapies," including Synanon (for drug addicts), Recovery Incorporated (for psychologically disturbed people), and Alcoholics Anonymous. (Mowrer notes that there are more than 265 groups of this kind listed in a directory, *Their Brother's Keepers*.[15] The American Conference of Therapeutic Self-Help Clubs publishes an official magazine, *Action*, describing some of the functions of these groups.)

While there is still a need for firm research evidence that these programs are effective, various reports (many of them admittedly impressionistic) point to improvement in the givers of help rather than in the recipients. Careful research evaluating these programs is needed, because there are numerous contaminating factors that may be contributing to their success, such as the leadership of the therapist, selection of subjects, and the newness or novelty of the program.

Although much of the evidence for the helper principle is observational and uncontrolled, there is one experimental investigation that provides at least indirect verification or support of the principle. In a study by King and Janis in which role playing was used, it was found that subjects who had to improvise a speech supporting a specific point of view tended to change their opinions in the directions of this view more than subjects who merely read the speech for an equivalent amount of time.[16] They describe this effect in terms of "self-persuasion through persuading others."

Volkman and Cressey formulate this principle as one of their five social-psychological principles for the rehabilitation of criminals:

> The most effective mechanism for exerting group pressure on members will be found in groups so organized that criminals are induced to join with non-criminals for the purpose of changing other criminals. A group in which criminal "A" joins with some non-criminals to change criminal "B" is probably most effective in changing criminal "A," not "B" . . . .[17]

Perhaps, then, the strategy ought to be to devise ways of creating more helpers! Or, to be more exact, to find ways to transform recipients of help into dispensers of help, thus reversing their roles, and to structure the situation so that recipients of help will be placed in roles requiring the giving of assistance.

In most of the programs mentioned, the helpers and the helped have had essentially the same problem or symptom. The approach is carried one step further in Recovery Incorporated, in which emotionally disturbed people help each other even though their symptoms may differ.

Therapy for the Poor

The helper principle probably has universal therapeutic application, but may be especially useful in low-income treatment projects for these two reasons:

1. It may circumvent the special inter-class role distance difficulties that arise from the middle-class-oriented therapy (and therapist) being at odds with the low-income clients' expectations and style. The alienation that many low-income clients feel toward professional treatment agents and the resulting rapport difficulties may be greatly reduced by utilizing a low-income person as a helper therapist.

For the same reason much wider employment of neighborhood-based nonprofessionals in hospitals and social agencies as aides or social-service technicians is recommended. Like the helper therapist, they are likely to have considerably less role distance from the low-income client than does the professional.

2. It may be a principle that is especially attuned to the cooperative trends in lower socioeconomic groups and cultures. In this sense it may be beneficial to both the helper (the model) and the helped.

Helper Therapy Mechanisms

What are the mechanisms whereby the helper benefits from his helping role? Brager notes the improved self-image that probably results from the fact that a person is doing something worth while in helping someone in need.[18] The King-Janis study suggests that becoming committed to a position through advocating it ("self-persuasion through persuading others") may be an important dimension associated with the helper role. Pearl notes that many helpers (such as the homework helpers) are "given a stake or concern in a system" and this contributes to their becoming "committed to the task in a way that brings about especially meaningful development of their own abilities."[19]

The mechanisms probably vary depending on the setting and task of the helper. Thus helpers, functioning in a therapeutic context, whether as professional therapeutic agents or as nonprofessional "peer therapists," may benefit from the importance and status associated with this role. They also receive support from the implicit thesis, "I must be well if I help others." People who themselves have problems (e.g., alcoholics, drug addicts, unwed mothers) should derive benefit from this formulation. Moreover, their new helper roles as such may serve as a major (distracting) source of involvement, thus diverting them from their problem and general self-concern. There is no question also that individual differences are important so that some people receive much greater satisfaction from "giving," "helping," "leading," "controlling," "cooperating," "persuading," and "mothering."

Helpers operating in a teaching context, again both as professionals and nonprofessionals, may profit from the cognitive mechanisms associated with learning through teaching. They need to learn the material better in order to teach it and more generalized academic sets may emerge from the teacher role. Finally, the status and prestige dimensions attached to the teacher role may stimulate learning.

The helper in the leader role may benefit from some of the same factors related to the teacher and therapist roles as well as the "self-persuasion through persuading others" mechanism and their "stake in the system." In essence, then, it would seem that the helper's gains are formed by the actual demands of the specific helper role (whether it is teacher, leader, or therapist), and by new feelings associated with the meaning and prestige of the role and the way he is treated because of the new role.

Cautions and Conditions

In a sense, the helper principle seems counter to the widely accepted psychological dictum that warns against therapist projection. The well-known danger, called to our attention by all of psychoanalytic theory and practice, indicates that a therapist with a specific problem may, unless he has understanding and control of this problem, project it to the person he is treating. Of course, in many helper situations this does not arise because both the treater and the treated suffer from the same malady. But in other cases when rehabilitated nonprofessional workers are hired to work with people who either have no specific problem or do not have the problems of the helper, the possibility of projection as well as psychological contagion has to be considered.

Two controlling devices are suggested to guard against the potential risk: (1) The helper should not be involved in any intensive treatment function unless he has considerable awareness of his problem and the projection issue; and (2) professional supervision is absolutely necessary. Perhaps one of the difficulties of the amateur therapeutic self-help programs is the anti-professionalism that frequently characterizes them.

There is another potential danger residing in the helper-therapy principle, especially if it is to be applied on a large scale. Much of the intrinsic value of the technique may depend on it operating in a relatively subconscious fashion. Once people know they are being placed in certain helping roles in order to be helped themselves, some of the power of the principle deriving from feeling of self-importance and the like may be reduced. That this is not entirely true is evident from role-playing situations in which the subjects know the object of the game but still are affected. Nevertheless, the question of large-scale manipulation of the principle, with the increased likelihood of mechanical and arbitrary application, does hold some danger that only careful observation and research can accurately evaluate.

Implications

The helper principle may have wide application in hospital groups (both in- and outpatient), prisons, correctional institutions, and so forth. Saul Scheidlinger suggests that the principle may have powerful implications for social work's understanding of the therapeutic process in all group therapy. Not only are individual group members aided through helping other members in the group, but the group as a whole may be greatly strengthened in manifold ways as it continually offers assistance to individual group members.

Sol Levine suggests that in a variety of types of habit change, such as efforts to curtail cigarette smoking, the helper principle may have considerable validity. Smokers who are cast in the role of persuading other smokers to stop smoking have themselves been found to benefit from their commitment to the new anti-smoking prescription.

The helper principle does not really require that only the helper profit or even that he benefit more than the person receiving help. Thus in a Flint, Michigan, study fourth graders receiving help benefited at least as much as the givers of help.[20] The helper principle only calls attention to the aid the helper receives from his helper role.

The helper principle has been utilized with varying degrees of awareness in many group situations. What we are calling for is more explicit use of this principle in an organized manner. Conscious planning directed toward the structuring of groups for the widest possible distribution of the helper role may be a decisive therapeutic intervention, a significant leadership training principle, and an important teaching device. It is probably no accident that it is often said that one of the best ways to learn is to teach. Perhaps also psychiatrists, social workers, and others in the helping professions are helping themselves more than is generally recognized!

New Family Approaches

Rachel Levine,[21] in addition to using role playing, has developed an unusual and apparently effective type of "treatment in homes" which she calls the technique of "Demonstration." In essence, the approach consists of the treatment agent bringing simple games, cards, and clay to the "multi-problem" home, and engaging as many members of the family as possible in these activities. When family conflicts arise around the games, they are discussed and worked with by the social worker right on the spot. Aside from the fact that this approach is much more involving than most office discussions, "it also eliminates the distortions which are common when conflict situations are reported after the fact and discussed in the office."[22]

Spiegel's approach to the family emphasizes "the importance of the extended family and the community to the functioning of the individual." He states:

> Although therapy concentrates mainly on the mother, father, and child, we attempt to see and make ourselves known to a wide assortment of relatives. This means that we become assimilated, to a certain extent, to the lineal chains of influence which bear upon the pathologic deviations in the family members. In addition, members of the therapeutic team become known, not simply as individuals, but also as members of a readily identifi-

able organization. This approximation of individuals and organizations reduces the fear of the strange, unknown group and, simultaneously, raises its prestige.[23]

Spiegel has developed some striking modifications in the traditional setting of psychotherapy. ". . .The therapists have at times attended family celebrations, have accompanied the father to his place of work, and have conducted therapeutic interviews in this setting, as well as in trucks, bars, and other unusual places."[24]

Sociotherapy and Involvement

Frequently an individual's psychological difficulties appear to diminish when he becomes involved in some commitment, activity, or social movement. This involvement can vary from a religious activity to a hobby, to a labor union, to participation in a block committee. Wittenberg found, for example, that participation in a neighborhood block committee led to marked personality development and growth in a woman on welfare, who despite some leadership potential had considerable personal difficulty.[25] Wittenberg's approach combined case work, group work, and community organization principles in a program directed toward "personality adjustment through social action," or what might be termed "sociotherapy." Here "the organization is the tool, while personality growth is the goal.[26] Essentially this is using whatever available healthy ego structure there is and building from there by using the environmental pressures as a catalytic agent."[27]

Many of today's new working-class clients, because they are members of Negro- or Spanish-speaking minority groups, have considerable interest in community organizations that represent their aspirations. Treatment agents accustomed to more clinical models tend to underemphasize the therapeutic possibilities of these types of involvement.

While certainly opposing any mechanical pressuring of all Negro clients to become interested in the Negro movement, we would argue that therapists should be alert to such possibilities whenever the client shows even slight interest in this direction. There are two reasons for advocating this model or orientation:

1. Use is made of a possible source of strength in the client and his traditions that is independent of the therapist. Continued dependence

and the tendency to deepen attention upon pathology so characteristic of much treatment are thus avoided.

2. A spread effect, a self-generator of positive change, is put into motion and it may lead the client to feel a growing sense of power and conviction which transfers to various areas of his life, his family, his friends, and the community, indirectly producing broad behavioral modifications and feedback effects.

These processes are not unrelated to the successes claimed by the Black Muslim movement in curtailing the use of drugs and alcohol among those members who previously had been active addicts and alcoholics. If their contentions are accurate, one must acknowledge that the effect of social ideology is quite impressive, regardless of one's particular convictions about the Muslim movement.

Marshall[28] points up the issue by noting that the social worker who just tries to change the drug addict "without offering him a faith in addition"—without embodying this change in a "central ideology" that might involve the addict—has a much harder task than the Muslim movement. It is striking that there appears to have been "a sharp decline in the incidence of crime among the Negro population of Montgomery, Alabama, during the year of the boycott (1955)."[29]

In countering the sociotherapeutic approach, it is sometimes contended that although a particular symptom may disappear, it is merely displaced and becomes expressed in a different form in the very nature of the new involvement. In support of this thesis, irrational, distorted, and inappropriate aspects of the client's behavior in the new activity are sought and cited. There is little doubt that this pattern operates on some occasions and perhaps partially in all such cases, but as an over-all criticism it appears far too oversimplified. It overlooks at least two important possibilities. One is that the new behavior may have emerged from or taken root in nonpathologic aspects of the patient's personality (the "conflict-free portion of the ego");[30] the other possibility—and perhaps more appealing to the traditional clinician—is the likelihood that the new behavior pattern may be a well-sublimated expression of the patient's character. Or a new dynamic may emerge from the novel experiences of involvement. In any case, there is much room for therapeutic guidance to insure against negative symptom displacement.

Unquestionably there are some dangers in this involvement approach, but perhaps it is time to err in new directions.

Pills and Needles as an Auxiliary Technique

Hollingshead and Redlich led the way in noting the low-income person's physical orientation toward treatment: most Class V clients believed that their problems were physically caused and should be physically (chemically, organically) treated via "pills and needles."[31]

Overall and Aronson studied low-income clients' expectations concerning psychotherapy: 70 per cent thought the doctor would be interested in their digestion, 78 per cent expected the doctor would ask them to describe the physical illnesses they had had, 55 per cent anticipated that the doctor would take their pulse and blood pressure, 45 per cent believed the doctor would tell them what kinds of food they should eat.[32]

In light of these findings, it may be in order to suggest greater consideration of all types of auxiliary physical treatment with low-income clients. Such auxiliary treatment might include the use of drugs (tranquilizers, LSD, sedatives, stimulants, hormones, vitamins), diets, massages, baths, heat treatment, breathing exercises, muscle-relaxation techniques,[33] the Somniatron,[34] sleep treatment (the new Soviet machine, electrosone, for inducing a full night's sleep in two hours is relevant).

To the low-income individual, pills, machines, massages are direct and knowable. Talk is vague and suspect. Often physical symptoms are involved in the emotional ailments of workers so that forms of medical treatment are especially attractive. Another advantage of medical treatment is that it can be explained to others—those who invariably inquire about one's ailments. How can talk therapy be explained?

Efforts of the National Institute of Mental Health and other groups to encourage the training of general practitioners for handling psychiatric problems in their usual medical rounds seem a positive trend. Such contact might enable low-income people to receive earlier psychiatric treatment. The break from the neighborhood physician to the special setting of the psychiatric clinic is a deep one for workers. In addition, treatment by a general practitioner clearly defines the distress as a "medical illness" and makes acceptance of treatment easier.

Unfortunately, there are still too few illustrations in psychiatry or community psychiatry where attempts are made to integrate the

physician and the psychotherapist in a program specifically attuned
for the new working class.[35]

Work with Children

Hertha Riese[36] reports an exciting approach to "educational therapy"
which appears to be quite successful with heavily deprived Negro
children who were rejected for treatment by all other clinics. This
approach combines an application of learning principles and techniques
with a modified psychodynamic approach.

> In child psychotherapy, *education* cannot be underestimated. It contributes
> to intellectual maturation and thus furnishes a safer ground for emotional
> growth. It is one means of promoting constancy of effort, and thus self-
> confidence, composure and poise. Analogous to play therapy in early child-
> hood, certain educational endeavors may provide material for psycho-
> therapy with the older child. We have had children assert that the teaching
> afforded in the Center has helped in solving their problems of maladjust-
> ment—their inability to learn having been their greatest worry and the
> cause of their fears, delinquency, isolation, and hostility.[37]

A most interesting parenthetic observation of Riese concerns the
strength of these deprived children:

> It remains one of our most unexpected, challenging and rewarding experi-
> ences that the most destitute and neglected children proved to have the
> greatest strength in adjusting to the conditions in the Educational Therapy
> Center and in coping with the menaces of their home and community.[38]

The use of selected films as discussion stimuli in the treatment of
delinquent boys seems quite promising. Anderson and Smith report
that the use of films that depict dramatic conflict which these boys
can understand seems to provide a therapeutic effect through helping
the youngsters "to express their inner emotions, to externalize
emotional tensions and be free of them; to face their fears . . . and to
discuss them quite freely."[39] In response to the films "they become
articulate and will express themselves freely. . . ." "Furthermore, the
hostile feelings which these boys have toward adults . . . seemed to
have undergone transference (shifting) to certain characters in the
films. Attitudes of suspicion and hostility were always at a minimum
following one of these films." Anderson and Smith also report a

decline in the number and violence of the fights in which these boys were involved.

Schwitzgebel's "change through being studied" approach to delinquents appears to have some promise. In essence, the technique consists of paying delinquent youngsters to talk into a tape recorder about their activities, fantasies, thoughts, and free associations.[40]

Pretraining for Treatment

Overall and Aronson state:

> One way of reducing cognitive inaccuracies is to attempt, during the initial phases of treatment, to reeducate the patient as to both his own and the therapist's role in treatment. Since a great proportion of dropouts occur after the initial interview, it would seem particularly important to raise the question of expectations during the first hour. Moreover, it may be necessary to encourage a direct expression of expectations so that both patient and therapist can more easily view and modify their roles.[41]

Listed here are some of the expectations or norms of treatment regarding which it may be useful to offer the low-income client "pretraining" (anticipatory socialization) before he enters directly into the therapeutic process:

1. To express personal feelings to a professional who is not a minister, a priest, or a medical doctor.

2. To expect no miracles and to know that most changes take time.

3. To recognize that talk can be useful.

4. To see that change requires work, that it does not necessarily come from the outside (the therapist).

5. To accept that some difficulties are self-produced, for example, by poor thinking or defense mechanisms.

6. To understand that some physical problems or ailments can be, in part, psychologically caused.

7. To accept some unstructuredness, nondirectiveness.

8. To realize that one can criticize and yet love and respect one's family.

9. To accept the fact that physical examination and treatment may not be essential features in the treatment of various difficulties. (In light of the Overall-Aronson findings regarding the low-income person's "physical" expectations regarding psychotherapy, pretraining in this area may be indispensable.)

Treatment Mechanism and Therapist Training

There is increasing evidence that a multiplicity of techniques can be effective if the client and the treatment agent believe in them. But—and here is the heart of the problem—the techniques that most low-income clients believe in are different from those that most middle-class practitioners believe in. Nothing could point more sharply to the need for treatment agents (including social workers) to be exposed to and trained in a wide variety of techniques congenial to low-income people (conditioning approaches, sleep therapy, muscle-relaxation techniques, role playing, hypnosis, drugs, directive therapies, etc.) rather than having a one-method approach.

Another solution is the combination of some of these techniques with the more cognitive, psychodynamic approaches so attractive to treatment agents. Reich combined muscle-relaxation techniques with psychoanalysis. Robertiello *et al.* moved to combine psychodramatic techniques with psychoanalysis. Drugs have been used adjunctively with "depth" treatments. Hypnosis has been combined with psychoanalysis to produce hypnoanalysis. Activity diagnosis and treatment have been utilized in a psychoanalytic context.

The treatment agent must accept the fact that he has to validate himself. The therapist's role should be clarified because the low-income individual is suspicious, and ambiguity feeds this suspicion. While religious and medical therapeutic motivations are grasped by the low-income client, social-service people are often seen as patronizing (do-gooders).

Some identification with the patient can be developed by having carefully directed and interpreted experience with low-income patients stressed in the therapist's training (not merely work at a city hospital), and by the therapist seeing the low-income patient in his best, freshest hours. As far as possible he should talk to the patient personally. The low-income patient usually wants some wholistic, not role-segmented, relationship. The therapist might select low-income individuals to work with whom he has some personal idiosyncratic feeling for, but he should avoid selecting only middle-class-like workers. He should find common interests with the patient (sports, movies, children, family, underdog); these are greater than imagined. Providing considerable reassurance and support from the beginning is important—give respect rather than love.

The Honest Approach

In addition to advance preparation of the therapist and client as a means of reducing distance and improving the therapeutic relationship, we believe that the relationship can also be strengthened by the "honest" approach. There are a number of reasons why an approach that strongly emphasizes honesty at every possible point may be especially important to the low-income client. Perhaps most important is the feeling of many of these clients that they have been widely manipulated by various institutions and agents in the society—the politicians, the newspapers, the social agencies. This has led to a pervasive alienation.

What is the meaning of the "honest" approach? Isn't all treatment honest?[42] No. In fact, most treatments cannot be completely honest all of the time. But different approaches can stress honesty and attempt in every way possible to limit variation from this theme. There are at least two fundamental limitations constraining against fully honest treatment: (1) The ego of the recipient or client may be unable to tolerate full honesty; (2) the tactics of the situation may require some limitation on a completely honest presentation of goals and means. (For example, a detached worker operating in a street gang, while he may endeavor to be as honest as possible, sometimes cannot fully achieve this goal, particularly in the early transitional phase of establishing a contact with the group.)

The following are some of the essential characteristics of an honest approach:

1. The therapeutic agent does not attempt by utilization of language, clothes, or manners to pretend to be "one of the boys."[43]

2. The treatment agent does not manipulate or lie to the client about either small or large things (he does not pretend to make a telephone call; he does not lie about the low-income youngsters' possibilities of obtaining a job, etc.).

3. The treatment agent directly and often ruthlessly exposes the manipulation and maneuvering of the individual or group. Criticism is open and direct and is considered a strong point in building toward

change; self-deception as well as interpersonal manipulation is exposed. (The treatment agent, of course, can be a group.)

4. The consequences of the negative behavior (e.g., drug addiction) are carefully and truthfully elaborated.

5. The honest treatment agent, while he may indicate his genuine "concern," is not oversympathetic or indulgent. He does not pretend to be a friend and his own critical feelings regarding the client's behavior are openly expressed.

6. The honest approach makes clear that the behavior change aimed for is not sought to please the treatment agent or the group and will not be rewarded in these terms.

7. The general approach is to discourage props and crutches and to demand effort, initiative, decision making, and responsibility. Thus with regard to the addict, the aim is to "de-institutionalize" and force the addict to deal with the responsibility of living in the community.

It is important to distinguish the honest approach from the "hard line." The honest approach is not punitive, authoritarian, moralistic, or is its aim adjustment to the norms of society. Awareness of reality consequences does not necessarily require an acceptance of that reality. The assumption is, however, that generally gang violence, addiction, and the like are not meaningful ways of changing reality.

Treatment Goals and Social Class

In contrast to the goals of insight and self-development in middle-class psychotherapy, the low-income patient hopes for visible, concrete, specific behavioral change and symptom reduction. It is especially important to him that his physical health improve. His concept of health is freedom from symptoms.

Removal of symptoms and improvement of their life situations are probably the two most generally anticipated goals of treatment for low-income clients. But to achieve them, it is often necessary for the therapist to consider related issues in the low-income person's life— issues related to ideology, values, and aspirations. Moreover, in order to develop and utilize the "strengths" of the client, the treatment agent will need to possess considerable familiarity with a range of the goals, hopes, traditions, and confusions of the old and new working classes. He cannot take for granted that these are the same as middle-class goals, or should he assume that because there are class differences in outlook and values that low-income clients do not have to be understood as individuals.

In particular, the therapist should know that while many low-income people desire middle-class occupations, most of them have considerable ambivalence about the competitive, prestige-oriented values that they feel are connected to these goals. Their occupational aspirations frequently have a different meaning and/or priority in their value system hierarchy.

Whenever the goals of low-income people appear to be similar to those of the middle class, they bear examination for different meanings, different contexts, different emphases. This is true because the central focus of middle-class life is different from that of the low-income individual. The major middle-class orientation, determined by job experience and the preparation for it in the educational system, is more often one of competitiveness, individualism, and prestige seeking. This does not tend to be the central value orientation of low-income culture.

But the low-income person is also concerned with status and prestige. The question is, what is the difference? The desire for status and prestige in the low-income person is very often connected with the simple desire for respect (some low-income youngsters think, in a misdirected way, that by committing violence they will win respect).

Then, too, conventional prestige is less imperative for the low-income person than it is for the middle-class person. His prestige goals compared to goals such as security are much less salient. This fact has been amply demonstrated in response to poll questions which ask: "Would you rather have a secure job or a job in which you might go further, but in which there is risk?" The class division which characterizes the responses is striking. The low-income person more often says he prefers the secure job; the middle-class person more often says, "I will take the risk."

The therapist who works with low-income populations has to have an awareness of these issues because they penetrate some of the major psychological problems. The therapist will have to recognize that some of the people he works with who are "lower class" (employed irregularly in unstable occupations) will want to become "working class" (employed in semiskilled and skilled occupations where employment is more stable). Other low-income clients may desire middle-class occupations but either might not desire or be strongly ambivalent toward the acquisition of many middle-class values. Still others may want to become "ultra middle class." In practically all cases the treatment agent will need to become proficient at interclass communication (indigenous nonprofessionals can play a crucial role here). While utilizing and accommodating to low-income traditions, styles, and strengths, the therapist must also recognize that in many areas the low-income person desires to change his ways; that he isn't necessarily happy with all his traditions, and that he has goals which are not working.

Finally, an especially important extra function of the treatment agent (be he guidance counselor, social worker, or psychiatrist) can lie in providing "know-how" for the low-income client; know-how about education, jobs, bureaucracy. One of the outstanding deficits of low-income people is their inadequate information about many of the mechanics of every-day life. Their lack of knowledge is a severe detriment to their total functioning and often overlaps with and heightens their psychological difficulties.

The Future

In the past decade, two trends have emerged in the field of psychiatry: a physiological trend highlighted by the appearance of a variety of new drugs; and an environmental-social trend reflected in community psychiatry, social psychiatry, milieu therapy, etc. These two developments appear to be in harmony with the treatment expectations and desires of low-income patients. Physiological and environmental psychiatry may not be relevant only to the expectations of the working classes but to their actual problems as well.

It may be that intrapsychic, psychodynamic treatment is now suited to middle-class expectations and problems, while social and physiological therapies are more appropriate for low-income problems. We believe this to be an oversimplification. Our outlook is that the emphasis in treatment should be class related, but that all individuals could probably benefit from treatment at the various levels: intrapsychic (and interpersonal), environmental, and physiological. Thus, low-income treatment programs might utilize social and physiological orientations as their starting point (and in general use them more extensively), but would nevertheless be concerned with internal psychological forces, and might perhaps give these factors greater attention as therapy progressed. On the other hand, therapy attuned for middle-class clients might begin with the psychological level and move outward toward the environment and "inward" toward the physiological.

In a sense, then, the emphasis on environmental and physiological causes, powered in part by the needs of low-income clientele, may contribute to the further development of a universal psychiatry with wider implications than our low-income focus might seem to imply. This conclusion is another illustration of our thesis that the new and old working classes are sparking activities and reorientations that are of benefit not only to them but to all of society.

NOTES

1. August Hollingshead and Fredrick C. Redlich, *Social Class and Mental Illness* (New York: John Wiley and Sons, 1958).

2. Norman Q. Brill and Hugh Storrow, "Social Class and Psychiatric Treatment," *Archives of General Psychiatry*, III (1963), 340–344.

3. William Haase, *Rorschach Diagnosis, Socio-economic Class, and Examiner Bias*. Unpublished doctoral dissertation, New York University, 1956.

4. *Ibid.*

5. See Rachel Levine, "A Short Story on the Long Waiting List," *Journal of Social Work*, VIII (1963), 20–23, for suggestions as to how to shorten intake procedure.

6. Cartoonlike tests, such as the Rosenzweig Frustration test, and simple picture selection instruments, such as the Szondi, may be especially valuable.

7. Jerome Beker *et al.*, "Situational Testing of Social Psychological Variables in Personality," in Frank Riessman, J. Cohen, and A. Pearl, eds., *Mental Health of the Poor* (New York: The Free Press of Glencoe, 1964).

8. Jerome K. Myers and Bertram H. Roberts, *Family and Class Dynamics in Mental Illness* (New York: John Wiley and Sons, 1959), p. 205.

9. Melvin L. Kohn, "Social Class and Parent-Child Relationships: An Interpretation," *American Journal of Sociology*, LXVIII (1963), 11.

10. *Ibid.*, p. 11.

11. Bruce F. Young and Morris Rosenberg, "Role Playing as a Participation Technique," *Journal of Social Issues*, V (1949), 42–45.

12. Gertrude Levit and Helen Jennings, "Learning through Role Playing," *How to Use Role Playing* (Washington: Adult Education Association, 1960), p. 10.

13. Frank Riessman, "The Revolution in Social Work: The New Nonprofessional, *Trans-action*, II, No. 1 (1965), 12–17.

14. In Chapter 14, we develop further one use of the nonprofessional in social service.

15. O. Hobart Mowrer, *The New Group Therapy* (New York: D. Van Nostrand, 1964), p. 4.

16. B. T. King and I. L. Janis, "Comparison of the Effectiveness of Improvised Versus Non-Improvised Role Playing in Producing Opinion Changes," *Human Relations*, I (1956), 177–186.

17. Rita Volman and Donald R. Cressey, "Differential Association and the Rehabilitation of Drug Addicts," *American Journal of Sociology*, LXIX (February 1963), 139.

18. George Brager, "The Indigenous Worker: A New Approach to the Social Work Technician," *Social Work*, X (April 1965), 33–40.

19. Arthur Pearl, "Youth in Lower Class Settings." Paper presented at the Fifth Symposium on Social Psychology, Norman, Oklahoma, 1964, p. 6.

20. Frank B. Hawkinshire, "Training Needs for Offenders Working in Community Treatment Programs," *Experiment in Culture Expansion* (Sacramento: State of California Department of Corrections, 1963), pp. 27–36.

21. Rachel Levine, "Treatment in the Homes," *Social Work*, IX (January 1964), 19–28.

22. *Ibid.*, p. 22. Levine also uses role playing in the home-treatment approach.

23. John P. Spiegel, "Some Cultural Aspects of Transference and Countertransference," in Jules H. Masserman, ed., *Individual and Familial Dynamics* (New York: Grune & Stratton, 1959), p. 180.

24. *Ibid.*, p. 161.

25. Rudolph Wittenberg, "Personality Adjustment through Social Action," *American Journal of Orthopsychiatry*, XVIII (1948), 207–221.

26. *Ibid.*, p. 208.

27. *Ibid.*, p. 220.

28. Kenneth Marshall, speech on Negro culture, given at Mobilization for Youth Training Program, September 12, 1962, p. 33.

29. Tom Kahn, *Unfinished Revolution* (New York: Igal Rodenko). Quoted by Jacob Fishman and Frederick Solomon, "Youth and Social Action," *American Journal of Orthopsychiatry*, XXXIII (1963), 876.

30. See John Cumming and Elaine Cumming, *Ego and Milieu* (New York: Atherton Press, 1962), pp. 13–14, for an illuminating application of Heinz Hartman's concept of a "conflict-free portion" of the ego.

31. Hollingshead and Redlich, *op. cit.*, pp. 340–345.

32. Betty Overall and H. Aronson, "Expectations of Psychotherapy in Patients of Lower Socio-economic Class," *American Journal of Orthopsychiatry*, XXXIII (1963), 425.

33. See Edward Jacobson, *Progressive Relaxation* (Chicago: University of Chicago, 1938).

34. The Somniatron purports to produce deep relaxation or sleep through electrodes affecting the cortex. (Reported by Lafayette Instrument Company, Indiana.)

35. See Michael Balint, *The Doctor, His Patient and the Illness* (New York: International University Press, 1957), for a profound discussion on the therapeutic potentials of the general physician-patient relationship.

36. Hertha Riese, *Heal the Hurt Child* (Chicago: Chicago University Press, 1962).

37. Hertha Riese, "Educational Therapy," *Psychiatry*, XIII (1950), 470–471.

38. Hertha Riese, "Educational Therapy, A Methodological Approach to the Problem of the 'Untreatable' Child," *Group Psychotherapy*, XII (1959), 61.

39. Celia M. Anderson and Carol C. Smith, "Film Experiment with Delinquent Boys," (New York: Film Library, New York University, and "600" Program, Board of Education, New York City, 1956), p. 30.

40. Robert Schwitzgebel, "Delinquents with Tape Recorders," *New Society* (January 1962).

41. Overall and Aronson; *op. cit.*, p. 430.

42. In this connection, see Seymour L. Halleck, "The Impact of Professional Dishonesty on Behaviour of Disturbed Adolescents," *Social Work*, VIII (1963), 48–55.

43. It is interesting to observe that practically all social workers working with addicts have acquired the language of the drug addict so that they speak of getting a "shot," getting "high," and so on.

V

Poverty and
Community Action

I3

❀   ❀   ❀

FIRST FORCE (A):
SERVICES AND PARTICIPATION

In this section we are concerned with the variety of agencies and pressures involved in community action to reduce poverty and improve neighborhoods. Three different types of forces are intermingled. The first force is that typified by the established social agencies in case work, clients, public housing, welfare, education, and remediation; it operates "inside" the social service network. The second force consists of groups attempting to produce changes in the systems of social and economic welfare by the strategy of external or "outside" militant pressure. The third force is to be found in the emerging (poverty-oriented) agencies that mediate between the inside established agencies and the outside pressure groups.

The war on poverty and the civil-rights movement have changed the context of action of the established agencies. Financially neglected in the fifties, the social-service agencies are discovering that funds are available if they are interested in the poor. Some agencies have rejected the new demands on them and want to continue as before but with better financing. The great majority of established agencies, however, are searching for greater relevance in programming today. In this chapter we suggest two approaches that could be taken—the support of neighborhood-service centers and the strengthening of consumer participation in the conduct of services. In the following chapter, we analyze a third line of advance for the traditional agencies—the wide-spread use of nonprofessionals.

Evidence abounds that the social services for "The Other America" are severely inadequate. Services are insufficient, frequently inappropriate or irrelevant, fragmented, and unsuited to the style of the poor, especially the minority poor. Since services are a substantial and rising component of the income of the poor, social agencies have great importance and their deficiencies are disturbing:

1. Existing services and facilities are deeply inadequate—whether in terms of cash allowances, the level or relevance of social services, or the availability of decent housing.

2. A crazy hodgepodge of private and public services exists with very little cooperation among them. "Hard-to-reach" clients are frequently the product of "hard-to-reach" agencies; "multi-problem families" may be a reflection of "single-purpose agencies."

3. Many agencies, despite their avowed goals, have not been primarily oriented to the poor; private agencies in the fifties and early sixties sought a new clientele in the middle class.

4. The orientation of much of social service is remedial and policing rather than preventive. Most welfare departments do little to increase the employment possibilities of their clientele. They frequently perform a police function with the poor. The concern with the morality of welfare recipients and the danger of people receiving it who are not legally eligible for it have made welfare a substitute policing system for low-income areas. In order to provide checks on the poor, the welfare worker becomes an investigator as she (or, less frequently, he) is called in New York City; her purpose is to check periodically on the behavior of those who are receiving "alms" from the government. This essentially becomes a police function, as little legitimate initiative can be undertaken by the poor person unless it is approved by the welfare investigators. Consequently, the poor, thought of as being ignorant, illiterate, and unimaginative, have developed a variety of ways of coping with the welfare worker; evasion is frequent as recipients become "welfare wise." And so we have a typical situation of a great deal of police and control efforts on one side and a considerable amount of matching efforts at evasion on the other. A stalemate is frequently reached with repugnance on the part of the authorities and lack of respect on the part of the recipients.

5. Routinization and bureaucratization characterize many services, private as well as public. The emphasis on the fiscal and moral side of

social services has led to welfare workers devoting a great percentage of time to filling out forms to determine which budget—Federal, state or local—should be charged for the expenses of individual clients. Little individualized attention is given to those who, to some extent, perform the function of serving as the clientele of the social agencies.

6. The personnel of many agencies are frequently not adequate for dealing with the problems of the poor. The more highly trained often are oriented to a psychoanalytic framework which has not been shaped for the specific problems of the poor. The less trained frequently do not see themselves (or are not permitted to see themselves) as more than clerks and bookkeepers.

7. A private government with limited checks has developed in many communities. Private agencies, soliciting funds on a mass basis from the community, are substitutes for public action. These agencies, run as they are by self-perpetuating boards of the Community Chests, United Funds, and the like, tend to be undemocratic and unrepresentative of those low-income areas in which they operate. The "tax base" of these agencies is regressive in as much as those at the lower end of the income scale tend to contribute a greater percentage of their income to community fund-raising drives than do those with higher incomes.

The maintenance of a private government of charity means that the community as a whole, and particularly the new working class, has limited effect upon the decisions which are made, especially the distribution of funds. Most Community Chest funds go to agencies which are not primarily oriented to the poor, even though many contributors to the fund believe this is the purpose of their contribution.

Moreover, the agencies have frequently operated as colonial administrators to the "natives" living in the poor areas of the large cities. "Natives" were scarcely brought into the operation; they had little part in making the basic decisions, and this was true even when, for practical reasons, a few of the more acceptable "colored natives" are brought into the lower levels of administration or are sprinkled through the board of directors. These practices have been changing, but not as much as the rhetoric of transformation implies.

Strongly put, the main impact of many social-welfare programs has been to provide enough services to keep the "natives" from becoming too distressed. The aim has been to "cool out" their anger rather than to help them out of poverty.

Social services—their financing, their control, and distribution—

must become recognized as the political problems they are, for fundamental questions of who gets what, and how this is determined, are involved.

8. There has been comparatively little attention among social-service professionals in helping communities of the poor to move to self-action and self-help. This is a crucial limitation of the existing orientation of most social agencies which are more concerned with using established community organizations than with building useful social and political action among the people who live in an area.

The Neighborhood Service Center

In response to the deficiencies of the service system, the poor have developed their own informal systems and traditions in order to cope and survive. Store-front churches, cellar clubs, home-town clubs, the extended family, the use of the street as a playground, the block party, the mutual assistance of siblings, music constructed from pots and pans, the informal know-how and self-help of the neighborhood, the use of peer learning, street language (hip, slang, etc.), the rent strike, and other forms of direct social action and protest are just a few illustrations of these forms of adaptation.

These adaptations of the poor are one of the strands of the movement toward neighborhood service centers, which could be a basic unit of the antipoverty war. Building on the strengths of established agencies and the poor, a new form is emerging of considerable significance. While the third-party agencies have frequently adopted the neighborhood-service center notion, it seems to us that its style and operations could be adopted by traditional agencies.

The basic format of the neighborhood-service center is an interesting combination of decentralization and centralization. Decentralization is an effort to make services more available to the poor by having agencies provide them through neighborhood facilities rather than through a central office. The centralization effort brings together a variety of services or access to services under one roof.

By increasing accessibility, the neighborhood-service center increases the visibility of social services and, hopefully, results in greater community awareness and participation. As more low-income people are brought into the service system, they may be able to demand the help that they need and become more sophisticated in their use of a service.

The neighborhood-service center goes beyond the traditional notion that giving a client information will enable him to be his own coordinator. By placing various services under one roof, a coordination by propinquity, the client is more likely to get immediately a wide gamut of services rather than having to travel distances to get to a service facility only to be placed on a waiting list. Through scope and concentration of activities the typical problems of the low-income service consumer can be reduced—being routed through and getting the delivery of services in a highly fragmented, incoherent social-service system.

These service centers can be utilized to develop any number of different types of programs: consumer-rights programs, legal rights, educational and tutorial programs, family planning, health services, mental-health services, housing, public welfare, job training and placement. Thus, they do not only bring together established agencies so they can work more effectively together, they can be a springboard for new kinds of activities.

Obviously, these centers will require many employees. The manpower needs cannot be met from the ranks of social-service professionals—nor would that be desirable if possible. The new role of the nonprofessional is rapidly expanding; we discuss this role in the following chapter.

We have observed in various parts of the country a number of neighborhood-service centers which are underutilized. This occurs when the facility is relatively inaccessible or unknown or where the center has achieved a reputation for nondelivery. For example, in one West Coast city the state employment office in a neighborhood-service center is well staffed but places few in jobs. An inauthentic program like this does not pull people in to use what purport to be "services!"

The neighborhood-service center is but one of many efforts that the established agencies can be involved in as they attempt to be more relevant and useful to the poverty movement. Nor is it free of many difficulties. But it is a way for established agencies to participate more effectively in the war on poverty either by participating in a center run by other agencies or in promoting such centers themselves.

The established agencies when they participate in neighborhood-service centers can be unresponsive in adapting to the new issues of the center. But the climate and stress of the neighborhood centers can mold traditional services in fresh and interesting ways.

The Client as Consumer Citizen

Another way of improving and adapting the social-service network is through the participation of the consumers of the services. Social services historically have typically been offered as a charity, a privilege rather than a right of the poor. Service users were treated as recipients and dependents without any decision-making involvement. The social-service world has not been a world of rights and democracy; it has not accepted the new income idea of participation in decision making as a new right.

A change is occurring. The Economic Opportunity Act, with its definition of community-action programs as programs developed, conducted, and administered with the maximum feasible participation of residents of the areas and members of low-income groups has, in effect, "legalized the poor as policy makers, program developers, program operators, and as program evaluators. It has provided a new perspective for all service agencies." Despite efforts to constrict this perspective, a new idea of continuing significance has been unleashed.

Traditional agencies can begin to involve their clients in the decision-making apparatus of the agency; in effect, changing the role of "client" to that of "citizen," where the individual has a right to service and a right to participate in decisions. Housing tenants can be represented and have a voice in the decisions of public-housing management. Neighborhood councils representing the poor can have a voice in sanitation and police protection. Parents and students should have a strong role in the schools and colleges. Welfare clients can have a voice in the administration of the welfare system. Neighborhood residents should have a role in the operation of community mental-health centers.

If appropriately implemented, involvement and self-determination of the poor can have very positive results. The consumer can be on the advisory committee of the agency; new relations with professionals could develop. The consumer as a participant can shape services that are adequate, appropriate, and utilized. The poor can become the constituency of the service system, providing support as well as informed criticism.

In the sixties, many established agencies began to break through their encrustations to pay attention again to the poor and to be concerned with the relevance and quality of their performance. But they have been slow to see the significance for themselves of the theme of participation. As a consequence, involvement of the poor has been more important an issue in the over-all conduct of the local war on poverty than in the operation of individual agencies. As we point out later, there are pressures for change and the first party forces can adapt more rapidly than they have in changing the role of their users. In the course of doing so, their services are likely to become better and more relevant.

What formerly existed as protest outside the system can now be brought into the system as organized representation. The rent strike has become legal in some jurisdictions; the demands of the welfare-rights groups can be introduced in the form of representative democracy with a forum and legitimate spokesmen. More generally, the users should have access to a useful grievance procedure and to the decision-making process.

Another way of involving the poor is by having them "surveyed" with regard to their reactions to public housing, welfare, education, social services. Their responses would be guidelines for policy changes. For example, residents in low-income housing projects could anonymously rate the housing manager (as students sometimes do faculty) and housing operations; this information would be available to the housing manager and his administrative superiors. This kind of market research on the reactions to the products and personnel of the social-service agencies could provide an important new perspective. The poor would be citizens or constituents where now they are powerless. Moreover, these surveys could be conducted by the poor themselves, functioning as nonprofessional research aides.

The involvement of the poor is no panacea for the ills and difficulties of the social-service world. Nor is this participation a substitute for trained, professional competence as some seem to imply. Effective involvement of the poor requires effective professionals rather than the withdrawal of all professionals. But the relations of the professional will change when he defines the service users as consumers and citizens rather than as "clients." Consumers and citizens have choices and rights, visible preferences and access to redress. There are strong tensions in this change, but we believe that this tension offers creative possibilities for the professional in his ability to make contact with those he seeks to help, and to shape agency activities so that they are more relevant to need and style.

In Negro areas particularly, the theme of participation has frequently assumed great militancy. The traditional agencies are being pressured to involve the residents in decisions rather than being content with providing what purports to be "service." The cry for "power" in many ghetto areas is a reflection of the feeling that within ghettos major service institutions have not brought the residents into the making of decisions. The development of rights to service and to participation as parts of the new income is a needed response to the hunger for independence and destiny control that service alone cannot meet. We believe that in the troubled realigning of power relations in the United States, the traditional as well as the new service organizations can make a substantial contribution by dealing as citizens and consumers with those who want help.

Actually, there is less and less choice for the agencies. For "no service without representation" is becoming the implicit demand in many ghettos. The social-service agencies will have to be learning how to respond to this pressure or find themselves a battle front.

In terms of our concept of the new income, social services have assumed great importance, especially in the lives of the poor. The established agencies and traditional professionals have a heavy responsibility, therefore, in delivering useful services. The new forms of the plane of living require new relations between professionals and agencies on the one hand and their users on the other. These relations are difficult to work out, but the involvement of users in the social-service decision-making apparatuses will be an important if frequently disturbing stimulus in reshaping and democraticizing the social-service world.

14

❀ ❀ ❀

FIRST FORCE (B):
NONPROFESSIONALS IN SOCIAL
WELFARE

In this chapter we take up the theme of the role of the nonprofessional that we introduced in chapters 9 and 12. The vast expansion of nonprofessional activity can be a most important way for the first force of traditional social-service agencies to improve their services.

The traditional view of the social services in America is that they are the prerogative of highly-trained professionals with complex specialized skills in the art of helping people. While this attitude has fostered improvements in the quality of service, it has, at the same time, severely limited the number of people trained to serve and has subtly produced gaps in communication with those in need.

How can the essential professional basis in a service relationship be preserved and still insure that the client's total needs are considered? One way is through building into the service structure functional roles for nonprofessionals. At the same time, this way may be the answer to another pressing question—manpower.

The Manpower Problem

Even with the phenomenal growth of the service professions and their training facilities, demand continues to exceed supply. The nonprofessional can serve, not as a stopgap, but as an intrinsic part of the service machinery, and can help meet the manpower shortage.

The use of nonprofessionals in capacities higher than the traditional volunteer started several years ago in the field of mental health. Dr. Margaret Rioch trained a selected group of intelligent, mature, middle-class women to be mental-health counselors.[1] J. D. Holzberg successfully used volunteer college students as companions to hospitalized schizophrenics.[2] In France, young men and women were trained as "educateurs" to work and live with small groups of mentally ill and emotionally disturbed children.[3] A number of existing facilities designed training programs for their psychiatric aides to extend the range of their work.[4] In educational systems and social-welfare structures there has been similar movement in this direction.

Most of these programs see the nonprofessional as an extension of the professional—an aide who can reduce the burden on the teacher, welfare worker, or clinician by doing some of the less technical tasks. In this capacity, he has customarily reflected aspects of the image of the professional. He is often recruited from the ranks of those with the same social background, the same attitudes and values, and, to some extent, the same educational background: middle-class housewives, college students, etc. These people are not the low-income, so-called "indigenous" nonprofessionals. The middle-class nonprofessional's role as an aide to the professional has in many ways eclipsed his function as an aide to the client. Even so, these problems have demonstrated the potential of the nonprofessional manpower resource.

Reaching the Unreached

There is a growing wave of plans to use the nonprofessional in more creative ways.[5] Schools throughout the country are using parents and other members of the community as "team mothers," parent-education coordinators, and in other similar roles. In some neighborhoods, Puerto Rican "informal leaders" are used as liaison between the schools and the Spanish-speaking community. The New York State Division for Youth and a number of other agencies employ former youthful offenders in interviewing and for related research tasks. Howard University's Community Apprentice Program has trained delinquent youths to be recreation, child-welfare, and research aides. Home-makers with minimal education and professional training are put to work by many social agencies in clients' homes. The Chicago Area Project uses low-income, nonprofessional organizers for community-action programs. Mobilization for Youth, in its diversified activities, employs nonprofessional leaders, case aides, parent-education aides, homemakers, and homework helpers, and many others. The Lincoln Hospital Health Service in New York trains mental-health aides for work in neighborhood-service centers.

Most of these new positions have come into being in programs for low-income groups. One reason is that these jobs offer employment opportunities and thus directly serve to reduce poverty. They transform dependent welfare cases into homemakers, former delinquents into researchers, and economically deprived students into tutors. More importantly, these new job categories represent a desire to reach the millions of poor.

As concern increased over social pathology, school dropouts, juvenile delinquency, drug addiction, and other deep-rooted problems, the difficulties of professionals in reaching the extremely disadvantaged were revealed. These difficulties were based in large measure on the past history of inappropriate and insufficient services for these people, and in part on the presumed low utilization of whatever services were offered. There was obvious need to make and maintain contact with those who have not been benefiting from the usual sources of service and help.

This is, perhaps, the basic problem the human-service professions face today. If it were the manpower shortage alone that had to be met, at least a partial solution would be to increase presently constituted services by using middle-class nonprofessional assistants. The deeper problem emerges when there is a deliberate seeking to help those who do not get critically needed services. There must be a change in the character of service, a real reaching out into the community, and determination to stay involved. This change can be effected by adding a new member to the "team"—the low-income or neighborhood nonprofessional. He can complement the professional not only by merely taking over lesser tasks, but by fulfilling newly created ones.

Only a crash program, on a scale large enough to be called a "movement," to recruit, train, and employ low-income nonprofessionals in new capacities can meet the problems of manpower, utilization, and need. These problems continue to grow, and threaten to engulf the promising plans for the future.

A major strategy for inside groups today is the rapid increase in the use of nonprofessionals, and we discuss in detail in this chapter a new kind of position—the expediter—that can provide important services to the poor. The effective use of nonprofessionals is not easy, and we attempt to deal with many problems in this chapter. The perspective within which we write is that the nonprofessional role can be an important source of employment for the poor and at the same time can provide needed services. Federal funds will be needed for increasing nonprofessional employment opportunities, but the willingness of professionals and agencies to promote nonprofessioal activity is of great importance.

The Expediter

The fragmentation of community social and health services, both public and private, is generally recognized as a major deterrent to their effective use by those who are in greatest need of them. The blue-collar worker or low-income person faced with scattered facilities, hampered by barriers of language, and embittered by the impersonal, officious, and institutionalized manner with which he is frequently met, often is overwhelmed and too often rejects, or is rejected by, the only sources of aid available to him. His problem gets worse. Only at the point of crisis does he or his family turn again for help.

There is no need to document the moral, social, or financial wastefulness of this situation. It is now being attacked at the most important level—community planning. One of the basic principles of both the new community antipoverty action programs and community mental-health programs is to provide a full range of services and to insure continuity of care or service to the client: (1) by making available a variety of services under a unified clinical and administrative program, and (2) by establishing a clear and workable pattern for interchange and cooperation among various community facilities and programs. This coordination and cooperation is not a simple administrative concern that can be easily handled with a new referral system. There must be a change in the basic attitude of the agency toward the client.

In the field of mental health it has been customary in this country to be content with merely making a referral without being concerned with whether or not the patient gets there. The principle seems to be that if you leave the responsibility to the patient, those who are "really" motivated will get there. This must be re-examined in the light of the experiences of lower socioeconomic clients. Generally, they are not sophisticated in maneuvering within the labyrinth of multifaceted medical and social agencies. They become lost in the process of referral and re-referral. Long waiting lists, unnecessary clinic delays, and inadequate treatment have imbued them with a sense of frustration and hostility, and sometimes despair. These feelings are so entrenched that new ways must be found to cope with them. The agencies must take upon themselves the responsibility for seeing that the individual patient gets to the service, or gets from one service to another, or even from one agency to another. Without the assumption of this responsibility, the concept of continuity of care or services will become a meaningless programmatic shibboleth. Nor can these problems be resolved through administrative improvements alone. A human link is needed.

> At one time, ward heelers performed the function of getting things done for individual citizens in difficulty. Civil service and bureaucratization have made these pressures less effective, particularly as the urban political machine has declined. A new intervener is needed. He is the wartime expediter but with some influence behind him which permits him to act as an effective source of pressure.[6]

The expediter is that needed social invention—the intervener. He would be the liaison between the client and the agency and outside resources. He would be the one to whom the client could appeal for help in finding the appropriate service, or in negotiating the service jungle.

Union counselors and veterans' service representatives have helped millions secure the benefits, health, and education services which were available to them but which they were not able to obtain by themselves. These two programs have demonstrated the value of designating someone whose primary function is that of liaison between the service agency and the client. The same function should be an essential component of every community action or community mental-health program, and the nonprofessional expediter can appropriately fill this role.

What Are the Expediter's Roles?

The expediter is a link between the client and community resources. As such, he performs the following roles:

Interpreter: interprets to the professionals the particular meaning or attitudes expressed in various subcultural ways of thinking and speaking; explains class patterns, values, or biases; interprets to the client a professional attitude or action; translates for the various nationality groups present in many communities.

Negotiator: intercedes for the client with a particular community agency in order to break through red tape to get appointments or benefits; negotiates for more expeditious service.

Attorney: required to act as a lay attorney to argue a case for a client who is not receiving the benefits to which he is entitled under the regulations of a specific agency.

Educator: informs clients of the kinds of services available to them, and their rights and responsibilities in receiving these services.

Instructor: teaches the client the best way to go about getting a particular service by, for example, suggesting to someone who is going to apply for a job how to dress or how to talk to the interviewer.

Helper: helps in the problem of getting a client to or from a particular service by going with the client, or by providing an escort or a baby-sitter.

The expediter expedites, facilitates, and improves service. Only indirectly does he participate in the healing process. In this respect, his job is differentiated from jobs of a similar nature (case aides, referral agents, counselors, and the like) in which the nonprofessional is used in a healing capacity. The nonprofessional can bring important qualities to the healing function. In these jobs, however, he plays different roles than the expediter does.

The case aide is a therapeutic agent. He intervenes in the client's life in a way that presupposes a corrective influence on the need which has brought the client to the service in the first place. On the other hand, the expediter is a service agent. He intervenes in the agency's life in a way that will assure the client that the therapeutic agent is made available, and continues to be available, throughout the period of his need. At times the case aide may perform some function of the expediter without risking his usefulness as a therapeutic agent. In fact, there are times when it might even enhance his healing role. The expediter, however, should be protected from performing direct therapeutic duties, such as case findings, counseling, etc. Agencies may tend to give more weight to these kinds of familiar functions and to encroach on the expediter's job to include them. This will devalue the expediter's role, overburden and confuse him, the client, and the agency about what his job really is.

The expediter is a service finder not a case finder. No nonprofessional worker should do case finding in the sense of evaluating a problem and making a referral to a specialized agency on the basis of that evaluation. For example, he is not qualified to determine if an action is a symptom of mental illness, or if an unemployed heart patient should be encouraged to go to an employment service or to the Department of Public Welfare. If he made such judgments, he could create additional problems for the client and he could undermine people's confidence in nonprofessional workers generally. The case aide, the homemaker, the child service worker, and all others should discuss these problems with their professional supervisors and be encouraged to bring these facts and observations to the professional's attention. The primary function of the nonprofessional is to find the service for the client, not the client for the service. He is employed to represent the client's interests against all the tendencies in every agency that may delay or deprive the client of services.

The Relationship between Professionals and Nonprofessionals

There are many problems involved in defining and developing the relationship of the nonprofessionals to the professionals, both within the agency and outside of it.

Professionals frequently are not clear about the role and the ability of nonprofessional workers. The agencies should carefully define the nonprofessionals' roles, tasks, and competencies to all professional personnel, including those in outside agencies, through memoranda and formal and informal meetings, both before the nonprofessionals join the staff and as their jobs develop. This will be a crucial point in determining the success of the nonprofessional program. The professionals will need to have the flexibility to appreciate and understand the nonprofessional roles and aptitudes, and to permit the reorganization of job structures. Great effort, therefore, must be put into preparing professionals for accepting the nonprofessional workers into the team structure, for utilizing them appropriately, and for allowing them to develop their own techniques in working with clients. While professionals may express this flexibility during the planning and training periods, the agency must watch to see that the voiced acceptance is being followed through in the actual operation.

There should also be careful preparation and training of the nonprofessional before initial contact with professionals. Their skill and confidence should be sufficiently developed so that they will feel comfortable. Relationships to professionals in other agencies should be held in abeyance until more skill has been acquired. Let the nonprofessional worker develop "practice" with professionals in his own agency first. The use of role-play practice might be quite advantageous in preparing nonprofessionals for interpersonal face-to-face meetings, telephone conversations, and other aspects of the relationship to professionals.

Sometimes, in accenting the value of the nonprofessional, a tendency arises to devalue the professionals and to emphasize one-sidedly their difficulties in reaching many of the poor. Both trainers and nonprofessional workers should be urged to guard against this reverse alienation. It is not proposed that nonprofessionals replace professionals. In fact, the employment of nonprofessional personnel will produce new roles for professionals as consultants, supervisors, teachers, and coordinators. The professional and nonprofessional should complement each other since each has a separate and important contribution to make toward achieving the common goal.

Professionals must understand that the nonprofessional worker is not a servant, but a server. Care must be taken that he is not given only menial tasks shunned by professionals. He will, of course, have to do such tasks, but he must also be assigned broader functions, expanding with his skills. Actually, from the very beginning nonprofessionals can do some meaningful work commensurate with the natural human-relations skills they possess, as in field work with people in the community.

Role Ambiguity: Who Am I?

Frequently, professionals assume that nonprofessionals identify with the poor and possess great warmth and feeling for the neighborhood of their origin. While many nonprofessionals exhibit some of these characteristics, they simultaneously possess other characteristics. Often, they see themselves as different from other members of the poor community whom they may view with pity, annoyance, or anger. Nevertheless, they have considerable knowledge of the neighborhood and its traditions and they communicate easily with many different types of people in the area. They both literally and figuratively talk the language of the poor and have some similarities in style, values, and traditions. In addition, nonprofessionals have a good deal of neighborhood know-how, savvy, and understanding. They are particularly good at functioning and communicating on an informal level. While they know the hidden assumptions of the neighborhood, it should not be assumed that they are always going to be friendly, cooperative, "concerned," or any of the romantic myths about the poor. Moreover, there are many different "types" of nonprofessionals: some are earthy, some are tough, some are angry, some are surprisingly articulate, some are slick, clever wheeler-dealers, and nearly all are greatly concerned about their new roles and their relationship to professionals.

It is most important to note, then, that nonprofessionals are frequently quite competitive with professionals. Some nonprofessionals think they are different from the poor and would be more effective than professionals if they had a chance. They are aware of the new ideology regarding nonprofessionals which calls attention to the special properties (e.g., style) which enable the nonprofessional to communicate with the low-income community in an effective manner. They feel this gives them something of an edge over professionals, and when combined with the training and knowledge they are acquiring in the professional structure, they will be "double smart," incorporating the intelligence based on their history with the new knowledge based on their training. Some nonprofessionals have imaginatively combined these two levels and are remarkably effective in dealing with problems at various levels; other nonprofessionals think they combine these two perspectives.

While nonprofessionals may be selected because of their informality, humor, earthiness, neighborliness—in other words, some of the "positive" characteristics of the resident population—the other side of the coin cannot be ignored. They may also possess those characteristics of low-income populations that interfere with effective helper roles. For example, they may behave with considerable moral indignation, punitiveness, and suspicion. Or they may be so open and friendly on occasion that the significance of confidentiality escapes them. Thus, while training will be building on their positive helping traits and potential skills, to some extent there must be an effort either to train out or control some of these other characteristics which operate against effectively playing the helping role in a social-service framework.

It should always be remembered that most nonprofessionals are probably not a representative "lower-class" population. In all likelihood the nonprofessional selection process sifts out people who can communicate with both the low-income group and the middle-class population. The nonprofessionals probably have considerably more ambition, drive, and envy than the poor, and less identification with them. It is, of course, possible to possess simultaneously some of these traits which appear to be mutually exclusive.

One of the greatest problems experienced by the nonprofessional is role ambiguity or lack of role identity: He does not know who he is or who he is becoming. He is no longer a simple member of the community if he ever was one, nor is he a professional. Actually, he is a highly marginal person. He may represent the poor, but he is not the poor. He uses his knowledge, his history, his past to bring a new voice of the poor into the system; but he, too, is now in the system. And he must be able to communicate and assist the professionals in his agency and in other agencies with whom he has relationships.

The nonprofessional is being asked in a sense to play a role differing from his accustomed role in the community. His style has in all likelihood been to talk to groups of people in the community, to help them express their anger, to mobilize them, and perhaps in some cases to bring them toward "second-force" groups—tenants' councils, civil-rights groups, and the like. But now he is employed "inside" the system by a government-supported operation, and he has to develop a different posture to the community and the agency with which he will be working. The new nonprofessional is being asked to play a two-way communication role. He is not being asked to organize the poor in order to smash the institutional structure. He will have to understand this thoroughly or else he will get into a great deal of trouble in his relationship with professionals and agencies as well as the people of the community. He may be rejected by the community as a "fink" or criticized by the agency structure as a misinformed hothead. He must learn to walk a narrow line.

There are unavoidable strains in this new role and they must be accepted openly and dealt with. In the pre-job training phase this new role should be defined from the beginning. But it will have little meaning to the nonprofessional except as a broad orientation base, until he is faced by the role conflicts in practice—until members of the community call him "fink" because he does not completely represent them and is not completely of them any more, or until he is criticized as a "hothead" by the agencies with whom he is dealing. For example: One of the aides at the Lincoln Project in speaking to a Welfare Department investigator about a client was asked who she was. The aide was annoyed and responded: "It does not matter who I am; my client is in great need—let's talk about that." She was acting as she had previously acted, as a neighbor or friend, angrily demanding the assistance of the agency; but this was an incorrect posture in her new role in relation to the Welfare Department and she was not accurately representing the stance of the Neighborhood Service Center Program. It is only through discussing this type of case that her own identity in relation to the nonprofessional role can begin to be clarified. But this is a long process, constantly fraught with strain and difficulty.

Role ambiguity is produced by many aspects of the situation. One is how the stance of the agency affects the relationship of the nonprofessional to the community and to the agency world. Another source of role confusion relates to the marginality of the nonprofessional's position; i.e., "nonprofessional" describes what he is not, but does not clearly indicate what he is. He is not simply a citizen or a volunteer participating in the organization, although the desire to have him represent the feelings of the neighborhood produces some similarity with the citizen advisory board role of the local resident. He is not the traditional kind of employee because his participation and neighborhood know-how and advice are sought; yet he is also an employee. He is not a professional, even though he does represent the agency and many people in the community may see the aide as a new kind of social worker. He is not a political-action organizer, even though he does develop groups in the community concerned with various types of change. He is an amalgam of all these various roles, and his trainers and supervisors must understand and try to clarify this new role.

But to repeat, the role itself has strains and contradictions, and the nonprofessional must be assisted to live within the framework of these dilemmas. He is the new marginal man. He must be selected with this in mind, trained and supervised in this fashion, and assisted in forging this new role.

Issues in Training the Nonprofessional

Training is basic to the effective use and development of nonprofessionals. If the nonprofessional movement is to grow, if the opportunity structure is to be opened up so that jobs can become careers and aides can rise ultimately to become professionals, major institutional changes will be needed: Civil-service requirements will have to be altered; the emphasis on educational credentials will have to be reduced; educational institutions will have to accredit on-the-job training; and many new trainers will have to be developed from among both professionals and subprofessionals.

The significance of training has not been fully grasped. National training institutes are only now emerging. There exists no national plan for the training of trainers, or for the retraining of professionals to work effectively with nonprofessionals.[7] The Job Corps has not been utilized for the development of training for nonprofessionals or their trainers. If the nonprofessional approach is to create more than jobs, if it is to develop genuine careers for the poor, moving them up the ladder step by step, authentic training is the key. Trainers must be trained in how to evaluate nonprofessionals; how to encourage participation; how to listen; how to supervise in new ways; how to provide functional on-the-job learning.

Jobs First—Training Built In

The traditional principle that long periods of training are necessary before an individual can be employed must be reversed; the motto should be "Jobs First—Training Built In." Nonprofessional human-service positions can begin with on-the-job training. Nonprofessionals learn essentially from doing plus systematic in-service training which can be phased in functionally as needed on the job. An interesting illustration of how this might be accomplished is provided by the Howard University Community Apprentice Program developed for "hard-core," functionally illiterate delinquents. One phase of this program was concerned with developing nonprofessional research aides. Initially the program was designed so that the research aides had as their first task to interview each other with a tape recorder. They learned only the simplest principles of interviewing in order to perform this task. Before long they recognized that they needed to know something about how to record the information and categorize it and later they needed some statistics in order to analyze it appropriately. As each of these needs became apparent, the appropriate training was introduced to develop the requisite skills.

The point is that training must be introduced functionally, on the job itself. The demand for long periods of training before the individual can even apply for a position is not adapted to the needs of the poor, the dropout, the delinquent functioning in a future world that has been unsure and in a school environment that has been unencouraging. The best way to educate many school dropouts is not to induce them back to school immediately, but to provide them with nonprofessional human-service jobs. This will provide the stimulus for obtaining the necessary education on the job and returning to the educational structures where appropriate and needed.

Basic education and skills that are badly needed by nonprofessionals (and all of the poor) should not be seen as merely remedial. Every effort should be made to cast them not as rehabilitation but habilitation. The assumption should be that people can be basically habilitated and developed at any time. In light of the new and extremely powerful educational technologies for developing literacy at all ages,[8] the historic pessimism which largely surrenders hope on other than preschool youngsters and sees all other assistance as merely remedial is to be highly questioned. Past approaches have been limited because recipients have not been involved, available technologies were inadequate, and the people's self-help energies were not utilized in combination with the best professional technology. Consequently a negative hopeless attitude prevailed. It is time to reverse all this.

The new nonprofessionals have different training needs because they have different goals. Some are career oriented, concerned with becoming a subprofessional and a professional. The second group is concerned largely with security within the nonprofessional job. A third is the "hard-core" poor, e.g., people who have been on welfare for many years, or have not had experience working, or have had difficulty with traditional work norms. Different training and supervisory structures are required for the three different groups. Phased, protected training structures, such as a Neighborhood Service Center base, are particularly relevant for the last-named group—the group that requires rehabilitative or habilitative work initially. Association with professionals may be more relevant for the more ambitious group.

Second-Chance U

An important danger in the expansion of the nonprofessional role is that the poor may become the source of cheap labor in the educational and social services with little chance of moving into the higher-paid, more responsible positions. Without openings at the top, we may be getting a black (or Spanish-language) nonprofessional class and a largely white professional class. This would be a disheartening outcome of the effort to provide more jobs for the poor and to improve the delivery of services.

Many of the nonprofessionals have the capability of considerable upgrading in their work responsibilities. Unless at least some of the nonprofessionals are in fact upgraded, there will be a piling up of the nonprofessionals in lower-level jobs. Incentives to development will be reduced if there is no place to go. The upgrading of nonprofessionals, therefore, becomes an important part of any program to augment their numbers. One escalator of occupational movement into real careers is by developing levels of nonprofessional jobs so that the more skilled nonprofessionals are supervising the less skilled. The other advance is through providing routes into the professional level in the educational and social services. This is difficult but not insuperable.

Programs will be increasingly needed to provide experiences which develop nonprofessionals and lead some of them into professional slots in the educational and social services. Special-service courses will not provide the educational credentials that are increasingly demanded today.

In effect, then, the development of a career line for the nonprofessional can become a new source of recruitment for the professions. Not only will this expand the number of professionals but, perhaps more importantly, it will influence the character of these professions. As individuals with quite different backgrounds than usual enter these professions, the excessive professionalism which frequently prevails will be challenged.

The upgraded former nonprofessionals will also be particularly useful in supervising and directing nonprofessionals. For with the expansion of nonprofessionals supervisory problems will grow.

Second-chance universities, like the one proposed for New York University, are needed to provide ways of getting education for the nonprofessionals so that they can become fully credentialed professionals. The objective is to provide a relevant and feasible college (and postgraduate) experience for nonprofessionals.

In the proposed model, most students at Second-Chance U would be selected by their educational or social-service agencies to go on to obtain a college degree and be supported by them while getting their degree. Other students will be adults from low-income backgrounds with an interest in going into work with the low-income. Many of the students will not have graduated from high school; the effort should be to provide them with both a high-school and college diploma through the Second-Chance U experience, rather than insisting on first qualifying through passing the equivalency examination or going back to secondary school.

The Second-Chance U approach is based on the notion that formal education is increasingly a discontinuous experience and that much education takes place outside of the formal educational agencies. In Chapter 6 we concluded that fewer and fewer individuals will be going through a continuous sixteen- or twenty-year experience for an A.B. or higher degree. This will be especially true of those from a low-income background as they move in greater numbers toward higher education. We should, therefore, look upon the nonprofessional role as one of the routes back into the educational (and occupational) main stream.

It is not enough to attract nonprofessionals to a degree program; the goal is to see that they complete the program and are effectively employed. Programs dealing with students with previous educational difficulties usually have high dropout rates. Increasing the completion rate requires accessibility, manageability, relevance and reward, remediation.

By accessibility we refer not only to physical location and transportation, but also to scheduling of courses so that they fit in with schedules and family demands. The program will set up variable class schedules so that the students can meet their varied demands. The widespread use of tutorials and independent work will make it easier to provide flexibility in scheduling.

By manageability we refer to the possibility of students' carrying a school load and being able to complete the program in a relatively short time. Several procedures could aid in reducing time: (a) Students could receive credit for their previous experience; (b) they could receive credit for their current supervised field work; (c) credit could be obtained on the basis of self-study and examination; (d) the usual academic calendar need not be followed and a twelve-months program could be adopted. The school load could vary from period to period so as to fit in with changing work responsibilities.

Relevance requires that colleges and universities not only be unorthodox in their admission procedures but be unorthodox and imaginative in curriculum and teaching. The colleges have to change if the nonprofessionals are to get the most out of the experience. Traditional curricula and courses are not likely to get the best out of nonprofessional and other students from low-income backgrounds.

The program should be oriented toward building a liberal-arts program around the interests and needs of this special group of students. Their concerns touch on vital issues of economics, psychology, sociology, anthropology, biology, history, philosophy, political science, and literature. This lever of interest and perspective should not be ignored. The aim should be to construct courses which build around their immediate interests and move out to a wider concern with broader issues. A division between "practical" and "liberal-arts" courses should be avoided; a new curriculum should be constructed which is relevant to what they are doing and want to do and which uses their experiences and concerns to move into broader issues. For example, the daily newspapers, commercial television, controversial articles, and fiction can be studied as social documents and used as introductions to broader issues.

While students should be expected to meet most of what is expected of a college graduate, they should not be forced into a typical program in order to come out at this point. They should be judged in terms of performance rather than on whether or not they have taken an orthodox package of courses.

Relevance, then, is a special theme—building on the nonprofessional experiences, going beyond immediate experiences, and then relating back to their experiences and possibilities. What they do or can do in their present and future positions can be viewed in a liberal-arts perspective, and the liberal-arts perspective can also be at least partially viewed in terms of relevance for the situation of the poor in contemporary America. The liberal arts have to be viewed in contemporary terms. This reinterpretation of "liberal arts" has very wide implication for college education generally, but it is especially pertinent to the educational prospects of the nonprofessional.

An important component of the program would be vital field placements. The nonprofessional job experience should be used as a learning tool and credit should be given for it.

For students with academic difficulties in reading, writing, expression, studying, special individual programs should be constructed as needed to help them. The aim is not to develop routes for sorting students out of the program but to build flexible arrangements for aiding students to complete the program and to go beyond.

Some of the graduates of the program will go on to graduate work. Programs should establish links to graduate-school programs (and perhaps build some special graduate curricula) to facilitate this move.

Many graduates will continue working with their present agencies. During the course of the program there should be constant consultation with the employing agency on the job experience and on planning the upgrading of the student on his job. This would involve helping the employing agency develop ways of utilizing the emerging abilities of the student. We want to avoid deepening the abilities of students without providing opportunities for their effective use.

Some graduates would have to leave their present agencies in order to have expanded opportunity. This step should be planned during their program and placements developed.

We need to multiply points and times of entry into the better-paying, credentialed jobs of American society. The upgrading of nonprofessionals can be one of the most important of the new routes to a more flexible and open society.

A Strategy of Change

The role of the nonprofessional can be "pasted on to existing practices without forcing any changes in them"; the tactic of using nonprofessional workers may not "readily answer the ideological issues of the changing ends and goals of social services today and tomorrow."[9]

If an agency wishes to utilize nonprofessionals in a negative fashion (i.e., not to change its goals but to reinforce them, not to serve the poor but to provide a façade), this can be done. The approach to failure is simple: recruiting and selecting the "wrong" kind of nonprofessionals; training them in the "wrong" way; using the nonprofessionals' skills to maintain the agency's status quo. These strategies could effectively destroy the purpose of a nonprofessional program; they might indirectly defeat the agency's program for working with the poor.

But given the current background of the manpower shortage, the antipoverty climate, and the criticism of social agencies' treatment of the poor, the utilization of nonprofessional personnel is likely to be a lever of change.

It is not the use of nonprofessional workers in the abstract which will foster change of agency outlook and program, but their employment in the context of other pressure[5] in the same direction; for example, government funding and support through the Economic Opportunity Act and the Community Mental Health Centers Act. The nonprofessional, working in this setting, can help pull together a variety of factors moving toward new agency orientation.

One factor is new technology. This can only be successful, however, in changing agency function in combination with other factors. But the view is that nonprofessionals carry within them the potential for influencing the reorganization of agency technology. It is the nonprofessional who can demonstrate new kinds of therapeutic intervention unavailable to the professional. He can be a companion, an active intervener, a provider of directive counseling, etc. In combination with professional objectivity and competence, and with over-all professional direction, this new unity of technology has enormous promise.

There is another very important aspect to the potential power of this new organization of personnel. The nonprofessional, as he makes a contribution to service, becomes more and more needed by the agency. His usefulness perpetuates his use, increasing the significance and power of his role. At the present time, the need for him in terms of serving the poor is stimulating many different agencies to consider the use of nonprofessional personnel. Some of their reasons are good and some are bad. Some want to give aides to the professionals, some want to serve the poor for ideological reasons, some want to provide employment for the poor, some want to try new things, some want publicity, and some want government funds. But they all add up to the possibility of widespread use of this type of personnel. Regardless of what reason was behind employing the uncredentialed worker in the first place, if he is given an opportunity to do a meaningful job, he will in time become indispensable to the agency and influence its functioning. Other agencies, not under pressure at this time to change their styles, will want to adopt the nonprofessional model once it is successfully demonstrated.

The introduction of nonprofessional workers into agency structures can be an effective strategy of change in the field of human services. It can meet many of the present needs: (a) It can markedly reduce the manpower shortage in the social-service fields; (b) it can help make the professional's role definitions more flexible, creating an alliance between professionals and nonprofessionals more fully to play their technical roles; (c) it can provide more, better, and "closer" service for the poor; (d) it can provide meaningful employment to the poor; (e) it can potentially provide millions of new jobs for the unemployed and underemployed in educational and social-service entities, a major growth industry in the United States.

The Politics of Nonprofessionalism

Two quite different charges have been made against the nonprofessional from a political perspective: (a) Hiring neighborhood people to play the nonprofessional role can be a way of "cooling out" the potential leaders of the low-income neighborhoods; (b) nonprofessionals do not accept the limits of the roles they can play as salaried employees of poverty agencies and attempt to move militantly on issues which endanger the continuation of their agencies.

We recognize the first as a danger, but in a period of rising concern about poverty and civil rights we think it less likely that the activists who become nonprofessionals will lose their militancy. Admittedly, our experience is limited, but in our talks with nonprofessionals in many parts of the United States we have been struck by the high level of militancy maintained by those nonprofessionals who were active before they joined the professional ranks.

Indeed, it may be that many nonprofessionals have been unwilling to accept the limitations of the role that is required of them by their employment in an established agency receiving public funds. While we believe that employees should not automatically assume the employers' definition of their roles, we do not believe that all aspects of one's citizenship aims can be played out in a setting of being an employee. The nonprofessional can push for a more vigorous policy by his agency, but he cannot go, as an employee, much beyond what the agency is willing to do. Thus, he may not be able to lead an attack on police brutality if his agency refuses to be involved in such issues.

But this limitation on job activities should not extend to off-the-job action. We urge a clear bill of rights for nonprofessionals which specifies that their employer does not infringe upon their activities when they are operating as citizens, not as employees. Some cities have begun to do this. This discrimination can often be a tenuous line as a nonprofessional is a citizen and employee in the same neighborhood, but we should not make employment a means of limiting the political rights of individuals, as has particularly happened in Southern poverty programs.

On the other hand, we do not believe that employment situations and personal political positions can be fully combined. Some mixing of inside-the-system pressures and outside positions can be useful in loosening up the system, but efforts at complete integration of the two approaches tend to result in losing out on what the inside approach can provide if programs are good—an immediate improvement in the circumstances of the poor.

Bringing nonprofessionals together into national groupings would be important in strengthening their roles. A national organization of nonprofessionals could take stands that individuals in programs cannot. It could play a leading role in pushing for increasing the number, the scope, and the upgrading of nonprofessionals.

The nonprofessional strategy for increasing jobs for the poor and for improving the delivery of needed services to the poor is only slowly capturing the imagination of civil-rights and other second-force groups. Nor has the nonprofessional strategy of redefining job tasks and skill requirements been applied adequately to private enterprise. We suggest that the nonprofessional strategy can be an important platform for outside groups in demanding significant change in the employment and well-being of low-income neighborhoods. Inside groups have begun to employ nonprofessionals, but in small numbers. A large-scale increase in nonprofessional employment—a million jobs —will require national pressure from outside to provide the funds and local pressure for upgrading. Many social-service agencies want to move; they need aid from outside. Wide ranging support is needed to increase funds for nonprofessional jobs, to spur job restructuring and job mobility. The nonprofessional idea can become an important movement for economic and social change in the United States. It is not as yet; it needs pressure to capitalize on the openings which now exist.

NOTES

NOTE: This chapter builds on an article written with Robert Reiff.

1. Margaret J. Rioch *et al.*, "NIMH Study in Training Mental Health Counselors," *American Journal of Orthopsychiatry*, XXXIII (1963), 678–689.

2. J. D. Holzberg, "The Companion Program: Implementing the Manpower Recommendations of the Joint Commission on Mental Illness and Health," *American Psychologist*, XVIII (1963), 224–226. Also J. D. Holzberg and R. H. Knapp, "The Social Interaction of College Students and Chronically Ill Mental Patients." Paper read at American Orthopsychiatric Association, Chicago, April 1964.

3. Southern Regional Educational Board, *European Mental Health Programs as Viewed by Mental Specialists and Legislators*, Atlanta, 1963.

4. Fort Logan Mental Health Center, *The Psychiatric Technician Training Program*, Denver, 1963.

5. L. J. Duhl, ed., *The Urban Condition* (New York: Basic Books, 1963); A. Pearl, "Guidance and Education for the Disadvantaged Child—The Need for Structural Change." Paper read at American Personnel and Guidance Association, San Francisco, March 1964; A. Pearl, "Youth in Lower Class Settings." Paper read at Fifth Symposium on Social Psychology, Norman, Oklahoma, March 1964; Ford Foundation, "The Great Cities School Improvement Studies" (New York, 1960), mimeographed.

6. S. M. Miller and M. Rein, "Change, Ferment and Ideology in the Social Services." *Proceedings*, Council of Social Work Education, 1964, pp. 26–27.

7. Supervisory staff, in addition to being recruited from among educators, social workers, and psychologists, might be sought from among Peace Corps returnees, nurses (especially psychiatric nurses), labor organizers and labor

educators, anthropologists, occupational therapists, and recent college graduates majoring in the social sciences. Training assistants must be recruited from among the nonprofessional aides.

8. The effective use of these techniques requires that they be built into the job structure—so that for designated periods during the work day (not afterhours) reading skills are developed and functionally related to job needs.

9. S. M. Miller and M. Rein, *op. cit.*

15

✿ ✿ ✿

SECOND FORCE:
PRESSURING FOR CHANGE

Social action has had a high place on the national agenda. The notion of organizing the poor in their own behalf has had support both within the social-welfare system, in federally supported community action antipoverty programs, and outside the system, in the militant conflict-centered approach of Saul Alinsky and the neighborhood-based models of the Students for Democratic Society and other "New Left" oriented groups.

While the theme of this section of the book is that there are many different routes to the improvement of the conditions of the poor, we do not underestimate the importance of social action. We disagree with its supporters who insist that no improvement is "real" unless it comes through conflict-centered social action. But that does not throw us in the camp of those who feel that professionals and community elites will usually make needed changes without pressure from "below" or outside the traditional channels. While interest in social action may wane in some periods, the long-run movement is toward greater social action. The appropriate role of pressure from the poor is therefore a continuing issue.

Models of Social Action

We feel that Saul Alinsky has made a contribution to American life in several ways. He has helped to bring religious groups into a concern with the problems of ghetto dwellers. In many situations he has forced out important issues in communities, upset tired equilibria, breathed vitality into rhetoric about local democracy, and made change possible. He has helped destroy the myth that the poor are an inert, unorganizable mass.

But we feel that his model is but one way of approaching community change, and we are not sure of the improvements in material life that have come out of his activities.[1] In our approach, we count returns more in terms of material improvements and the opportunity of becoming non-poor than do those who are primarily concerned with reducing the feelings of powerlessness of the poor.[2] Nonetheless, we see much in the idea of social action appropriately used. But not all situations demand it; nor are all official acts enemy actions.

The crucial questions are when is social action necessary and what forms should it take? We cannot pretend to have satisfactorily answered these questions even for ourselves since as authors we have disagreements, but we think that we can analyze some issues so that second-force action from outside the system can be more effectively discussed.

In this chapter we compare two major social-action approaches being developed "outside of the system"—Alinsky and the New Left groups. We indicate some possible relationships between developments taking place outside and those occurring within the governmental system. Our underlying hypothesis is that both the intra-government and extra-government developments may profit from conscious consideration of each other.

Both Alinsky and the New Left have much in common. They both function outside of the governmental and professional systems. They both appeal to the alienated poor, stressing citizens' rights. Both have a "now" emphasis, begin from below, and are neighborhood based. They emphasize American grass-roots traditions, feel that the poor require an outside organizational force to organize them, stress militant appeals and direct action. Both have been stimulated by the civil-rights movement and the concern with "maximum feasible participation" that was manifested by the Community Action Program's staff in the first days of the Office of Economic Opportunity. Both approaches have received considerable press attention and have captured at one time or another the imagination of large numbers of people across the land. Neither has a well-developed, long-range strategy nor much analysis of developments taking place in the society. Neither has presented a significant national program affecting employment, education, housing, welfare, drug addiction.[3]

Both emphasize the value of conflict as the exclusive lever of movement in the society. Both strongly deprecate developments taking place within the system including most phases of the antipoverty movement. Both reject movements from "above" and have strong anti-official authority and anti-leadership biases, frequently identifying all official leadership with irrational leadership and authoritarianism.

Both serve a valuable role as critics, highlighting the dangers associated with the new developments taking place within the system. Alinsky as the "gadfly" of the antipoverty war has charged that "the new Federal charter will not foster what its main-stream critics most fear: an authentic social revolution."[4]

Both the New Left and Alinsky are essentially anti-ideological, although each has developed some vague new ideology. Both want the poor to have a voice in the things that affect them. Neither has developed much thinking or strategy for the emergence of a movement although Students for a Democratic Society (SDS) vaguely planned at one point to consolidate local neighborhood groups at some later time. Alinsky, because of his national reputation and press, developed a wave of imitation for a time, so that in some cities which believed themselves to be riot prone (Rochester, Kansas City) Alinsky-influenced programs emerged.

Neither approach seems to have much perspective regarding the forces that brought them to national attention. (The tools of the sociology of knowledge have not been utilized by them.) Hence, Alinsky rarely discusses the significance of the antipoverty movement in powering the new interest he obtained for a while. In a larger context, neither recognizes the significant context of a highly affluent society that apparently tolerates considerable more "radicalism" and "radicals" than in the fifties. Why radicals should receive such a good press is a question that does not seem to have arisen for the new radicals.

More important is the failure to consider the potential relevance for radical social action of major trends in the larger society: occupational change and the new role of education; urbanism and the decline of the local political club; the new tolerance in the business community of Keynesian approaches and the rapid growth of the gross national product; the failure of traditional psychotherapeutic approaches for the alienated low-income populations and the concomitant interest in new forms of sociotherapy for the poor; the significant cleavages within "the establishment" and the existence of many establishments; the increased role of the Federal government in dealing with manifold urban problems and the potential alliances of the Federal government and the cities. Finally, new possibilities opened up on the domestic scene; programs in education, recreation, anti-poverty, mental health, health, and housing emerged. With limited awareness, both Alinsky and the New Left moved into the openings provided by the early civil-rights successes and by the widespread Federal anti-poverty legislation.

Both approaches seem to have lingering leftovers from the psychology and radicalism of the thirties (most surprising for the young Left!). Thus they frequently imply that all gains for the have-nots must be achieved at the expense of the haves and that these gains must be achieved by making the haves uncomfortable. There is little understanding of how developments within the system can be utilized by movements functioning outside of the system. That the antipoverty community-action programs may be organizing segments of the poor that are not attracted to Alinsky or the New Left is not looked upon favorably, even though these segments of less militant, less vocal poor may provide a later source of support for Alinsky and the student movement.

Nor is there realization that the nonprofessional human-service jobs that we discussed in the previous chapter can be utilized as a wedge for demanding millions of jobs and careers for the poor. The new Federal antipoverty focus on providing more adequate services to the poor and expediting service delivery through employing large numbers of new nonprofessional manpower provides the possibility of important anti-bureaucratic breakthroughs in service delivery.

Significant potential coalition with outside groups such as Alinsky and the New Left is possible here, particularly with the outsiders prodding the inside groups to achieve their avowed objectives more effectively. For there is considerable concern both within the system and outside it for the humanizing of bureaucracy, limiting bureaucratic discretion, guaranteeing the voice of the recipients of service, and guarding their dignity and rights. Moreover, improved service for the poor does not seem to come at the expense of taking anything away from the rich. This will perhaps be most striking in the health field.

Other hangovers from the thirties are reflected in Alinsky's radical posturing ("I am a professional radical"), his tough-guy imitation of John L. Lewis ("This is war."), and the vague socialism of the New Left in which the socialist principles are not particularly attuned to new developments in American society. Their theoretic armamentarium relies on fairly vague traditional socialism in the economic and political areas.

Both programs are fundamentally concerned with what might be called citizens' rights vis-à-vis non-humane bureaucracy. A citizen's rights movement could incorporate many of the demands of both the Alinsky group and the New Left and probably could bring in developments taking place among a variety of groups throughout the country, such as the welfare-rights movement, the Citizen's Crusade against Poverty, the civil-rights groups, the grass-roots independent antipoverty groups. All these forces are concerned with the broadened view of the new income: citizen's rights in relation to the bureaucratic structures of welfare, education, and protection (police).

The usefulness of a second-force approach does not mean that poverty-oriented, inside-the-system groups should adopt this posture. Indeed, we feel that many official poverty agencies brought unproductive trouble upon themselves by acting as though they could ignore the constraints of being a governmentally-supported agency and could compete with nongovernmental poverty groups organized on the conflict model. *The conflict model may not only be unuseful in certain situations; it may be only minimally usable by some groups.*

Differences between Alinsky and the New Left

Alinsky and the New Left differ in tactical emphases, groups appealed to, traditions, and philosophic roots. But the major differences relate to the highly moral, principled, noncompromising orientation of the New Left. This is in marked contrast to the far more pragmatic, tactics-oriented focus of Alinsky. To some extent, when sections of the New Left move toward coalition politics, this difference is reduced.

But the basic ethos of SDS is essentially focused on idealistic principles and positions which are supported even when this is not tactically or organizationally rewarding. Thus the New Left took a strong position on peace in Vietnam even when this position had little national appeal. In contrast, Alinsky has eschewed international policy questions and sticks to issues and grievances that can be utilized in mounting a successful local campaign. He is more concerned with local success and stable organization; only rarely will he espouse a position which is widely unpopular. The New Left, supported by youthful zeal and positive idealism, has no such limitations in the causes it espouses. Under certain circumstances, principledness can become pragmatically successful (the tactics of principledness), and many of the objectives of the New Left have been won. The unrelenting, uncompromising, dedicated, vivid demands of the New Left even in the peace area have received surprising national attention. The Berkeley rebellion has provided a model for college youth to imitate throughout the nation.

Another difference relates to Alinsky's stress on power and organization in contrast to the New Left which repudiates power and instead emphasizes acting together reciprocally.

The Relationship of the Inside and the Outside

There are many potentially fruitful lines of relationship between those forces working within the governmental structures and the outside social activists. Each group has its own focus and its own blinders, but certain over-all goals which may be held in common can provide a source of joint effort or at least interchange of ideas and perspective. Thus, professionals concerned with involving the poor in the antipoverty programs may have something to learn from the participatory democracy concepts of the New Left, even though these concepts cannot be fully applied within the system. Moreover, the uncompromising principledness of the student movement provides a valuable object lesson for those who live more pragmatically within the system.

Professionals also have much to learn from the brilliant tactics of Alinsky. His approach to voter registration campaigns ("Vote for power," rather than a citizen "duty" appeal) is likely to be much more effective with large sections of the poor and the minority groups than traditional approaches.

On the other hand, many poor are unattracted by the Alinsky conflict model. The selective pull within the low-income communities of the conflict approach tends to be ignored by the Alinsky adherents. Only some of the poor find the conflict model compelling.

To the extent that the outsiders are effective in their demands for the poor, they move the center of gravity farther to the "left" and thus may provide the insiders with more leverage in mediating the demands of the poor with the traditional agencies and power structures. This is evident in the rent strike which later became legal in New York State, whereas at one time it was a special militant tactic available only to groups outside the system. The outsider's success with the rent strike has much to do with the current legitimation of this tactic. The importance of the civil-rights groups in the poverty programs in San Francisco and Seattle could have influenced antipoverty forces in these cities and provided greater flexibility for groups committed to the poor and working within the system. Alinsky's criticisms have been highly influential in raising questions regarding the representatives of the poor in the antipoverty programs in large urban centers.

The groups outside the system also can deal with sensitive areas in their criticism of the bureaucracies. Thus, welfare-rights associations and groups concerned with police protection and police brutality can be developed more fully outside the system. Since insiders need to mediate between agencies such as the police and the welfare department and the poor, they cannot adopt as militant a stance toward these agencies. Moreover, the outside groups can pay more attention to getting legal assistance to large numbers of people.

Groups outside the system can provide the clout necessary for winning the national programs that might be developed in housing, jobs (new careers for the poor), education, and urban development.

It is in this national arena that Alinsky has been especially ineffective. Alinsky's work in the forties and fifties occurred in a national atmosphere of little new social legislation and fiscal tightness in social welfare. This experience has not prepared him for the legislative onslaught of the mid-sixties. Expansion of funds and proliferation of programs in education, welfare, health, and the like have occurred. Returns for the poor from these new activities are inadequate. But these programs are new resources in the scene. It is not enough to speak of the poverty programs as "political pornography," as has Alinsky, without indicating more effective ways of using existing programs and offering new or alternative programs. New resources are available; their useful employment is the issue. Outside pressure is needed for their expansion and improvement.

The Alinsky and New Left groups have failed to play this role. The local approach of both SDS, and especially Alinsky, has discouraged them from dealing with national issues. But only some of the problems of the poor can be solved through neighborhood, or even city, changes. Increasingly, national action is needed. Neighborhood agitation for more inspections for housing violations will not increase the housing supply. Only Federal action will. Similarly, unemployment and underemployment will be solved mainly through governmental activities. Organizing on immediate neighborhood issues is obviously needed, but the great strategic skill that frequently seems to be missing in social action is tying up local issues to broader questions of national policy—where the needed funds are.

Our orientation is that second-force groups should play a much more forceful, sophisticated role in affecting the distribution, use, and increase of new resources. In the absence of informed, effective pressure from action groups, these resources tend to be inadequate, shore up existing activities with little change, frequently are oriented to the wrong problems, and are poorly utilized in low-quality programs. Since the established agencies can react in a variety of ways to pressure, some specificity in demands is needed. For example, many school systems have responded to pressure to improve education for the disadvantaged by adding on a "preschool program" without any other changes—an action doomed to failure. (See Chapter 7).

It is our belief that the poverty program has not been stronger in impact because action groups have focused on only one element, the "maximum feasible participation" theme, and neglected the programmatic side of what kinds of decisions should be made. *Power without program can lead to little material improvement in people's lives, just as program without power can lead to paternalism and "cooling out."* We recognize that "material improvements" are not enough for those for whom participation, control, and power have become important. But opportunity to become non-poor is desired by the poor, and programs built around this theme are perhaps the best way to organize many sections of the poor and develop meaningful power.

The militant social actionists can grow in political strength by beginning to organize the poor that had previously been unavailable to them; that is, those of the poor who have been unattracted by militant direct-action appeals. Community-action programs within the system are organizing this more inactive poor and moving some of them along to more advanced forms of organization, providing a new recruitment pool for the groups functioning outside the system.

People working within the system are probably more alert to developments that could provide new demands by the activists on the outside. Thus, the demand by nonmilitants for millions of nonprofessional new careers for the poor could provide an important arena of cooperation for the two forces, the insiders and the outsiders. Similarly, in education, where Federal money is providing the ground for major changes in the educational system, groups outside are demanding a voice in how the schools are to be run.

Only through communication between at least some segments of the forces operating outside and inside can vital new programs and demands be developed and social-action strategy be combined with other strategies of change, strategies that must include: neighborhood law firms, antipoverty community-action programs, basic legislation such as the Community Mental Health Act, and new ideology that deals with the neglected issues of inequality and human decency.

The different strategies of change converge as well as conflict. Social actionists functioning outside of the system and many social planners functioning within the system have much to gain from mutual contact and exploration. From this relationship a much more rounded and effective strategy of change may emerge, together with the necessary theoretic base.

A particularly crucial activity for social scientists is in aiding civil rights and other groups to carry out a useful role in escalating antipoverty efforts. At one level the need is for the second-force groups to play a more forceful and informed role at national levels. For example, during the first twenty years following the Employment Act of 1946, no civil-rights group testified during the important annual congressional hearings on the President's Economic Report which sets the objectives and tone of Federal economic policies. The civil-rights groups did not pursue the connection between their efforts to improve the conditions of Negroes and the poor and general economic policy.

At another level, the outlook and programs of national organizations should lead to and benefit from actions of their local chapters. Programs in different cities should be tied together so that they have cumulative impact, feeding and being fed by the policies and activities of the national organizations. It is in helping action groups to develop a more effective stance in effecting the utilization of the new resources (and in increasing resources) in the poverty field that social planners and social scientists can learn from and contribute to the activities of the second-force groups.

The antipoverty movement has the possibility of significant achievements. These gains have begun to occur in certain limited though important areas, but a massive impact on improving the conditions of the poor has not been accomplished. The second-force groups can play an important role in insisting on better programs and much more funds.

Some of the dangers of a weak war on poverty that second-force groups can help to overcome are: funds inadequate to do the job, welfare succumbing to welfare expenditures; the nonprofessional and professional competing and not fully articulate with each other; services provided without representation and representation provided without power and influence; participation not spread to all of the service areas— welfare, housing, etc.; emphasis on changing people rather than institutions, the positives in the life of the poor ignored; jobs provided without upgrading and without training ("lock in" will result); providing services as a substitute for assuring a decent income to the poor and the opportunity to become non-poor; the demand for services outstripping the supply, resulting in frustration and disillusion—agencies might become alienated because the increasing demands of the poor for service outstrip the resources provided by government; the evolving neighborhood service centers converted into integrating links for the traditional agencies but not utilized to develop the voice, participation, and base of the poor; developments taking place within the system not articulate with the demands of groups functioning outside the governmental system; no one laying claim to the antipoverty movement, no one organizing the nonprofessionals, and the antipoverty movement remaining at a token level rather than providing millions of jobs, careers, widespread representation and participation, and the fulfillment of entitlements and rights; antipoverty programs functioning as socio-therapy rather than institutional change.

This is an agenda for action in the war on poverty. The second-force groups have failed to apply themselves to these crucial issues.

The Failure of the Second Force

For the most part, groups functioning outside the system such as the civil-rights groups, the Alinsky-organized neighborhoods, the students' groups, the trade-unions, the welfare-rights groups, the rent strikers, and the intellectuals have failed to claim the antipoverty openings. They have remained skeptical, cautious, aloof, fearing cooptation, distrustful of the role of the government. Much of this hesitation has been warranted, but not all of it. Even the administrators and agents of the antipoverty legislation within the system have failed to capitalize fully on the possibilities or to develop a useful ideology.

Most of the groups functioning outside the system have demanded greater participation and voice, have registered protests, but have not developed specific antipoverty programs. There is much protest without program. The civil-rights groups have not developed major educational plans or housing programs or large-scale demands for nonprofessional jobs and careers. Nor have they fully developed demands for representation of the poor in a wide variety of areas: housing, welfare, social service, and education. They have restricted themselves largely to the role of general critics rather than putting forth large, significant programs. Nor has there been a developing coalition among the various groups functioning outside of the system, joint action which might be led by the civil-rights movement, transforming itself into a citizens' rights movement, uniting the churches, the unions, the Alinsky groups, and the developing neighborhood-service center constituencies of the poor being organized directly through the local poverty agencies. There has been little attention to organizing the large numbers of nonprofessionals who are now employed and who will be employed; many very much want to be organized both in unions and potentially in a movement that goes beyond unions.

The role of the outside groups is extremely important in expanding the antipoverty movement and avoiding the many dangers in government programs. Citizens' rights groups can demand jobs, training, and careers for the nonprofessionals, and the fulfillment of the rights and entitlements of the poor. They can demand that wage scales be appropriate. They can insure that neighborhood-service centers become the base for participation by the poor; that clients become members; that neighborhood meetings are held and attended; that the poor get adequate incomes, that training results in jobs; that job opportunities are constructed for the poor by government and private employers; that the voice of the poor is heard and heeded.

Outside groups can make sure that the antipoverty movement does not become just another form of tokenism, and that the goals of careers, rights, and participation are achieved.

Emerging in the United States, fitfully but discernibly, is the equivalent of a Wagner Act for the poor. The Wagner Act (or the National Labor Relations Act) in the thirties provided a mechanism for gaining collective-bargaining rights for workers—a requirement that employers bargain in full faith with representatives of their employees and that employees be protected as they attempted to organize themselves. Community-action programs are becoming the arena in which the poor can organize to demand rights of negotiation with agencies and therefore participate in the decisions which affect their neighborhoods—whether these decisions affect the physical rebuilding of the area or the kinds of programs of training or social service or education that are desirable there.

As we argue in the next chapter, official community-action agencies can usually only be limited *direct* and forceful representatives of the poor. The constructive use of external pressure and organizing is needed so that the poor can have an independent voice and strength. Second-force groups can perform this role. But they need policy, strategy, flexibility, and allies as well as militancy.

NOTES

1. In saying that we are not sure of the material gains from Alinsky's programs we are not indulging in an academic backhanded slap. We really do not know what the results have been. Alinsky and his supporters may say that that is our fault, but no one has objectively told the story of what results from his conflict model.

2. Warren Haggstrom, an Alinsky-oriented social worker, has presented the powerlessness theme in his "The Power of the Poor," in Frank Riessman, Jerome Cohen, and Arthur Pearl, eds., *Mental Health of the Poor* (New York: The Free Press of Glencoe, 1965).

3. Although using the Alinsky and New Left approaches as types of conflict models, we recognize considerable variations among programs that purport to be following either model.

4. *Newsweek*, September 13, 1965.

16

❊　❊　❊

THE THIRD-FORCE
STRATEGY

The community-action programs (CAP) of the war on poverty have pursued a variety of strategies: a precursor organization such as Mobilization for Youth (which has continued as an official CAP agency in the New York City program) for a while pursued a vigorous policy of advocacy with and for the poor, including strong criticisms of the police and local schools. In San Francisco, the Western Addition office of the city poverty program at one stage centered on efforts to organize the Negro residents into an effective political force; political opposition led to a redirecting of the program toward straight services. Other programs have been essentially financial conduits to existing social-service and educational agencies, with little effort to change existing agencies and practices, or to mobilize the poor.

In this chapter we present a strategy for antipoverty community-action programs that promotes change in social-service activities without inevitably promoting great disturbance in communities. We recognize that in many communities more can be expected and gained from pov-

This chapter was written with Martin Rein.

erty programs. An aggressive program of legal rights can be pushed; the boundaries of permissible action can be expanded without throttling reactions. But in a larger number of programs, the third-party approach outlined here is the only viable one. It provides a way of improving agency function without great struggle. It produces improvements in the living conditions of individuals very immediately. But—it does not solve all the problems of political powerlessness, nor does it produce a radical redistribution of resources toward aiding the poor nor a sharp improvement in the employment prospects of the area, although it can increase the number of nonprofessional jobs.

Obviously, then, the third-party strategy has limits. But many community-action programs have been unsuccessful in directly improving the conditions of the residents. Large-scale ambitions about changing the "power base" or "challenging the establishment" frequently do not produce results. Moreover, what is possible to do with government money is circumscribed. Much that is desirable is unlikely to take place within official community-action programs; they can provide an arena of action, but what can be done under official auspices with "establishment" money is limited.

In the effort to be more than an effective service to and with the poor, many local poverty agencies have failed to be anything at all: they are not effective political machines nor do they provide effective services.

The third-party approach, then, is a way of getting immediate returns from the use of community-action funds. It does not solve all the problems of poverty. While it does attempt to introduce change in existing agencies, it does not seek to overturn these agencies. It is a modest approach; that is its limitation—that is its hope.

In this chapter we address ourselves mainly to the militant view of what community-action programs should be rather than to the more tradition-oriented agencies and professionals who do not want these programs to exert much influence in their localities. We do this because we are oriented to change in the social-service network as are those with a militant stance, but we fear that the radical posture discussed in the preceding chapter has sometimes inhibited the achievement of important goals that community-action agencies could attain. Federal and local governments will be assigning changing roles to community-action programs or community corporations; the following analysis is aimed at depicting the recurring issues in any type of community action by governmentally supported groups.

The Third-Party Strategy

The third-party strategy sees the local poverty agencies as intervening between the poor who represent the demand side of the social-service market system and the established community institutions who represent the suppliers of service. As a third party they fully represent neither, but rather they are an attempt to produce a better juncture between both. They can be seen in terms of a strategy for bringing together the citizen and the bureaucracy; the techniques of "linkage" are an attempt to provide greater coherence in a highly fragmented system. The need for third-party innovations arises from the inequities created by our bureaucratic and political system in which functions are specialized, authority is widely dispersed, and bureaucracies become autonomous and unresponsive to changing human needs.

The demand for action has been stimulated by the rise of the civil-rights movement and the planning explosion that provided the context for national social-welfare policy in the sixties. The poor are being organized by various second-party action groups which have an independence that cannot be emulated by publicly sponsored agencies. These independent political groups can more easily appeal to potentially militant indigenous leaders and propel aggressive social protest with considerable freedom and with no threat of withdrawal of public funds.

Consequently, in many cities governmentally sponsored community-action programs oriented toward the poor would do better to adopt a "third-party" strategy rather than a strategy of organizing the militant poor. The CAPs can organize those sections of the poor who are not attracted to the protest models of Alinsky, the civil-rights groups, and other independent-action committees. They can develop indigenous leaders who would not be developed via the protest route. They can attempt to function as advocates of the poor, negotiating with the institutional structures of welfare, housing, police, and the like.

The third-party strategy suggested here depends on new resources being poured into the social and educational network and on pressure from more militant second-force groups functioning outside of the system. The third-party orientation is essentially an "inside strategy," working within the system to be changed. Its legitimacy within the system gives it the possibility of impact at the same time that it limits the forms of impact.

Such third-party interventions are not new. Health and welfare councils and the information and referral agencies created by them represent an antecedent form of third-party intervention. The political club, the trade-union counselor, and the veterans' representative have also created their own third-party interveners to help their respective constituencies utilize the service system. The Citizens' Advice bureaus in England and the Ombudsman—the complaints man in the Scandinavian countries— are illustrative of the European experience. A brief comparison of the American and European experience provides a perspective for understanding the structure and function of local CAPs.

The American Structures

The traditional approach in America attempted to resolve the problems of fragmentation by two unrelated approaches. On the supply end it was concerned with voluntary cooperation among "suppliers." The case conference is one example of the process that attempts to resolve discontinuities and conflicting prescriptions as they apply to the single case. Voluntary welfare councils also tried to bring about coherent policies. Representatives of suppliers met to try to resolve community rather than individual problems by joint deliberations and common study. They assumed that individual agency policy would change as these representatives came to learn the nature of the problem through a process of study and discussion. Occasionally this forum for self-education took the form of coordination in connection with joint projects. Change was to be created by the education of leaders who could rise above the interests of the agencies they represented and and dispassionately promote changes that provided greater coherence in the tangle of social-service domains and privileges.

Welfare councils were also concerned with demand, as witness the various kinds of information and referral services. At times these services were available for special-interest groups. Benefits counselors of the United Mine Workers counseled union members on the use of welfare services. Some political leaders employed personnel to help grease the welfare machinery, not only for those loyal to the machine, but in the hope of promoting new alliances to the broader community as well. Such favors help to build indebtednesses that in turn promote political loyalty. Welfare councils frequently publish a directory of most community services and refer individuals who call for advice to the "appropriate" agency.

The principle of coordination by consumer education governed the operation of these services. The consumer was given information about his needs (an X ray for tuberculosis, a medical examination, a counseling interview) and about the services that were available to accommodate his needs. It was assumed implicitly that knowledge would lead to increased use of service. On special occasions the worker supplemented the education of the consumer by facilitating the services. Lack of coordination was viewed as an information failure that more knowledge could mend. Conflicting interests and vested interests were both regarded as alien to sound professional practice and were underestimated as an issue in service referrals.

Scattered available information suggests that these procedures produced low arrival and delivery of services. Emphasizing the routing of clients through the system naturally emphasizes the importance of diagnostic work. A New York study reveals that 66 per cent of the voluntary mental-health services in 1962 provided only diagnostic and psychological evaluation. Of the 5,851 children who had contact with psychiatric clinics "only 14 per cent . . . received a service defined by the clinics themselves as 'treatment.' "[1] Problem clarification substitutes for actual service.

Until recently the welfare-council approach dominated the thinking of most professional coordinating and referral systems. Contrast the assumptions of the traditional approach with those of the CAPs (actual performance may be different). Six dichotomies emerge. They dramatize the differences but may overstate and exaggerate what is more often difference of degree rather than kind. Nevertheless, the differences in emphasis are important.

First, the traditional approach more often than not started with the assumption of resource constancy—how to distribute a stable or shrinking resource base. The abiding assumption was scarcity. In contrast, CAPs are based on the availability of potentially large new sources of funds. They can serve as a newly created mechanism for the redistribution of income and services. New commitments of the Federal government to distribute its largesse to local communities in such areas as housing subsidies, education (once regarded as a remote arena for Federal aid because of the church-state issue), poverty programs, training and retraining, and so on, have markedly modified the earlier policies of attrition.

The traditional approach was chiefly concerned with duplication and overlap. Waste, inefficiency, and competition among services were widely regarded as an evil that contributed to the growth of social problems and that aggravated the rational use of service resources. The solution was greater coordination and efficiency. Cost accounting and centralization of services were sought—the application of business technology to welfare was the model. While CAPs also stress efficiency, they are by contrast much more concerned with effectiveness. Today's concerns are with product as well as cost accountability. Are programs achieving what they set out to do? Do children learn to read? Do youth get jobs? In other words, today's rhetoric and agenda have shifted— quality and relevance of service to the consumer have become central issues of social policy.

The traditional approach abandoned or neglected its prime commitment to selectivity, the provision of services to low-income populations, in favor of community-wide service. Community agencies affiliated with traditional coordinating structures such as settlement houses and family agencies defined their function as service to the total community, not only to those in poverty. Scarcity of funds made fee charging for all clients attractive, and professional practice turned away from serving high-risk clients. Both trends contributed to the disengagement of voluntary agencies from the poor. The CAP approach assumed that the major emphasis must be on the distribution of services to the poor. While other groups may also receive services, the CAP model is committed to the repeal of the "Iron Law of Welfare" (those in greatest need fail to receive quality community services).[2] The principle of selectivity has now replaced the earlier emphasis on universal services for the entire community.

The traditional approach was committed to "good causes"—the distribution of acceptable benefactions—rather than to "issues" that involve a conflict over ends (e.g., social class integration) and means (e.g., birth control).[3] The professionals sought to protect the prestige and reputation of the sponsor by avoiding controversy and conflict. By contrast, CAPs are more concerned with consumer protection and in many cities are more willing to risk controversy.

The traditional approach was concerned with a limited range of interventions. Education and training were not regarded as acceptable social-welfare functions. Intellectual justification for this position could be found in Wilensky and Lebeaux's important distinction between institutional and residual, which left education outside the domain of social welfare because it was institutionalized.[4] Moreover, special planning was largely concerned with the voluntary agencies, although there was much self-criticism for the failure to coordinate and to work with public agencies that, after all, controlled the major expenditures in social services. The new approach, on the contrary, guided by a theory of the poverty cycle, is committed to a broad range of intervention, especially in the opportunity structures—education and work. Both were almost completely ignored by the traditional voluntary-planning structures, which concerned themselves primarily with recreation, health, welfare.

The traditional planning approach derived its legitimacy from social and economic elites. It was assumed that they acted in the "best interests" of the total community. According to the tradition of noblesse oblige, elites brought an obligation and a special competence in coping with community problems. Their advantaged position allowed them to maintain a dispassionate interest in the good of the whole community. The harmony of community interest rather than conflict and vested interests was the accepted orthodoxy. In contrast, the new approach derives its legitimacy from political government and may be more directly responsive to the consumer, to the electorate, and to public opinion than the elites were. Interest groups are recognized. The political process accepts conflict as natural and will acknowledge the claims of the poor as their power increases.

CAPs represent a new coalition, uneasy at best, between government and popular democracy. Insistence on "the maximum feasible involvement of the poor" as a condition for the receipt of federal funds strengthened this tendency. (Public planning is threatening voluntary planning, much as government responsibility for dispensing relief in the thirties challenged the function of the family agencies and propelled them into new directions.)

But both the traditional and the new approaches share a common dilemma, which sets the limits on the kinds of intervention they propose. Both approaches are committed to increasing coherence and rationality without decreasing the autonomy of social-welfare agencies. Both do not wish to infringe on the authority of established community institutions to define their function and carry out their mission. Contemporary social planning in the United States is unwilling to intervene in the free-for-all of decentralized democracy. Curiously, then, social welfare remains the last bastion of laissez faire and free enterprise. Social planning has not been able to reconcile its advocacy of direction and coordination with its faith in the vitality of an un-directed, individualistic, market-oriented society.

This self-imposed philosophical constraint on planning leads to a special type of social planning at the local level, one directed at creating the "cement" that binds distributors and consumers.[5] Attaining coherence and rationality in the supply-and-demand system has captured the interest of the planners. Resolving the dilemmas of receiving, screening, routing, and coordinating consumer demand into a highly fragmented and incoherent social-service supply system has become the agenda of social planning.

The CAPs have introduced some important innovations in the form of the "third-party" planning that derive largely from the assumptions listed above. Before examining their working assumptions, which have largely remained implicit, let us turn to the European experience.

The European Experience

THE BRITISH SYSTEM

The Citizens' Advice Bureau was initiated in England during World War II in response to "the trials and the bewilderments of those who were bombed, of those who needed help but did not know what help there was nor where to get it."[6] In the postwar period Lord Beveridge regarded the bureau not only as a way of getting advice, but protection as well. He proposed that one of its aims be "to help protect the citizens against the public authority when the latter, through mistake or stupidity, is acting wrongly."[7] Today each bureau is autonomous, although accredited by a national office. In 70 per cent of the bureaus, all staff are unpaid. The budgets of the bureau are met by both volun-tary contributions and public subsidy and are independently run. More than 400 bureaus receive about one and a quarter million inquiries yearly. More than half the requests concern family affairs and housing.

The bureaus have not attempted to serve as a means of protecting citizens against bureaucratic discretion as might be inferred from the statement by Beveridge. But as part of a national organization they are in a position to do more than simply advise individuals—they can attempt to promote and modify legislation on behalf of the citizen. The information they receive is in some measure a reflection of public experience with the service bureaucracy. Also, the British use of a national organization giving service to local bureaus is one way of developing a common body of experience. A national or regional body can disseminate information, train personnel, and thus strengthen the quality of the service.

Some analysts have argued that case workers in American communities could serve a similar function, advising their clients about community resources and funneling to welfare councils special problems that require reform. The argument is plausible, indeed convincing; only the experience has been found wanting! The idea of consumer protection against an indifferent or hostile bureaucracy is alien to traditional agencies, which define consumers as clients and professionals as acting in the best interests of their clients. More recently, Alfred Kahn has argued for adapting British practice to the United States by developing information centers that would be useful to all groups in the community, not only to the poor.

THE OMBUDSMAN

The Ombudsman originated in Sweden in 1809; in 1919 the constitution of Finland created such an office. Since the mid-fifties it has been adopted by Denmark, Norway, and New Zealand. England is adopting the system and Congressman Henry Reuss (Democrat—Wisconsin) has proposed a modification of the system for the United States.[8]

The Ombudsman receives complaints from citizens who feel that they have been mistreated by government officials. He is appointed by Parliament for a limited term of office and is an "insider" with full access to confidential files. Although he can prosecute public officials, he seldom resorts to such extreme measures. More likely he notifies the department in question of his criticism and occasionally makes his findings known to the newspapers. Not surprisingly, his recommendations are accepted and acted upon. The Ombudsman is chiefly concerned with those situations in which the bureaucracy exceeds its authority and fails to follow approved procedures, i.e., the problem of administrative abuse. His responsibilities extend to all agencies of central government—only occasionally does he examine complaints against local government. He does not need to receive a complaint before he acts, for he can investigate at his own discretion.

In the Scandinavian countries, the Ombudsman received approximately 1,200 complaints in 1964. The commonest complaints are against institutions of constraint—the police, the prisons, the mental hospitals, and the courts (contrast this with Citizens' Advice Bureaus, which refer cases mainly to service institutions). About two-thirds of the complaints are dismissed as not warranting further investigation. In only 10 per cent of the cases has there been an official criticism of government by the Ombudsman.[9]

Thus, third-party interventions in the European experience seem to be concerned largely with citizen education and the abuse of authority. They do not constitute, per se, a special machinery to protect the interests of the consumer. The citizen is by and large not defined as an interest group in need of protection against the abuse of administrative discretion. They do, however, differ from traditional American information and referral systems in that they are broadly concerned with institutional performance and its modifications. They also differ in their definition of the service recipients: the Citizens' Advice Bureau, like the traditional American services, is concerned with the un-informed, the Ombudsman with the aggrieved, and the Community Action Program with the alienated.

But the common link that binds all these programs is the restless problem of bureaucratic society—how to make bureaucracy respon-sive to the citizen consumer, protecting his rights while serving his needs. The third-party strategy for local CAPs attempts to join the needs of the alienated consumer and the social-service bureaucracies.

Community-Action Programs

Community-action programs are simultaneously concerned with the expansion of consumer demand among the poor as well as with the development and modification of agency resources, purposes, and technology. What distinguished the CAPs from the traditional American and European approaches is their commitment to respond to both the supply and the demand side of the service equation. In so doing they help reduce fragmentation, increase the coherence of the welfare system, and facilitate the more humane and equitable distri-bution of resources.

Community-action programs increase consumer demand through use of a variety of new and old techniques. More people are brought into the service system, new client groups are created, and old clients not only request additional services to which they are entitled but become more effective in obtaining what they seek.

First, decentralization through the neighborhood-service center structure provides access and visibility. As a consequence, reaching out to the low-income community is greatly extended. This decentralization promotes easy access in the local neighborhood and is intended to improve neighborhood participation and thus demand.

Decentralization has another side. The neighborhood bases (acting as one-stop centers) attempt to overcome fragmentation by placing the various services under one roof, thus enhancing the physical possibility of increased coordination and integration. The effect of this new structuring—coordination by propinquity—has the potential of increasing and fusing the supply of services; it should also make demand more effective. If efficiently organized, the neighborhood base cannot only meet demand more effectively but can also encourage the maximum use of services through coordination, reduction of red tape, greater communication, liaison, and so on. A common intake can serve to route clients to services more efficiently as well as to reduce the intake effort of the many different services. One intensive intake procedure should be much more effective and shorter than five different ones.

Second, as an expediter the new nonprofessional staff aide is introduced in an effort to connect the client to the varied services in the system more efficiently. The aide does not simply provide consumer education by information and referral; rather, he actually facilitates the delivery of the service by playing a variety of roles, including those of intervener, interpreter, helper, negotiator, escort, and baby-sitter. What hitherto was "supplied" by the traditional structures through information is now provided through direct assistance, through action. The expediter does things by example; he provides a model, support, follow-up to insure rapid service delivery. He cuts through red tape and gets rid of bottlenecks. These are legitimate roles, as far as the client is concerned, based on his nonprofessional peer status, his residence in the neighborhood, his similarity in style, and his background, and also through his connections with the agencies provided by the CAP. His ability to expedite matters is further increased by extralegal "wheeler-dealer" skills which are semi-legitimated, as is true in the Citizens' Advice Bureaus in England. He is encouraged to find ways around the problem and can utilize his knowledge of the informal system of the neighborhood as well as the formal system of the agencies. What was previously attempted through information and referral the expediter can now achieve by guaranteeing the arrival of the client, speaking for him, following up on obtaining the service, and so on.

Expediting can be reinforced by the development of community-action groups of welfare clients to request changes in welfare practices. For example, bringing together mothers who are having trouble with their children may increase demand indirectly in that the group may request the services of school psychologists and child-guidance specialists as consultants or group leaders; the organization of literacy groups that request assistance from the Board of Education also increases demand; clean-up campaigns require greater assistance from the Sanitation Department as well as the police; health campaigns for prenatal assistance for pregnant women increase the demand for services on the part of the Health Department and the hospitals; anti-drug addiction campaigns involve the Police Department and other agencies in increased efforts.

The use of advisory committees that involve the poor can increase demand for more relevant services and put pressure on the system at various points. This may be true whether these committees acquire significant power or remain more in the form of structures for the expression of consumer preferences.

Finally, the over-all improved coordination and integration of services should eventually lead to greater demand, bring more clients into the service system, and increase the demands of the clients already in the system. By guaranteeing that a checkup at a mobile health truck leads to appropriate medical assistance, the utilization of the checkup service is likely to be heightened considerably. Moreover, the numbers of people who then require specific medical aid will be increased, placing further pressures on the service-dispensing system. As word gets around in the neighborhood regarding the improved services, this leads to a greater demand. People who were previously somewhat doubtful about requesting these services will be brought into the system.

These new techniques and approaches of the CAPs in expanding consumer demands are far beyond the traditional information and referral services. But if local CAPs only increase demand and do not attempt to increase the supply of service provided by established agencies, difficulties will surely arise. Fortunately the CAPs should have available to them numerous avenues for aiding the suppliers of services, especially if second-force groups effectively mass pressure around relevant and specific demands.

Traditional welfare councils attempted to reduce fragmentation of services through voluntary joint deliberations and common study. By contrast, the modern CAPs have available much more powerful incentives for defragmentation, which still leave the agencies their autonomy. The new one-stop neighborhood centers (see Chapter 12) and the nonprofessional manpower (see Chapter 13) can furnish the energy to increase the resources of the agency system and to permit much greater integration without loss of agency independence. The decentralized neighborhood centers can provide screening and a common intake that will save valuable time and energy for the receiving agencies. Under the traditional system, agencies had little assurance that the people referred elsewhere ever arrived there, or if they did get there, that they received expeditious treatment. The new neighborhood-service center can provide this integrating link, as well as receive the type of clients who were not previously served by the original agency.

In addition, the CAPs can help the agencies that supply the services by providing some or all of the following: funds through subcontracting and coapplications for special grants; manpower, including both shared nonprofessionals and professionals; training and knowledge in the use of nonprofessionals and small neighborhood-center extensions; prestige through alliance with such institutions as universities; assistance in increasing the self-help resources of the community and its informal systems (although to some extent this may increase demands on the former agencies, in another important sense it adds to the total service supplies of the neighborhood).

It is important that CAPs become aware of their potential power as third-party interveners, that they aid the supplier as well as the potential consumer of service. Their ability to reinforce and substantiate agency requests for funds, their closeness to the community, their prestige, their variety of services—all these factors can potentially increase the resources of the established agency.

Within the third-party framework that we have proposed CAPs can accomplish a great deal more than they have been able to realize thus far. CAP agencies can help the poor form consumer cooperatives and credit unions, develop planned-parenthood programs, organize health services enabling, for example, pregnant women to obtain the necessary prenatal services that will assist in longer life for their children.

CAPs can make a contribution to increasing the cohesion of the neighborhood by assisting people to get to know each other better through parties and socials and through the development of various types of groups. They can greatly increase the self-help power of the area and the involvement and interest of people who are typically not appealed to by militant, protest, direct-action approaches. CAPs can also provide professional and subprofessional legal aid to assist in guaranteeing the legal rights of the poor.

CAP agencies can furnish information to the poor to assist them to become far more effective clients in the service system. To some extent, information is power. CAPs can train members of the community in service-giving procedures, and this know-how represents perhaps even more power for people in the community.

The CAPs can greatly add to the integration of services such as is now being developed by the one-door neighborhood health centers which will tie together a great variety of health services at a local base. (Comprehensiveness, continuity, coordination, and decentralization are important goals in this design.) CAPs can play a major role in the coordination of all fragmented services, not only those that exist in one area such as health. They can help to connect welfare, housing, health, and recreation. Expediters and facilitators are needed all through the disconnected service system, each of whose agencies wishes to preserve its autonomy. CAPs can utilize their legitimacy and personnel (not only nonprofessionals, but professionals at various middle and top levels) to facilitate service integration. They can even utilize a modified type of Ombudsman. They can call on their implicit mandate and legitimacy, which gives them the right to help obtain more effective services for the poor.

Problems

But the demanding strategy of drawing together an indifferent supplier with a strengthened demand system has inherent in it certain problems that deserve special comment.

1. Green tape. One of the great dangers in the expediter model is "green tape." Here the expediter does not change the red tape in the

system but rather circumvents it; that is, the client receives special attention because of his connection with the particular power structure (historically the political club, currently the CAP). This does not lead to the development of the system toward more expeditious service for all; rather, the system remains intact. Moreover, nothing happens for the clients who do not have access to the expediter.

We favor a model in which the role of the CAP expediter is oriented toward expanding the system in order to achieve more equitable distribution of services for all clients in need. Although the development of this change is produced for particular clients who have a relationship to the expediter, system change is the goal, not specially favored service for the few. At first precedents are developed from cases being expedited, but these precedents must be firmly internalized in the system independent of the operation of the CAP. Thus, attention must be given to the method of translating the privileges won by the ad-hoc expediting approach into system change—permanent practice supported by new rulings, laws, practices, agreements, and arrangements. In other words, new forms of organization and function have to be worked out to implement firmly and codify the modifications of the system as they develop.

2. The dilemma of cooling out. There is a danger that nonprofessionals will make legitimate a service that is not in the client's best interests—the third-party structure may coopt potential opposition and neutralize discontent. The client is taught how to adjust to an unfair system. The client is taught acceptance of "reality," which in the end means the status quo. (Community organization programs stimulated by service agencies such as schools, housing authorities, settlement houses, and so forth have been most vulnerable to this problem.)

A related dilemma is that supplier cooperation is sought, but the agenda of reform is forsaken as cooperation becomes an end in itself. Product accountability is overlooked as the third party becomes "cooled out" in exchange for its survival and enhancement as a viable organization. As a result, institutional change as a goal is neglected.

There is also the danger that emphasis on services and service delivery can leave untouched the redistribution of power toward Negro and other poor minority groups. The scramble over services control may also accentuate conflicts in neighborhoods without providing a useful arena for resolution.

3. Losing "neutrality." The task of the third party has been defined

as that of an insider-outsider—accepted as an insider by the suppliers, but nevertheless acting as an outsider to them, supporting consumer needs and encouraging organizational change. In practice these tasks may conflict. The interests of the demand and supply sides of the equation are not always congruent. On occasion diplomacy, tact, and skill in negotiation may strain human ingenuity with the result that the third party may be forced to choose sides.

4. Third party as competitor. An awkward tension will arise if the third party captures resources and becomes a service supplier. Despite its best intentions it may be forced to act as a sponsor of a neighborhood law firm, an employment program, or a consumer-education program. Such situations may arise because it is easier to by-pass the indifference or lack of competence of established institutions by creating new or parallel services. The third party is likely to be viewed as a competitor for available resources. A choice may have to be made between the need for change and the fear of competition.

Progress cannot be achieved without certain costs. Today's reform becomes the conservative institution of tomorrow. We are confident that for each dilemma counterstrategies can be developed if they are sought.

Why Have the CAPs Failed to Reorient?

These four difficult problems explain some of the reasons why CAP agencies have failed to move toward an effective third-party strategy.[10] But they do not explain all of the reluctance or hesitation in making the move. A recurring difficulty is one which faces all who wish to make important changes—the role of reform and the assessment of possibilities and limits.

Many who have sought significant changes in the American social-service labyrinth have failed to understand the mandate of CAP and confuse it with an outside-the-system radicalism. As this became less and less tenable, they have not pursued the difficult road of attempting to shape a CAP program that can produce important changes in the situation of the now-poor.

The advocates of militant CAP programs have also failed to understand the CAP mandate and have confused it with an outside-the-system radicalism. Frequently, CAP groups have thought they needed to overthrow a negative system and have attempted to imitate tactics of political organization. But it is extremely doubtful that political organization can long take place within a government-supported framework. To some extent the activist context which propelled the development of the antipoverty movement has limited the perspective of some CAP agencies. They have been unable to envision methods of change other than highly activist ones.

Most CAP groups have either adopted the militant posture or else have been concerned with providing only minimal assistance and information to the poor, staying within the narrow perspective of tradition-bound agencies. Because they do not understand what they can do within the system, CAP approaches have frequently been haphazard, undeveloped, primitive, confused, lacking in direction and ideology, performed halfheartedly. This is understandable because the CAP groups were born rapidly in an activist ferment surrounded by much publicity but with a vague mandate. Moreover, social-agency experience and social work training in the United States have not evolved methods and programs for this new role.

Often they have assumed, with traditional radicals, that a monolithic establishment has a finite amount of power which must be taken away from it if the poor are to profit in any way. Hence, some CAP agencies rapidly encountered backlash simply because of their posture long before they could actually accomplish very much. Traditional political groups, led by the mayors, have been immediately fearful and unadaptive.

In essence, militant CAP groups have not been able to understand the new potential "give" in the system, the give which has been stimulated by the affluence of the society, pressured by a civil-rights movement (functioning outside the system) which demands change. CAPs have not understood that far-reaching changes may be attainable within the system through new types of personnel, new methods, new structures, new conceptualizations, and their own new authority.

Not only have many CAPs failed to learn how they could work with existing agencies to assist and change them, but they have also failed to recognize how they could utilize and respond to various groups (the second force) functioning outside the system (without imitating them).

CAPs have access to segments of the poor that other outside-the-system groups cannot easily reach. They can assist agencies without attacking them, and they may be able to change these agencies without overthrowing them. They may gain revenues of great magnitude, but will they be ready to use them effectively?

The third-party strategy may not lead to grand revolutionary zeal, but resounding failures do not necessarily benefit the poor.

This chapter has discussed four different third-party interventions, including two approaches utilized in the United States and two that evolved abroad. In the European experience third-party interventions seem largely to be concerned with citizen education, policy development, and the abuse of authority. The major American experience prior to the antipoverty community-action programs was concerned with consumer education and voluntary interagency cooperation. The CAPs are more oriented toward new methods of developing consumer demand and consumer protection. They are also concerned with new forms for achieving coordination among agencies and suppliers of service, while maintaining the traditional autonomy of the individual agencies.

Critics may well argue that CAPs cannot serve simultaneously as an authentic spokesman for the poor and as an agent of established power. Sooner or later they will be forced to choose sides and, if they compromise their client commitments, the CAPs will have lost their purpose and the potential support of the poor. But if the agencies are alienated, they will reject the CAPs. The resolution requires combining a program of modified consumer advocacy with an effort to assist the traditional agencies.

The CAPs represent a new alliance of the public and private agencies and the poor. They must serve both groups. They have, in essence, two clients. That is their dilemma; that is their possibility.

The relationship between the outside groups and inside third-party groups will certainly not be static. These outside groups frequently produce demands and crises to which the CAPs should develop responses. Thus a CAP program functioning in an area where there has been widespread criticism of the police, such as Watts or Oakland, can propose the employment of policy-community subprofessional aides. These aides, as has been illustrated in Richmond, California, can reduce tensions and improve relationships. Or in areas where a particularly inadequate school system is sharply attacked by second-force groups, the CAPs could help propose and develop relevant school programs.

Other kinds of connections between the inside and outside groups are emerging. Civil-rights leaders could be invited to join local boards. Clients of CAPs may move toward direct participation in political-action groups.

But the two forces, although they should articulate with each other, have separate functions and goals. Alinsky can organize for vastly increased demand. So can civil-rights groups. Functioning within the system on government money, CAPs do not have this freedom. Without grass roots and civil-rights pressures, however, CAPs may not be able to make the vital connections in the social-service system. They may only expand demand without increasing quality services.

One mandate of CAPs is to overcome the difficulties separating the poor from the traditional agencies, which are frequently slow to move. How this is done will vary from community to community and will depend upon regional and local political climates, as well as the specific ideologies and orientations of the local CAP group. A major factor will be the power structure of the community. If well-organized, strong groups exert pressure outside of the system (such as an Alinsky-organized group or student-Left led group), the third-force group will be moved toward the demand side. If there is a strong demand from community groups for control of funds, the demand side would be stressed by the third-force groups. On the other hand, if traditional voluntary agencies and/or public agencies were in command of the local CAP, the emphasis would be much more on the supply side. Moreover, the way in which federal funders apply pressures to local programs in the response to the larger political pressures on it will shape the varying emphases on supply or demand in different CAPs throughout the country.

The third force is therefore in a tenuous role, torn between the needs of the poor and the constraints on the formal agencies, sensitively responsive to pressures from outside the system as well as within it. This responsiveness must always seek to achieve some degree of balance between the supply and demand sides or else risk alienation from either the poor or the formal agencies. The focus must be on increasing the sensitivity of the bureaucracies to the poor, reducing their discretionary powers, and enabling better coordination without loss of autonomy.

In serving as a third party, community-action programs can find a new orientation to give purpose to their work. They can tackle the intractable problem of how to make large-scale formal organizations respond humanely and effectively to the needs of the citizen in a bureaucratic society. This mission requires a willingness to push established agencies when they are slow to move and a recognition that as a third-party agency there are limits to such pressure.

The first year of the poverty program was marked in many communities by a militancy against traditional agencies with little effective CAP programming. The product frequently was antagonism without results. In the next years, the established agencies in many communities played a bigger role in the programs and moderated the push for change.

The third-party strategy calls for neither perpetual militancy nor chronic acquiescence. It pays attention to the structure of pressures on it and attempts to move effectively within its possibilities. It pushes the boundaries of its mission but does not attempt to break them. It does not accept the notion that change can come about only through militant action. But it does not deny the importance of militancy even when it recognizes that such action may not be fully available to it because of its governmental character.

The third-party strategy offers social delivery, not a social movement or a comforting continuation of past programs. It is limited, which makes it practicable. And practicality should neither be revered nor scorned. Exploiting the possibilities of an insider-outsider role may sometimes have more gains than fruitlessly insisting on a militancy of action where it can result neither in the delivery of services, nor the mobilization of the poor, nor the augmentation of resources. A mechanical insistence on militancy can be self-defeating. On the other hand, a conventional commitment to staying within narrow limits of established systems can result in busy work without improving the conditions of the poor and moving toward the reduction of poverty. The suggestion here is that there are times and places for a third-party strategy.

NOTES

1. Sylvan Furman *et al.,* "Social Factors in the Flow of Children to Outpatient Psychiatric Facilities." Paper presented at the American Public Health Association, Annual Meeting, November 1963, mimeographed, p. 5; and Furman, "Suggestions for Refocusing Child Guidance Clinics," *Children,* XII (July–August 1965).

2. Martin Rein, "The Strange Case of Public Dependency," *Trans-action,* II, No. 3 (March 1965), 16–23.

3. Peter B. Clark and James Q. Wilson, "Incentive Systems: A Theory of Organizations," *Administrative Science Quarterly*, VI (September 1961), 129–166.

4. Harold Wilensky and Charles N. Lebeaux, *Industrial Society and Social Welfare* (New York: Russell Sage Foundation, 1950).

5. The CAPs also attempt to integrate the distributors of service with each other through the local multiservice centers, and here, too, their autonomy is left intact.

6. See Richard Titmuss, *Problems of Social Policy* (London: Longmans Green and Co., 1950), p. 291, and Alfred J. Kahn *et al.*, *Neighborhood Information Center: A Study and Some Proposals* (New York: Columbia School of Social Work, 1966), pp. 16–36.

7. Mildred Zucker, "The English System of Citizens' Advice Bureaus," *Conference Proceedings of the Extension of Legal Services to the Poor* (Washington, D. C.: Government Printing Office, November 1964).

8. See, for example, Mildred Zucker, "Citizens Advice Bureaus: The British Way," *Social Work*, X (October 1965), 85–91, and Alfred Kahn *et al.*, *op. cit.*

9. These observations are based largely on an unpublished report by Peter Marris, "A Report on the Scandinavian Ombudsman and the British Citizens' Advice Bureaus," Public Affairs Program, Ford Foundation, 1965.

10. We are not here concerned with why the "traditionalists" do not move. Obviously, interest, inertia, and power are involved as well as the absence of a feeling of urgency.

V I

Social Science
and Social Policy

I 7

❀ ❀ ❀

SOCIAL CHANGE VERSUS THE "PSYCHIATRIC WORLD VIEW"

The new working classes are generating a series of crises for the school, mental hospital, and social agency with their established middle-class outlook, traditions, and structure. The poor have long been alienated from the teacher, the psychiatrist, and the social worker, but a new element has emerged to force change. Today's active poor have a number of potentially power-producing qualities that make them more difficult to ignore: They are concentrating in heavy proportions in the suburb-segregated metropolis and they are "colored," fusing together on ethnic as well as economic issues.

This potential might is beginning to be appreciated by social scientists and other intellectuals.

Social scientists can play an extremely important role during this period, charting new paths, developing programs, and providing active support and leadership. It may be useful in this context to examine the intellectual atmosphere of the forties and fifties, particularly the "psychiatric world view" emerging in those years. Despite the partial decline of this world view, it has considerable lingering power and serves, we contend, to curtail ardor, involvement, and commitment. Moreover, some of its defects are precisely those displayed by many intellectuals in their dealings with broader issues and may be instructive for that reason. In today's rapid social change and intellectual doubts, we may be ripe for a self-critical analysis of this psychiatric world view, preparatory to deeper participation in the social changes that lie ahead.[1]

The Psychiatric World View

Formerly, authoritarian thinking and behavior were considered in political and ideological terms; in the fifties they came to be described in terms of the "authoritarian personality."

Crime and juvenile delinquency were seen mainly as reflections of family instability and personality maladjustment. Criticism of basic features of the society was formulated in terms of "the neurotic conflicts of our times." Communist bureaucracy and political rebelliousness alike were analyzed as reflections of distorted relationships to parents. Segregation and discrimination were viewed largely in terms of their pathological personality effects upon the Negro. Learning problems of children were attributed to psychological conflicts or emotional blocks.[2]

Psychiatric categories functioned as both cause and effect, as independent variable and dependent variable alike. Discrimination caused personality problems while educational difficulties were the result of need conflicts. At times it almost seemed as if discrimination and prejudice would have been acceptable had they not produced deleterious personality consequences!

So ran thought in the age of psychiatry, which defined almost everything in psychological terms. Although it may not have been clear that we had a neurotic culture, it became increasingly evident that we were living in a "psychiatric culture."[3]

All kinds of problems—social, medical, educational, political—were interpreted through the new psychiatric world view. Problems were not searchingly examined to determine their variety of causes or whether and how psychological causes might play a role. Rather, presumed psychological diagnoses were readily given and typically went unquestioned.

This world view was costly in at least two ways: It deflected analysis and action away from nonpsychodynamic (for example, social) approaches and it often contaminated the original problem by introducing inappropriate modes of attack.[4]

But it did much more: It sponsored new values, new goals, new models of man.

The New Hero and the Pathology of Moderation

A new hero emerged in the age of psychiatry. He had a number of interesting attributes. He was expressive and calm, free and well balanced, self-actualized and moderate, autonomous and cooperative. He was neither intense nor overemotional; a good team man, he was a productive being. He evidenced his ability to work, love, and relate to people. Through it all he was an individualist—not a conformist.

The new hero was thoughtful, knew and accepted himself, and possessed just the right amount of extroversion and introversion. He cared about people and society. He was democratic, anti-authoritarian, and anti-bureaucratic. He had a mild interest in politics, and strongly rejected the masses and mass culture—one of his few strong feelings. He was not too overtly competitive, disliked conspicuous consumption, and favored sex equality. He preferred relatively permissive—although currently more balanced—child rearing and education.

Our new hero did not get burningly angry, nor was he known for his passionate convictions or intense ardor. He was, in sum, the new, well-adjusted, upper middle-class man.[5]

Contemporary psychiatry in the United States typically questions extreme, intense behavior. This questioning arises, in part, out of psychiatry's fundamental concern with pathological self-damaging behavior, which is often extreme. On the other hand, many healthy urges of the patient are underdeveloped and therefore unlikely to manifest themselves in intense form. Thus, unwittingly, psychiatry has come to look with suspicion on very strongly held beliefs and urges, often characterizing them as resistances or reaction formations.

In practice this stress on equilibrium—the middle road—has led to a number of difficulties that would be more obvious were this orientation less compatible with today's bias in favor of moderation.

Frank Barron, in a fascinating article on the psychology of imagination,[6] pointed out that, judged by the criteria for health prescribed by modern psychiatry, a large number of creative scientists and artists would be abnormal. Much of the behavior of many creative people is characterized by intensity, turbulence, and lack of calm.

Barron notes "the apocalyptic rages of Beethoven, the savage indignation of Jonathan Swift, the terrible loneliness of Van Gogh, the criminality of Rimbaud, the shameless preenings of Baudelaire, the stoical despair of Emily Brontë, the excruciating psychical and spiritual pain endured by Heine," and asks, "Could it be that these creative people had been in need of psychotherapy?" He further observes that, in the typical criteria offered for mental health, he heard "warmth mentioned, but not heat; spontaneity, not passion. No one had spoken of willfulness, fierce self-assertion, hatred of an established order."

An important criticism that can be leveled at twentieth-century psychiatry is that it has not sufficiently developed a high order of creative people. More often it has striven for "balanced" people who have rid themselves of their earlier neurotic intensities but have not replaced them by new constructive zeal.[7]

Too often the implicit advice is to avoid soaring for "unrealistic" heights. The implicit motto seems frequently to be "Better to have never tried than to have tried and lost."

Which Motives Are Questioned?

One of the subtle avenues through which the new hero values penetrate through the psychiatric milieu to the public at large is that of the questioning of some motives and the unquestioning of others.

In psychotherapy, patients express various ideas, feelings, impulses, attitudes, many of which are implicitly or explicitly questioned by the therapist who encourages the patient to delve beneath the surface and uncover the motivational origins of these feelings, preparatory to changing them. A large number of feelings and beliefs would typically be questioned and analyzed: intense ambition, authoritarian views, strong anticapitalist leanings, prejudices, hostile feelings, a revolutionary wish, or a deep belief in religion.

But when an individual, whether he is in therapy or not, expresses a need to develop himself, or a democratic impulse, or any of the attributes of the new hero, the motives underlying these feelings are not typically sought for or uncovered. Their acceptability is usually considered self-evident.

True, democratic, cooperative, warm feelings are not always

interpreted as genuine motives but as disguises for other kinds of motives. However, if they are seen as an individual's true motives, they are not inspected further, whereas authoritarian, revolutionary, and traditional beliefs would not be accepted as genuine motives. Not only are the personality attributes and motives of the new hero unprobed, his values remain unchallenged.

This value bias is one of the most important ways in which psychotherapy has been incorporated into our middle-class world view. Our quarrel with the value penetration of psychotherapy is its unconscious projection of the values of the professional upper middle class. Many may be intrinsically related to psychological well-being, but this must be carefully demonstrated, not tacitly assumed. Furthermore, because these values are unconsciously projected, there is little if any consideration of the possibility that a wide variety of other values might be consistent with psychological health. A pluralistic outlook is not part of the psychiatric world view.

The "New Ideology"

The psychotherapeutic world view was intimately related to a number of trends and movements extremely popular in the forties and fifties and cannot be fully understood apart from them. Those trends included progressive education, the child-rearing movement, the sexual "revolution," the high regard for creativity, and the great interest and sway of the writings of David Riesman, Erich Fromm, and William H. Whyte.[8]

Instead of analyzing each of these views separately, it is useful to investigate their social origins as a group, as a "new ideology."[9] Such a sociological analysis of the rise of the new ideology as a whole may provide clues to the extra-scientific reasons for its flourishing development.[10]

While it may be difficult to place precisely, it seems fairly evident that the new ideology arose after the Great Depression and spread most rapidly with the end of World War II. This new world view had its greatest appeal in intellectual professional circles, and from there spread to large portions of the middle class, particularly the new upper middle class of professionals and managers.

A number of traditional middle-class ideals were seriously challenged, one of the first being the Protestant Ethic, with its emphasis on hard work and repressive control of emotion as the keystone of success. Criticism of traditional education's emphasis on discipline, authority, and order was no longer restricted to the narrow group of John Dewey's disciples. (Just as psychoanalysis began with Freud some years before it captured the American middle class, so progressive education arose long before it became an institution in the forties.)

This period brought with it the emphasis on child rearing not for the child's sake alone but, in Harold Orlansky's phrase, as a "revolution in the nursery"—an important instrument of social change and the key to future adult happiness and productiveness. New methods of child rearing developed, accenting permissiveness and expression and de-emphasizing discipline and the control of emotion.

This era was also marked by a great stress on sex education, an attack on traditional morality, and ultimately by demands by more extremist wings (Wilhelm Reich, Paul Goodman) for a "sexual revolution" as the key to change.

The psychodynamic world view was part of the same picture. It attempted to weaken the traditional superego values of the old middle class on the grounds that a good deal of neurotic difficulty stems from an overly severe superego. It espoused greater emotional expression, self-acceptance, and self-actualization. It was primarily concerned with individual, nonsocial methods of change.

All these movements had much in common. They represented a rejection of certain traditional middle-class mores, especially discipline, industriousness, diligence, and emotional control. The old middle-class values of freedom and individualism were reformulated as demands for emotional expression and permissiveness. Creativity, self-actualization, and individual autonomy became the key goals, rather than competitive success.

The new ideology also tended to favor introspection and strength through consciousness, knowledge, awareness. Thus, with regard to sex there was more concern with providing information (sex education) than with solutions or guides to the morality issues. The attack on secrecy, the appearance of the Kinsey Report, were part of the same trend. The preference for "talking things out" and "accepting yourself" fits in here. Parlor psychoanalysis with its public self-examinations served the same need. Consciousness was equated with power and control. To understand one's problems gave a measure of control, and all the movements comprising the new ideology reflected this need for control, more particularly ego control.

Social Roots

What social variables contributed to the sweep and power of this new world view with its ardorless hero and its emphasis on the non-social, individual etiology of social phenomena? Why did it arise in the forties and fifties, rather than the thirties?

The Great Depression stimulated much social thinking of a radical bent. American capitalism itself was questioned and the Soviet Union was looked upon with much interest in many intellectual quarters. The widespread realization of the moral and democratic failure of the Soviet world coincided with the end of the depression and the resurgence of American capitalism. At the same time capitalism no longer had the surging vitality and forward march that had marked its historic rise. The values necessary in capitalism's earlier days that propelled the old middle class—"pull in your belt," "work hard," "don't fool around"— were no longer indispensable to modern bureaucratic, sales-oriented capitalism. The problem of traditional capitalism was production; the problems of modern capitalism are distribution and organization. The values that characterized the former were no longer useful; in fact, at times they were downright inconvenient.

Along with this change came the decline in importance of the old middle class of small businessmen and independent farmers and the concomitant rise of the new middle class, with two different segments and two somewhat different value-orientations. On the one hand was the organization man and the sales group; on the other, the professional intellectual stratum.

These two groups required values alien to the old entrepreneurial middle class, and, to some extent, different from each other. Riesman's and Fromm's categories neatly describe the different orientations of these strata: the inner-directed man is the old middle class with what Fromm described as a compulsive dedication to work, the hoarding orientation, and the accompanying superego values of the Protestant Ethic; the other-directed man is the new salesman, the organization man portrayed by Fromm as the "exchange," market-focused personality, conforming not to basic traditions but to trends and other people.

And then there is Riesman's autonomous man, Fromm's productive character type, Maslow's self-actualized man, the new hero of the intellectual professional, searching to be free. Autonomous man opposes equally the stuffy compulsiveness of the old tradition-bound middle class and the new conformism of the bureaucratic salesman. He chooses, instead, the values of creativity, freedom, self-development, expression; at times these values have merged with permissiveness, anarchy, laissez faire, rampant individualism. A de-emphasis on organization, discipline, and inhibition emerged because organization and order, after all, can easily become identified with bureaucratic regulation and pedantic compulsivity.

Bureaucracy's Need for Creativity

Despite the constrictions upon freedom and creativity emanating from "bureaucracy," there was, surprisingly enough, a great need for creativity and some measure of freedom on the part of the industrial bureaucracy itself. This is what the new ideologists such as Riesman, Fromm, and Whyte failed to grasp adequately.

They appeared to think that the call for creativity, which is a crucial feature of the new ideology, simply reflected social criticism, and was basically an anti-bureaucratic complaint. Permissiveness, expressiveness, political ardorlessness contribute to the kind of creativity required today by the corporation and the professions. The tasks facing these occupations require ingenuity, a facile shifting from one activity to another, getting along with others without being completely trammeled by cooperation, a capacity to grapple with the new. And it is not only the 2 per cent of the labor force in research who face such tasks; both business executives dealing with great technological changes and swiftly changing markets and professionals grappling with rapidly evolving skill demands and increasingly employed in large-scale bureaucracies have these problems.[11]

The new ideology with its stress on individual flexibility and creativity is functional, then, for occupational success. No wonder the cries of Fromm, Whyte, Riesman, and others for nonconformity were warmly and easily accepted. Some corporation presidents wrote of their desire to employ mavericks; college presidents demanded non-conformist students (but not on their campuses!); slick magazines published attacks on the cult of conformity. Rigid conformity may be all right for clerks but not for executives and professionals. Consequently, a variety of groups in society assault conformity and praise creativity and independence.

The new ideology replaced the old individualism with a tempered and psychologized new individualism. Independence and self-development (the modern displacement for success striving) are still the core, although the individual recognizes that he may have to cooperate to be acceptable. The individualist shows imagination with the tasks he is assigned but does not deeply question the institution that assigns them. He is more concerned with his family's emotional health than before and carefully allots time for his family. He abhors injustice and violence, but they are not his responsibility. He is a busy citizen involved in the complex of suburban committees because he wants to feel that he has some control over the events directly impinging on his family; the local tax rate and the obsessive concern with the education of his children are more compelling issues than racial equality.

True, some criticism still lingered, but more and more it became a rather vague criticism of "society" and "the culture." More important, a quiet presumption grew that, whatever was wrong with it, the society was a given entity. Adjustments would have to be made within its basic framework, even if the starting point of analysis was a criticism of the "contradictions of the culture." The ills of society had to be cured without basic reorganizations. More individualistic solutions such as psychotherapy became popular. If social change was impossible, it was best to concentrate on individual improvement. The age of psychologism was born. Child development and education took on enormous importance because they were a form of action, seemingly under the individual's control, which could bring great improvement without raising the question of societal change.

The New Unconscious

Despite the psychological self-consciousness of the architects of the new ideology, they have not developed an awareness of their own role in society and how it contributes to the shaping of their value preferences. Thus, the neo-Freudians as well as the progressive educators talked a great deal about man's needs for self-expression, creativity, and the like; they had little awareness that they were expressing their own special needs in a particular historical period, emerging from their specific position in relation to the bureaucratization of society. In ethnocentric fashion, without perspective, they supposed their own needs and values represented a universal model of man or human nature. Unwittingly, for the rejected life-and-death instincts of Freud, they substituted the notion of "basic needs" for productivity, creativity, self-actualization, autonomy. They committed the age-old error of intellectuals so well exemplified by Mannheim in *Ideology, and Utopia*—the error of assuming that, although other ideas may be socially produced, their own were pure and above cultural influence. The extra-scientific factors that might be affecting them, their own professional bias and particular experience, were not scrutinized carefully.

The absence of perspective among the new ideology makers provides a key to understanding many of their difficulties, as well as the distortions and abuses that have arisen as their ideas have been put into practice. The abuses of the age of psychiatry are shown in a new light. The tendency to psychologize problems, the parlor psychoanalysts, the new models of human nature with the projected middle-class needs of creativity and self-expression (with self-actualization at the apex), the alienation of the new working classes from psychotherapy, the failure to seek for nonpsychiatric methods of change—all these and many more are far easier to comprehend if the psychiatric movement is seen, not only as a mode of treatment, but as one expression of the ideology of the new middle class.

Progressive education also illustrates the impact of implicit assumptions. Critics have decried the excesses and distortions of progressive education. Excesses are often related to unexamined assumptions, and in this instance the assumptions are best understood in connection with what progressive education de-emphasized, namely, discipline, authority, tradition, routine hard work—values increasingly alien to the new middle class in its frantic search for the much-demanded creativity. In contrast it emphasized expression, freedom, intrinsically satisfying work—values increasingly important to the new middle class. No wonder then that, as progressive education was experienced by more and more middle-class people, the values it de-emphasized tended to be more and more neglected, although they had not been ignored in the original writings of progressive educators. Those values that were peripheral in the original system of progressive education were neglected or distorted in later practice, because the hidden social meaning—the congeniality with new middle-class needs—came more into play as the system became an institution. The seeds of the later errors can be found in part in the original ideology, but if the movement had had greater social self-awareness, many of its excesses might have been discarded long before sputnik so dramatically, and perhaps excessively, revealed them.

Conclusion

The psychiatric world view arose in the forties with the post-depression resurgence of the American economy and was propelled forward by the rapidly expanding and increasingly powerful professional stratum. This view was linked to other ideological movements (the New Ideology) such as child rearing, progressive education, and sex education. All were basically ego-centered philosophies with a powerful emphasis on ego control. Placing less hope in broad societal change than was done in the thirties, the new middle class focused on those elements that seemed subject to direct individual control: the family, child rearing, sex behavior, education, development of the self (through self-understanding), and emotional expression. Moreover, the flexibility that derives from ego control is more useful for the development of the creativity needed by the professional than would have been the inhibiting, binding control of the tradition-bound superego.

The psychiatric world view and the new ideology reflect the occupational and advancement needs of the professional stratum in a period of retreat from broad social change and passionate political involvement.

These world views, while perhaps well adapted to the occupational aspirations of the professional, are not suited to the possibilities of social change in the present period.

This context, we believe, furnishes a framework within which to comprehend the halting involvement of social scientists and intellectuals in currently developing social changes. The blinders acquired during the age of psychiatry in the forties and fifties still limit intense commitment and the search for far-reaching social change. Since the limitation of commitment is seen as sophistication, wholehearted involvement is withheld. The psychological mode of thinking has not developed a vocabulary of social change, let alone a theory. For example, the intricate writings on prejudice and discrimination with their heavy psychological bent have been made largely irrelevant by the events of the sixties. These hesitations and blinders are residues of the past intruding into the swiftly changing American political landscape with its new needs for the contributions of intellectuals.

We do not believe that their contribution requires direct participation in social movements (they need not march on Washington). Nor does it require the anarchistic total rejection that frequently characterizes the radicalism of Paul Goodman, for example.

We do believe that the professional's most significant contribution is likely to lie in the application of his skills (analysis, research, conceptualization) to the problems of social change, thus linking his professional interests and his social conscience. Here the great danger stems from professional parochialism,[12] whereby particular professional formulations, rather than the problems at hand, dominate in shaping the nature of the contribution. We hope that the professional's contribution will be conditioned more by the requisites of social change than by particular professional inclinations and that the professions will themselves change so that they will be increasingly relevant to the central domestic issues of our time.[13]

In essence, we need intellectual involvement with a problem-centered technology, rather than method-centered, prestige-oriented professionalism.[14]

NOTES

1. It should be noted that the phenomenon of the intellectual engagé was not completely absent in the fifties: witness C. Wright Mills. Mills, however, was relatively isolated (although not ignored!) in social-science circles.

2. See, for example:

T. W. Adorno et al., The Authoritarian Personality (New York: Harper & Bros., 1950).

D. Bingham, "Problems of Personality Development among Negro Children," in C. Kluckhohn and H. Murray, eds., Nature, Society and Culture (New York: Alfred Knopf, 1953).

P. Blanchard, "Cases Illustrating Psychoanalytic Contributions to the Problems of Reading Disabilities," in E. Hartley, H. Birch, and R. Hartley, eds., *Outside Readings in Psychology* (New York: Thomas Y. Crowell, 1955).

K. Horney, *The Neurotic Personality of Our Time* (New York: W. W. Norton, 1939).

A. Johnson, "Juvenile Delinquency," in S. Arieti, ed., *American Handbook of Psychiatry* (New York: Basic Books, 1959), pp. 840–855. On page 855 is cited a list of references reflecting a psychiatric view of delinquency, including the works of A. Eichhorn, K. R. Eisler, K. Friedlander, W. Healy, S. A. Szurek, and E. Weiss.

A. Kardiner and L. Ovesey, *The Mark of Oppression* (New York: World Publishing, 1951).

G. J. Pearson, *Psychoanalysis and the Education of the Child* (New York: W. W. Norton, 1951).

3. Strictly speaking, "psychological terms" is an incorrect formulation because psychodynamic, psychoanalytic explanations emphasizing unconscious causes became the vogue. In this chapter the word "psychiatry" covers the gamut of psychoanalytical orientations. While we later refer to the processes of psychotherapy, our major concern is with inappropriate generalizations of these basically psychological views to the society at large.

4. An important question not addressed here concerns the appropriate use of psychological levels of explanation in analyzing various problems, including social problems.

5. The passionate commitment of many intellectuals to Adlai Stevenson in 1952 and 1956 is an interesting exception. As the political symbol of much of the new hero ideology, standing in contrast to the old-fashioned traditional style of Eisenhower, Stevenson overcame many intellectuals' reluctance to be political believers.

6. Frank Barron, "The Psychology of Imagination," *Scientific American* (1958), 151–166.

7. Psychiatry has not fully faced the enormous problem of developing energy, intensity, and fervor in people. The underlying assumption is that if the neurotic conflict tying up the energy is removed, then the person will be able to go on fairly easily to be productive. This assumption is actually a derivative of Freud's libido theory, which has been rejected by most modern schools of therapy. According to this theory the individual has just so much energy, and this constant amount is either bound up in conflict or available for constructive sublimation. Unfortunately, insufficient attention has been focused on how to redirect the energy after it has been released from conflict. Much more crucial, however, is the slight concern for methods of increasing the total energy of the individual, because the traditional libidinal model, with its constant energy assumption, has tacitly remained.

8. In the sixties, David Riesman and Erich Fromm became intensely concerned with issues of peace. It is their earlier work to which we refer.

9. An interesting related trend developed in the late fifties in the "end of ideology" thesis of Daniel Bell and Seymour Martin Lipset. This trend was part of the same pattern reflecting the "end" of involvement, strong belief, intensity, far-ranging goals, and deep social criticism. It was a philosophy of accommodation, consensus, and pragmatism.

10. The social origins and social functions of a system cannot reductionistically be employed as tests of its validity. Our concern with the social basis of the new ideology is rather to illuminate the specific extra-scientific reasons for the un-

critical acceptance of these ideas. For example, the institutionalization of psycho-therapy has been little affected by the generally unfavorable scientific evidence regarding its value.

11. At the same time that it requires creativity and imagination, modern bureaucracy also attempts to limit and control them both consciously and un-consciously, and herein lies the clash with the intellectual. Thus the new ideology reflects bureaucracy's need for creativity and at the same time struggles against the anti-creative, restrictive controls of bureaucracy, which have become identified with discipline, authority, and conformity per se.

12. We think that some of the involvement of social scientists in the peace movement has been characterized by this parochialism: e.g., the psychologists who are very much concerned with showing how their specific conflict-reducing paradigms might be beneficial in reducing world conflict.

13. A fascinating area for study would be the Negro revolution, with its variety of leaders rather than one charismatic all-powerful leader, its cross-class character, its remarkable tactics, slogans, organization, and discipline, and the relationship between the integrationist and nationalist trends.

14. The last chapter develops an approach to a more policy-relevant social science.

18

❀   ❀   ❀

TECHNOLOGY AND POLICY

Two Agendas

This book is directed toward both professionals and citizens. It seeks to influence professionals' behavior in two ways: by improving their technology, the way they work with clients and pupils; by involving professionals more profoundly in the development of social policy and social change.

Underlying both the technology and the policy orientation is the basic assumption that a link is needed between professionals and a developing, stirring, progressive underclass—the new working class. Each without the other will be inadequate; the professional will be static, credential- and guild-oriented; his work will remain frequently precious and irrelevant. He will float in the status quo of the particular technology that has emerged in his field at a particular time. The needs and fervor of a clamoring underclass furnish direction, verve, and an orientation toward problems and content rather than status, form, and tradition. The energy that sparks the development of new ideas and the creativity of the professional frequently comes from the needs of the outsider, the implicit critic. Furthermore, the backing of a broad spectrum of citizens is needed if policy ideas are to become practices.

The rising underclass needs the professional to help develop breadth, perspective, and program. To believe otherwise is to romanticize and glamorize the poor. Without leadership and direction, some of which must come from professionals, the poor will remain undirected, "spontaneous," and frustrated. Complaints will evolve without program and organization; the danger is militant posturing without direction and ideology.

While we believe that a segment of the poor or new working class frequently provides the opening or the crucial level for change, this opening is not enough. The realization of opportunity requires a linkage that goes beyond the poor. It is this belief that leads us to emphasize the positive contribution of the underclass, while rejecting well-intended but sentimental folklore that implies that the poor have all the answers, that they should run all the programs by themselves, that because they have experienced poverty they know all about how to deal with it, or that poverty is a positive, happy state of life.

Our view of history sees a much more pluralistic grouping with segments of the professionals and segments of the underclass providing the central dynamic in the present period. Youth groups, labor, churches, and other groups of the society will be involved in this broad coalition at various points.

What is the significance of the technology, the practice of the professional, in relation to our two broad agendas? In the present period some of the most important policy questions center around education, health, jobs, social services, participation. Politics will increasingly focus on the questions of "the new income"—improvement of education for the disadvantaged (and all classes), more effective organization of social services, better provisioning of jobs and income, the institutionalization of new rights.

The practice of professionals is a fundamental policy question with long-range implications. Simultaneously, it is a significant question of technology, because it is only through the development of appropriate technology and practice that the poor can be educated, can receive useful services, can be helped to grow and become involved. Thus, policy and technology questions frequently overlap, as do our two audiences (professionals involved in practice and professionals and citizens involved in social change).

The Development of Expanded Technologies

In this book a major goal has been the expansion of the variety of approaches utilized by the professional. We have assumed that his methods and practices are frequently too narrow, and not entirely appropriate for low-income populations. Consequently, our orientation toward technology is frequently not to negate what the professional is doing, but to expand it. For example, the use of students as tutors is directed toward the broadening of teaching methodology, rather than toward the replacement of teachers by peers.

The underlying assumption is that professional approaches frequently become less relevant to the needs of the populace because of the commitment to traditions, vested interest, learned technologies, and credentialism. Furthermore, professional schools frequently train in relation to a particular viewpoint; thus, one social-work school will emphasize Rank, another Freud, another Sullivan, but rarely is a wide range of technology and method taught. Moreover, social science in attempting to emulate physical science seeks the one "correct" scientific approach. This physical-science model narrows the range of technology and tactics.

We believe there is a great need for professionals to be trained far more inductively in the field and for theory to be built on this type of clinical experience. Do not doctors learn more about doctoring through their internship and resident experience than through the preceding classroom years? Perhaps these and other professional programs would be more pertinent if they were built upon clinical experience from the beginning as is the case at Western Reserve Medical School.

Perhaps it is worth while to indicate our differences with conventional professional social-science perspectives. For these differences have affected the texture of this book. While having the highest respect for the professionals' commitment to scientific knowledge, system, perspective, and specialization, we nevertheless do not want to overestimate the professional orientation. We think professionals frequently have much to learn from common sense, intuition, and the people they serve. Professionals can also learn from "fringe" systems such as Alcoholics Anonymous, SYNANON, psychotherapeutic existentialism, etc.

Our own identification is frequently with the new, the developing. In a sense, as outsiders within any particular profession, we have some of the advantages of the marginal man—the independent perspective and ambivalence that produce a critical stance. More important, perhaps, is our activist approach of using social science in order to produce change, rather than simply to study phenomena. Thus, one source of our orientation toward the culture of poverty theory is that, as a concept, it appears to be pessimistic about the possibility of movement. It sees the low-income population as being fatalistic, apathetic, difficult to move. It does not reveal levers of motion. Our activist approach leads to an emphasis on utilization of the strengths and the positives of the underclass as one source for movement. Marx declared that the task is not to understand history but to change it. *Our belief is that one best understands history by trying to change it.*

As social science has entered the applied fields (for example, in medical sociology or educational sociology), its first major endeavor has been a description of discrimination, either against an ethnic or a low-income population; witness the work of David Caplovitz,[1] Patricia Sexton,[2] August Hollingshead, and Fredrick Redlich.[3] This perspective forms an extremely important part of applied social science, but we have generally assumed these conditions of discrimination. We have emphasized instead methods of overcoming them through utilizing the strengths of the poor, through style match, role playing, neighborhood store fronts, nonprofessionals, etc.

We have taken as problematic the relationship between practitioners and clients. We look at the ingredients of the relationship rather than assuming that the present packaging is the most appropriate way of conducting the varied sets of relationships involved in practitioners' functioning. Consequently, we have looked at the nonprofessional peer as a way of providing new kinds of learning experiences for many students. Instead of thinking that teaching is done only by teachers in the traditional teaching ways, we offer the possibility that there are many different ways of learning, and, consequently, many different kinds of people who can perform effective roles in aiding people to learn. Similarly, in looking at the psychotherapeutic relationship, we argue that there are many different ways of helping individuals. Some of these involve the use of psychiatrists in additional ways, but there are many other alternative formulations and possibilities available in terms of much more direct aid by people other than the psychiatrist.

We do not assume that the present complex of relationships is necessarily optimal. We argue for much more flexibility, imagination, and innovation in spotting the kinds of relationships which are important and for developing new categories of personnel to fill them.

As our society becomes more oriented toward social services, it becomes increasingly important to develop a wider number of people to perform the multitude of tasks needed to make this a more humane society. If we insist upon a limited number of people of high education as the major focus in the social services, there is no chance of providing adequate services.

Our argument insists upon the significance of technology. At a time when there is much discussion of institutional imbalances and inadequacies, it is sometimes unrecognized how important it is to improve the performance of professionals (and paraprofessionals) at the level of the job that they are to do. While it may be necessary to change institutions in drastic ways, there is a dearth of knowledge and understanding of how to perform certain tasks more effectively. Much of our work has moved along this particular line.

Contrasting Approaches

It is interesting to contrast the action-technology approach we have been advocating with other approaches in the areas of education, social service, and mental health. In education, for example, the usual demands are for more teachers, preparation of children for the school via Headstart programs, special services through psychologists, guidance counselors, and the like. In mental health, many new approaches have developed, such as walk-in clinics, group and family approaches, day hospitals. The great danger is that they may be pouring old practices into new formats. What practices and technologies are to be developed in these walk-in clinics, day hospitals, and group approaches? What will the greater numbers of teachers do? How will the teaching machines be utilized to develop contact with the low-income population? How will earlier preparation through Headstart affect the inadequate school systems? How will the special services modify pedagogy and teaching practice in the classroom?

The typical approach in education is largely more of the same, rather than a reorganization of process around new methods and techniques. The mental-health approach provides new forms but it is unclear how the process and technology are to differ. The walk-in clinics appear to be providing brief psychotherapy—more of the same traditional package only in shorter form.

In social work, role playing and demonstration approaches can be added to classical case-work intervention in order to make it more palatable for low-income populations.[4] Unfortunately, there is little consideration of the possibility that social case work as a whole may not be the appropriate treatment of choice for many problems of low-income people. Thus Hollis' emphasis is additive and mildly corrective. No reorganization of the process is offered.

The various interventions that are popular are either compensatory, based on presumed deficits or weaknesses in the low-income population, or additive, such as Hollis' approach, or form centered, such as the walk-in clinic which attempts to develop methods of reach without changing the fundamental services to be offered. Seldom are practice or technology taken as the basic problematic. There has been little emphasis on finding functional equivalents or basically reorganizing practice.

Unfortunately, criticism of professional orientations is frequently met with the response that one is being anti-professional. Quite the contrary. A genuine professionalism must include efforts to raise professional practice beyond the point where it is. A basic intellectual canon recognizes, of course, the need for the growth of knowledge and modification of it, based upon testing it in practice and changing it by learning from many varieties of experience.

A strategic element in our sociology of technology is obviously an emphasis on the class factor and a recognition that the development of the technology may be sharpened by observing its difficulties at its weakest point, namely, in relation to the new working class. Our basic assumption is that what is good for the poor may turn out to be good for large numbers of people in the society at large. Focusing on the poor provides an avenue for the expansion of social technology and the practice of the profession.

In contrast to the educational sociologists, the medical sociologists, etc., we have been less concerned with a generalized analysis of the system in which education and treatment take place and more concerned with specific processes, methods, techniques. Hence we are concerned with developing an action theory, a sociology of professional practice which, though varying from discipline to discipline, will have a common core of fundamental elements. This theory embraces an understanding of the strengths and limitations of the professional role and envisions ways of expanding professional technology. The professional must be ready to change and to adapt to some of the demands of accountability.

Finally, we believe that more professionals should be committed to a broader concern than simply studying the social scene. In this sense we have been influenced by the Freudian and Marxian traditions. An interesting illustration of the contrasting static pessimism of much social-science research can be observed in the view that low-income people will be very unlikely to accept birth-control approaches, presumably because they are less interested in planning, do not have sufficient time perspective, are more apathetic, are less interested in health measures, etc. Studies made in the abstract, that is, without available birth-control clinics, frequently support this type of conclusion. Action sociology, as noted above, discovered a very different result. When services and clinics became available, accessible, and convenient, large numbers of poor people swept forward to obtain the new birth-control techniques.[5]

Social Policy

A number of policy assumptions guide this book. As we have said, a basic one is that segments of the poor, the underclass, or the have-nots have an important role to play in stimulating progress. We assume that groups in power rarely recognize and seek to change the deep deficiencies that emerge as their system becomes stabilized. Striving for stability and organization, they tend to emphasize the functional aspects of society and to overlook the dysfunctional elements which may be producing the conditions for change and reorganization. If the established power groups remain aloof too long from these tensions toward institutional change, they may be subject to revolutionary overthrow. If, on the other hand, they respond to these critical forces they may attempt to incorporate them in the system and thus continue in power by sharing some dimensions of power or by expanding power. The changes that ensue will then be more subtle and will reflect not a direct expression of the criticism of the underclass, but rather a more distilled integration of the new forces and the existing system.

For the most part the American system has functioned in this latter fashion as the power groups have been remarkably resilient, responding to pressures of various underclasses (e.g., the labor movement in the thirties) and providing many, though insufficient, openings for change within the capitalist form of society.

Accepting this general framework for the moment, our posture is largely that of *radical reform*. We have been concerned that the maneuverability of the system be utilized to its fullest extent for the development of large-scale institutional reforms, building on the needs of the new working class.

In this sense, our position is different from many of the New Left, who demand the complete recasting of society. We differ from the New Left (and from Alinsky) in that we see the possibility of expanding the power of the upperclass without necessarily removing the power of the upperclass; that is, we do not see a finite amount of power (a zero sum game) in which the poor must take it from the rich.

We are also distinctly different from the new reformers led by Lipset, Moynihan, Glazer, *et al.*, who largely seem to see reform coming from within the system itself and underestimate the significance of a critical underclass pressing for change.

We seek to expand the rights of the poor and we want to see American society improved at the same time. We do not merely want to bring the poor into the American main stream, but to improve that main stream by building new rights of participation, by increasing the rights of direction and control over bureaucracy for all, by humanizing the organizations which structure our activities, by improving the school system for all by making the university become relevant to the poor, by reducing inequalities, and by the independent, critical monitoring of the affairs of society.

While we think agitation and conflict are important parts of efforts to achieve great changes, we also believe that great changes have begun to take place in the United States. Conflict and confrontation are means; we do not avoid them, we do not necessarily always embrace them.

Our program is one of radical reform rather than of revolution. We feel that many Americans are searching for a perspective on class and policy which moves beyond welfare amelioralism without embracing a revolutionary zeal which appears to be ineffective in an affluent society. We believe that the fear of revolutionary apocalyptism is leading many people away from efforts at deep reform of society.

In our perspective, both an inside and outside strategy are needed. We do not believe that only an outside strategy, and only an outside strategy of conflict, can be useful. Nor do we think that those who play the inside role of attempting to improve the conditions for the development of effective action for the poor, nor those who move between both worlds (as we do), are inevitably cop outs, escaping the "real" action.

Intellectuals can help develop responsive programs and policy by working both within the system and outside the system, both as representatives of government and as technical consultants for groups such as the civil-rights forces, welfare-rights groups, new-careers movement, etc. Unless the rising new groups have links with committed professionals, the demands of the new working class will remain undeveloped, frustrated, and chaotic. Unless the rising group of professionals and intellectuals, those who are criticizing the traditional, professional establishments, develop connections with the rising underclass, their ideas and ideology will lack fire, fervor, and relevance, remaining watery reflections of traditional thinking. The rising intellectual must respond to the mandate for creativity, change, and new ideas. In order to do this, he must be tuned to the ferment and new developments in the society, in particular to the demands and spirit of the critical underclass. This responsiveness does not imply a blanket and uncritical acceptance of the demands of the new working classes.

It should be clear why we oppose both the vulgarized versions of the culture of poverty concept of the poor and the contrary romantic tendency of depicting poverty as purifying and intellectually rewarding. The new intellectuals must provide some of the leadership, expression, and ideology for the poor and with the poor. We take this as our charge, as we believe others such as Richard Cloward, Michael Harrington, Preston Wilcox, and Bayard Rustin do. They see themselves as providing necessary ideology for the development of social movements which include the new working class as a significant element.

The policy reflections of our over-all viewpoint are found throughout the book. Thus in section II on education we noted that the integration movement's demand for improved education resulted in vastly expanded educational expenditures for all children in the United States; the quality-education demand of the new working class provided the opening for the development of education as a whole. We observed, however, that this demand was diverted away from integrated education and we discussed critically some of the strategic and policy reasons why this occurred.

In the field of mental health, we argued against the one-sided psychiatric world view, which we believe diverted people from supporting needed social change and moved them toward a highly introspective, self-oriented perspective.[6] Our concern was to attempt to formulate some lines for the development of new mental-health technology. Hence we stress the significance of role playing, sociotherapeutic approaches, new diagnostic tools, the helper-therapy principles, counseling that emphasized know-how about the system rather than an introspective and historical orientation, and the special significance of the nonprofessional. We think the latter is especially important, because he carries within him the possibility for new peer interventions, needed subjective approaches to counterbalance the necessary distance and objective of the professional, special ability to reach people on a large-scale basis in poor neighborhoods, a built-in carrier of the culture and idiom and language of the people to be treated.

Professional theory and technology must be developed in combination with the nonprofessionals and the receivers of service themselves, whether poor or non-poor. In the present transitional stage in which professional technology is inadequate, greater reliance may have to be placed on most sensitive listening to the receivers of service and the nonprofessional workers. This, of course, produces special strains among the three groups as professionals are wary about giving up their traditional proprietary rights and doubt the wisdom of the militant spokesmen of the new working class; and the poor and the nonprofessionals voice strong criticisms of the inappropriateness of professional expertise.

Summary and Conclusions

1. Basic difficulties that characterize our society in the areas of education, services, rights, and bureaucracy are frequently more dramatically felt and responded to by segments of the new working class, particularly the Negro poor.

2. Our concern for the poor does not in any way reflect a romantic admiration of poverty. Aside from humanitarian considerations, this interest rests on the belief that a segment of the poor is a crucial source of progress for other groups in relation to major institutional problems. When the poor are stirred into action, they frequently strongly oppose institutions and practices which are unhealthy for other groups. Thus, the minority poor has been sharpest in its concern about the limitations of the welfare system, bureaucratic discretion,

pseudo-morality, lack of participation, and legal rights. Segments of the poor, particularly because they are outside the system, sharpen perspective in many ways. They demand change. Those in power are rarely self-correcting in as deep a fashion.

3. The professional and the poor need each other. The poor will help the professional to make his techniques more appropriate, less formal, less credential based, more problem oriented. The failures of professional techniques in treating mental illness, in education, and in developing policy in a great variety of areas are all too well known. Professionals and all of us in the middle class need the vitality, criticism, and activism of the poor. In turn, the poor need connections with professionals in order to develop policy and technology useful in meeting their needs. The poor are not the exclusive repository of understanding about the ways of dealing with poverty.

4. We have opposed that segment of the antipoverty movement that stresses changing the poor to fit institutions rather than changing institutions to involve the poor. We believe, however, that it is necessary not only to change institutions to fit people, but also that the most effective way of developing change is to utilize the positives in the traditions, style, culture, and ways of the poor as one crucial lever in bringing about the needed structural changes. Those in the antipoverty movement who have utilized neighborhood-service center store fronts and indigenous nonprofessional workers are building on the traditions of the poor in introducing deep-seated changes in the delivery, character, and quality of services in America.

5. We believe that other social classes would benefit from the extensions of technology that we have suggested to improve the conditions of the new working class in education, mental-health practices, and service delivery. For example, the failure of psychiatry in treating severe mental illness is well known. Its congeniality with the temper of the upper middle-class neurotic has perhaps obscured the fact that its methods are frequently not curative here either. The concern with developing more appropriate mental-health approaches for low-income populations may have enormous implications for better treatment for all. Similarly, peer intervention, especially useful with the poor, has implications for the treatment of all patients, as does the process of sociotherapy which proposes indirect models as an additional tool for mental-health improvement. The kinds of changes we have proposed in education for the disadvantaged might likewise have a powerful revitalizing effect upon the entire educational system: use of nonpro-

fessionals to aid all teachers; development of expanded teaching technology utilizing more styles of learning again widens the teaching base. Or the use of new decentralized community-based service forms (such as the Citizens' Advice Bureaus in England) may have an important anti-bureaucratic effect on service delivery for all groups of the population. Our emphasis on rights and participation is useful for middle-class groups as well. New models which emphasize the development of manpower through providing jobs first with training built in have major implications for the development of needed paraprofessional manpower that would release professionals to concentrate on creative tasks.

6. Our concern with the relationship of technology to policy is based upon our change bias and our awareness that institutional change does not simply come about through decree or legislation. It frequently requires technology to implement it, as well as in some cases to trigger it. We differ from most social scientists in that we have an explicit change bias rather than an abstract or purist approach to problems. We are far more problem based and concerned with the effects of action intervention. Social-science analysis is frequently too static and based upon the input of very small variables reflecting a less affluent age.

Our suggestions have been directed for the most part to professionals and to social scientists functioning inside governmental and professional systems. Our remarks have attempted to connect these groups with the forces of change emanating from outside their systems. The demands of the civil-rights movement, the upsurge of youth, and the fact of the new working class all reflect in sharpened form the difficulties and alienation in the larger society.

We believe that as the underclass becomes a part of the society it is not only changed and adjusted to the old, but it changes and adjusts the old. The labor movement, which today has lost some of its traditional impact and ideological power, in its heyday produced tremendous changes for the entire society, while itself becoming absorbed within that society. The new working class may bring similar and possibly even greater changes to all of us.

Issues of professional practice increasingly permeate our lives. Thus, by addressing ourselves to the problems of education, social services, mental health, community action, we have touched on sensitive problems for all Americans. Politics and policy, as well as technology, are basic to practice. The crucial issues of today require a citizens' perspective along with a professional perspective. These are new, potentially creative tensions in which the new working classes are forcing out vital questions. New content in professional practice and new linkages between professionals and citizens are needed.

NOTES

1. David Caplovitz, *The Poor Pay More* (New York: The Free Press of Glencoe, 1963).

2. Patricia Sexton, *Education and Income* (New York: Viking Press, 1961).

3. August B. Hollingshead and Fredrick Redlich, *Social Class and Mental Illness* (New York: John Wiley and Sons, 1958).

4. Florence Hollis, *Social Casework* (October 1965).

5. See Adelaide Cromwell and Frederic Jaffe, *Negro Fertility and Family Size Preferences: Implications for Programming of Health and Social Services* (New York: Planned Parenthood, 1966).

6. It is interesting to observe the reaction that seems to have developed in response to the general critique (not ours alone) of the psychiatric world view and the new emphasis on the need for social change and social action. Many social scientists have been highly responsive to the need for social action and social change. Unfortunately, however, their emphasis has been largely ideological and they have not developed appropriate technology, program, and scientific theory to accompany their new feelings and commitment. Thus some social scientists have come to recognize their deficiencies in failing to anticipate the civil-rights revolt and their general lack of understanding of poverty and the poor. But they have not yet developed significant theory and conceptualizations in these important new areas.

ACKNOWLEDGMENTS

Earlier drafts of many chapters appeared in various journals and collections of essays. We are grateful to Ira Harrison, Elliot Mishler, Martin Rein, Robert Rieff, and Sylvia Scribner, the co-authors of some of these earlier drafts, and to the publishers and editors of the following articles for their permission to reprint, rework, or use selections for this book:

"The American Lower Class: A Typological Approach," *Social Research* (Spring 1964), pp. 1–22.

"Child Centered Radicalism: The New Pre-School Mythology," *American Child* (April 1966).

"A Comparison of Two Social Action Approaches: Saul Alinsky and the New Student Left," *New York State Psychologist*, XVIII, No. 2 (April 1964).

"Dropouts: A Political Problem," in Daniel Schreiber, ed., *The School Dropout* (Washington, D. C.: National Education Association, 1964).

"The Ebb and Flow in the School Integration Movement," *Integrated Education*, IV, No. 5 (October–November 1966), 8–18.

"The Indigenous Non-Professional," *American Journal of Orthopsychiatry*, XXXVII, No. 4 (July 1967). Robert Rieff, co-author.

"The New Anti-Poverty Ideology," *Teachers College Record*, LXVI, No. 2 (November 1966), 107–119.

"New Approaches to Mental Health Treatment for Low Income People," *Social Work Practice* (1965). Also presented at the National Conference on Social Welfare, 92nd Annual Forum.

"The 'New' Working Class," in Irving L. Horowitz, ed., *The New Sociology: Essays on Social Values and Social Theory in Honor of C. Wright Mills.* Copyright © 1964 by Oxford University Press, Inc. Reprinted by permission.

"Poverty, Inequality and Policy," in Howard S. Becker, ed., *Social*

Problems: A Modern Approach (New York: John Wiley, 1966). Martin Rein, co-author.

"School Dropouts and American Society," *New Society,* London (November 7, 1963).

"The Search for an Educational Revolution," in C. W. Hunnicutt, ed., *Urban Education and Cultural Deprivation* (Syracuse: Syracuse University Press, 1965).

"Social Change versus the 'Psychiatric World View,'" *American Journal of Orthopsychiatry,* XXXIV, No. 1 (January 1964). Copyright © 1964 by the American Orthopsychiatric Association, Inc. Reprinted by permission.

"Social Class, Mental Illness, and American Psychiatry," *Milbank Memorial Fund Quarterly* (April 1959). Elliot Mishler, co-author.

"Standards for an Affluent Society," in Gerald Somers, ed., *Towards Freedom from Want* (Madison, Wisc.: Industrial Relations Research Association, 1968).

"A Strategy for Anti-Poverty Community Work Action Programs," *Social Work,* XI, No. 2 (April 1966). Reprinted by permission of the National Association of Social Workers. Martin Rein, co-author.

"Strategy for Change," *American Child* (April 1966).

"Teachers of the Poor," in C. W. Hunnicutt, ed., *Urban Education and Cultural Deprivation* (Syracuse: Syracuse University Press, 1965).

"The Third Force: An Anti-Poverty Ideology," *American Child* (November 1965). Martin Rein, co-author.

"Types of Dropouts: The Unemployables," in Arthur B. Shostak and William Gomberg, eds., *Blue Collar World* (Englewood Cliffs, N.J.: Prentice-Hall, 1964). Ira Harrison, co-author.

"The 'Underutilization' of Mental Health Services by Workers in Low Income Groups," *American Journal of Psychiatry,* CXXI (1965), 798–801. Copyright © 1965 by the American Psychiatric Association. Reprinted by permission. Sylvia Scribner, co-author.

INDEX